THE
GUARLFORD
STORY

THE GUARLFORD STORY

Don Hill
Eric Jones
Janet Lomas
Peter Mayner
Rosemary McCulloch
Michael Skinner

The Guarlford History Group

Published in the United Kingdom, 2005, by
The Guarlford History Group.
4 Bamford Close
Guarlford
Malvern
WR13 6PF

© The Guarlford History Group

ISBN 0-9550498-0-6

Book design and photograph restoration by Michael Skinner

Printed in England by
Print Plus
126 Widemarsh Street
Hereford
HR4 9HN

DEDICATION

This book is dedicated to Joan Bradshaw, historian of Guarlford, whose researches and writing have provided so much inspiration and material for the present account. The authors of 'The Guarlford Story' are greatly indebted to Joan for all that she has done to record and sustain the life of this village over many years.

THE AUTHORS

Donald J Hill

Don was born in Richmond, Yorkshire. After leaving school, he enlisted in the army as an apprentice and then went on to serve as soldier and electronics engineer in the Royal Electrical and Mechanical Engineers (REME) until retirement in the rank of major in 1991. In 1979, while working at the REME establishment in Malvern, he and his wife Barbara came to live in Guarlford, but did not take up permanent residence until 1986. For many years, he has been treasurer, then churchwarden to Guarlford Church and Chairman of the Village Hall Committee. Past activities include Village Fete organiser, Madresfield Parish Clerk and Madresfield School Governor. He is also treasurer to the Malvern branches of two Service charities, SSAFA Forces Help and the Royal British Legion.

Dr Eric H Jones

Born in Oxford and brought up in Cardiff, Eric was educated at three universities, including the University of Texas, U.S.A. His interest in American literature led to the award in 1973 of a Ph.D. for a thesis on the poetry and fiction of Sylvia Plath, completed with essential moral and typing support from his wife, Siti. They both came to live in Guarlford in 1976 for Eric to take up appointment as Head of English and Drama at what is now University College Worcester in January 1977. In the mid-1990s he made a career move to become the first Director of the College's International Office. Subsequent visits overseas on behalf of both the College and the British Council included destinations in China, India, Malaysia, the U.S.A., and various European countries. Committed to Guarlford as a community over many years since the Silver Jubilee of 1977, he has been actively involved as a Parish Councillor and in other ways for more than twenty-five years. Wider interests include international travel, the countryside – especially National Parks – the National Trust, and art history.

Janet Lomas

Janet and her husband farm the Home Farm of the Madresfield Estate, farming both sides of the Madresfield and Guarlford parish boundary. Her interest in local history began at home, where there is a wealth of historic interest and archaeological features. Janet has been Guarlford Parish Council's appointed tree warden for eight years, and is a keen wildlife conservationist, working both as a local volunteer for several national and local organisations and also as a full-time farm conservation adviser with the Herefordshire Farming and Wildlife Advisory Group (FWAG). As well as advising farmers on wildlife conservation, her work with FWAG involves promoting conservation of the historic landscape.

Dr Peter E Mayner

Peter has lived all his life within the original Guarlford parish boundary and for the last forty-eight years at Cherry Orchard. Educated at Haileybury College, the original East India Company's college, and then Trinity College, Cambridge and Birmingham University, where he studied medicine, he also gained his Royal Air Force Volunteer Reserve wings with the Birmingham University Air Squadron. He developed an interest in underwater archaeology through founding membership of scuba diving clubs at the two universities. Peter worked in local hospitals after qualifying, prior to joining the Peninsular and Oriental Steam Navigation Company. Extensive travel around the world culminated in service 'under fire' as Company Medical Officer in the Falklands Conflict when the 'S.S. Canberra' was requisitioned. After twenty years at sea, he was forced by ill health to retire home to Guarlford, where he is Chairman of the Parish Council and pursues interests including music and the Chairmanship of the English Symphony Orchestra's 'Friends', the National Trust, rugby, cricket and wine-making!

Rosemary McCulloch

Rosemary moved to Malvern in 1978, when her husband Angus transferred to the Royal Signals and Radar Establishment from the Signals Research and Development Establishment, Christchurch. Their three sons attended Madresfield School, where Rosemary served as a Parent Governor, and she also helped the Reverend David Martin to start the Benefice Junior Church in 1982. She has an Honours degree in English from the University of Wales, Bangor, and, after being Supervisor of Lansdowne Playgroup, taught in Malvern, mainly at the Chase High School, as a supply teacher for many years. With many interests, mostly concerned with family and community life - topics which she enjoyed researching for the present book - Rosemary has also been President of Guarlford Women's Institute since November 1998.

J Michael Skinner

After completing National Service in the Royal Signals, Michael came to Malvern in 1952 to join the Radar Research and Development Establishment at Leigh Sinton. He remained with the establishment through its many amalgamations and name changes until he retired in 1990 from full-time service from what had become the Royal Signals and Radar Establishment. He continued working part-time to represent the UK on both the Steering Committee and Project Management Board of an international NATO research project on automated Information Fusion and Visualisation. This was a particularly rewarding time as it involved visiting and working with very friendly and co-operative scientists and engineers from Canada, Denmark, France, Germany, Italy and the Netherlands. He finally retired in 2000, after the successful completion of the project. Michael moved to Guarlford with his family in 1971 and became involved in village life as Secretary to the Silver Jubilee Committee, Secretary and Trustee of the Village Hall, and, in 1980, Parish Clerk.

ACKNOWLEDGEMENTS

The authors are deeply indebted to the Local Heritage Initiative (LHI) whose advice and grant have made possible the creation and publication of this book.

The Local Heritage Initiative is a national grant scheme that helps local groups to investigate, explain and care for their landscape, traditions and culture. The LHI was developed by the Countryside Agency and is funded by the Heritage Lottery Fund and the Nationwide Building Society.

The Guarlford History Group (GHG) would also like to thank both the Elmley Foundation for providing the resources to purchase equipment, which will enable the GHG to give presentations on its research and projects to local schools and groups and the Guarlford Parish Council for donating its Community Pride prize money as start-up funding for the project.

This book could not have been written without the help and enthusiasm of the present and former parishioners of Guarlford for not only agreeing to be interviewed but also for searching out and making available their old family photographs and giving permission for both their accounts of Guarlford village life and their family and other photographs to be included in this 'Story of Guarlford'. The authors would like to express their thanks to all the under mentioned for their invaluable help and apologise if anyone has been omitted or if there have been any inaccuracies in the accounts.

Mr C Attwood	Mrs P Bayliss	Mr S G Beard	Mrs M Bennett
Mrs D Bick	Mr D Bladder	Mr H Bladder	Mr G Bott
Miss J Bradshaw	Mr K Chester	Mrs J Clark	Mrs J M Crisp
Mrs C E Dring	Mrs E Dunn	Mrs P Fairhurst	Mr J Gammond
Mrs L Gilroy	Mr R Gilroy	Mr C Hayes	Mrs D Hayes
Mr D Hewins	Mr D Hill	Mr P Hughes	Mrs M Hunaban
Mr C Hyde	Mr B Iles	Mr E Jenkins	Mrs J Kershaw
Miss P Jones	Mr E Lane	Mr J Little	Mrs E Llewelyn
Mrs C Lockley	Dr P E Mayner	Mr A Medcalf	Mrs R McCulloch
Mr S Micklethwait	Miss C Moody	Miss J Newell	Plough & Harrow
Mrs M Omar	Mr A Rose	Mrs M Rutter	Mr J M Skinner
Mr M Simpson	Mrs M R Thomas	Mrs S Thorne	Mr A Tummey
Mrs M Waldron	Mrs J Ward	Mrs C Weaver	Mrs S Wheeler
Mr C R Williams	Mrs R Williams	Mr K Woolley	Sir Jerry Wiggin
Mr B Wyndham	Mr A Young	Mr J Young	
Commander Ratcliff's grandchildren			

The authors would also like to record their appreciation for the help provided by the Madresfield Church of England School, the Worcestershire Record Office and the Worcestershire Historic Environment and Archaeology Service.

The photographs shown in Figures 7.8 and 7.9 are Crown Copyright, they were taken by the Telecommunications Research Establishment (TRE), Malvern, and are reproduced by kind permission of its successor the Defence Science and Technology Laboratories (Dstl), MOD. The photographs shown in Figures 3.8, 7.12, 8.7, 8.9, 8.10 and 10.5, are reproduced by the kind permission of the *Malvern Gazette, Berrows Newspapers.*

The photographs reproduced in Figures 2.17, 3.0, 4.12, 4.14 and 9.2 were taken by Mr C D Walton, the Barnard's Green Photographer, and are reproduced by kind permission of his daughter Mrs J Preece.

The map shown on the cover and in Figures 5.2 and 8.6 is in the public domain and is reproduced by courtesy of the Ordnance Survey; it is an extract taken from the 1832 Ordnance Survey Map, which was published at the Tower of London on 11th February 1832 by Lieutenant Colonel Colby of the Royal Engineers.

The Foley 1744 Estate map shown in Figure 1.1 is also in the public domain and is reproduced by courtesy of The Worcestershire Record Office and by Messrs Davis, Foster and Finley, Solicitors, who donated it to the Record Office.

Finally, the authors are very grateful to Tony and Shirley Goddard for carrying out the very necessary and onerous task of proof reading this book.

Local Heritage *initiative*

FOREWORD

Inspired by our local historian and life-long resident Joan Bradshaw, our Guarlford story has had quite a long gestation. The project gathered momentum after our village millennium pond and churchyard restoration schemes were awarded the second prize in the Worcestershire Community Pride Competition of 2002.

The Guarlford Parish Council subsequently decided to set up a committee to research, write and publish our village history, using the prize money. In addition to this, we have received a generous donation from the Elmley Foundation; and in 2004 we successfully applied for Lottery funding through the Local Heritage Initiative and were awarded a substantial sum for a project which is seen to benefit the whole community.

The committee of volunteers has met regularly since 2003 to manage the project in its various aspects: the interviews, research, gathering and restoration of photographs, and then writing and formatting the text and finally designing and creating the page layouts. We intend to set up an archive of photographs and interviews in due course to include much that we were unable to fit into this book. The archive may then be expanded by future generations of villagers.

This has been a fascinating project for all of us. I personally have enjoyed speculating upon the origin and meaning of such names as 'Twopence' and 'Tenpence Morley', 'Penny' and 'Splash' meadows on the old tithe map. I have also found my Saturday morning sessions in a local hostelry, with a group that I have christened the 'Village Elders', especially rewarding.

I hope that you will derive as much pleasure in reading our village story as we have gained from producing it.

Dr P E Mayner

Chairman
Guarlford Parish Council

CONTENTS

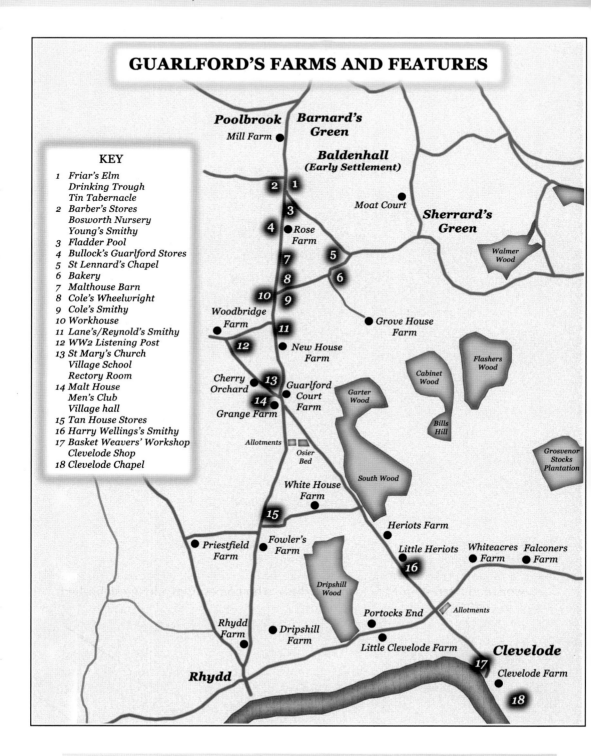

GUARLFORD'S FARMS AND FEATURES

KEY

1 Friar's Elm
   Drinking Trough
   Tin Tabernacle
2 Barber's Stores
   Bosworth Nursery
   Young's Smithy
3 Fladder Pool
4 Bullock's Guarlford Stores
5 St Lennard's Chapel
6 Bakery
7 Malthouse Barn
8 Cole's Wheelwright
9 Cole's Smithy
10 Workhouse
11 Lane's/Reynold's Smithy
12 WW2 Listening Post
13 St Mary's Church
   Village School
   Rectory Room
14 Malt House
   Men's Club
   Village hall
15 Tan House Stores
16 Harry Wellings's Smithy
17 Basket Weavers' Workshop
   Clevelode Shop
18 Clevelode Chapel

Poolbrook
Mill Farm

Barnard's Green

Baldenhall
(Early Settlement)

Moat Court

Sherrard's Green

Walmer Wood

Rose Farm

Woodbridge Farm

Grove House Farm

Flashers Wood

New House Farm

Cabinet Wood

Cherry Orchard

Guarlford Court Farm

Garter Wood

Grange Farm

Bills Hill

Grosvenor Stocks Plantation

Allotments

Osier Bed

South Wood

White House Farm

Heriots Farm

Priestfield Farm

Fowler's Farm

Little Heriots

Whiteacres Farm

Falconers Farm

Dripshill Wood

Allotments

Portocks End

Rhydd Farm

Dripshill Farm

Little Clevelode Farm

Clevelode

Clevelode Farm

Rhydd

INTRODUCTION

Lady Beauchamp opening the Parish Fete, c.1910

In her account of the origins of Baldenhall and Guarlford, Joan Bradshaw quotes 'Coriander', writing in the *Malvern News* in December, 1963: "I have been discovering what an interesting place the parish of Guarlford is. I feel that the study of its people, and its past and present history, could be a life's work." While it has been virtually a life's work and interest for Miss Joan Bradshaw, who comes from a long-established village family, and we are indebted to her for providing many of the sources of this History, the present authors embarked upon their work in the early years of a new century, the twenty-first, conscious of the need to record Guarlford's story while much of it could still be found in the memories of the village's older residents. Following Guarlford's celebration of the new millennium and then, in 2002, of the Queen's Golden Jubilee, it seemed the right moment to try to capture something of the history and distinctive character of this small Worcestershire village.

Though Guarlford shares much with every other English village, particularly of course in its agricultural past, there is also a history which is unique to each place. It is this distinctiveness, this uniqueness, which we endeavour to trace here, using documentary sources, old maps, photographs and, above all, the memories of those whose families have lived in Guarlford for many generations. What is it about this place, which makes it different from other English villages? The answer must be found in the lives and history of the people and families who have made their lives here over the centuries and their interactions with one another.

While the main emphasis of the History falls on the late nineteenth century and the whole of the twentieth century, both because this relatively recent period is best remembered and also because it is the time of Guarlford's life as a village which is most likely to be of interest to our readers, it is no less important to trace, as far as possible, the earlier history of the settlement, so that there is a more complete picture of the slow evolution over the centuries to the Guarlford we know today. The History therefore looks at the earliest traces of this place in the archaeological record, then goes on to the medieval records of the village as far as they exist, to the rise and fall of Baldenhall, and to the evolution of the place and place name which finally became 'Guarlford'. As time passes, the historical record becomes progressively fuller and maps, in particular, help in providing a framework for establishing the patterns of ownership and settlement, the Foley Estate map of 1744 being one important example. Certain features and buildings give shape to the local landscape, most prominently Guarlford Court, while national events such as the seventeenth century's Civil War at least came near to the village and left some mark, albeit small.

In his book, *Rural Life in Victorian England*, G. E. Mingay says: "In the nineteenth century the English countryside saw more rapid and remarkable changes than had been wrought in perhaps all the preceding centuries."(p.9) Guarlford, however, was not very directly affected by the industrialisation which so transformed the physical and social landscape in other parts of England, and the county of Worcestershire remained predominantly agricultural; but forces of change were at work that would culminate eventually in the first of the World Wars, an industrialised war, causing casualties even in this quiet corner of the country. Life in nineteenth-century Guarlford, then, was the last long phase of relative stability, before the following century's upheavals and, arguably, the biggest watershed of all, the Second World War, after which the old ways, certainties, and close-knit community life were never the same again. It had been a community which had its prominent families and major landowners, such as the Foleys, whose property embraced so much of Malvern, and it had been a community defined to a considerable extent by the local farms, farm owners, workers and families. One of the oldest farms, for instance, and one whose history is quite fully documented, is Woodbridge Farm, purchased by the Lane family in 1775 and in their ownership until very recently, when all but a few acres were sold. Other farms such as Fowler's, Dripshill, Grove House, New House and Little Clevelode provide the backdrop against which Guarlford families lived and worked. Life and work were hard, wages were meagre, and expectations modest; but, in common with all their fellow countrymen and women throughout England, those who spent the whole of their lives here and who rarely ventured beyond the confines of the village also had their pleasures and community-based pastimes, not knowing or owning the motor cars and television sets which today open up a much wider world. The church of St Mary the Virgin and the chapels gave, with the Christian calendar, a structure and a meaning to life for which many in the present might experience a kind of nostalgia, a longing for a spiritual home in a predominantly secular age; the village school gave its children the security of having the essential knowledge and skills needed in later working life. Both in the case of the church and the school there was a source of continuity in village life, a continuity also provided, in particular, by the long incumbency of two Rectors of the parish, John Bateman Wathen, Rector for forty-eight years, and Frederick John Newson, Rector for fifty years.

Guarlford Churchyard, 1917 and 2003

Village life in the nineteenth and twentieth centuries is generally well documented, and from the turn of the nineteenth century onwards there is an increasingly rich harvest of photographs that has been gathered to provide a vivid visual account of the changing scene, a generally tidy and orderly-looking one in various settings outside homes and farms, with the people in photographs taking an obvious pride in their appearance. Shops, businesses, clubs and societies all add to the texture and tapestry of Guarlford life, together with times of entertainment such as fetes and whist drives;

and so, too, do moments of drama and tragedy such as the moving photograph of the burial of one of the Panting brothers, brought back to Guarlford for a military funeral, and that of the RAF Beaufighter which crashed in Guarlford in the Second World War. Moreover, since 1894, there are the minutes of the Parish Council to give another narrative of local events and concerns, with the Women's Institute also providing a further perspective through its records.

The last twenty-five years have not seen great changes in themselves, rather they have seen the consolidation of the changes that had already taken place. With the exception of the Men's Club during this period, a meeting place that had been housed in part of the former Malt House, the physical appearance as well as the general character of Guarlford have changed comparatively little. Community life, though inevitably and sadly not as vigorous as in the past, continues, another part of the Malt House, the Village Hall, providing the parish with an invaluable meeting place for Harvest Festivals and other occasions. The Rectory field is still the setting for the annual fete, while Cherry Orchard has seen recent Millennium and Golden Jubilee celebrations. Pride in the appearance of the village was recognised by a Worcestershire County Council award in 2002 for a restoration of the pond in the village centre, a centre, which had been a gathering point for the young for many years.

Those who live in Guarlford today, like the inhabitants of ancient settlements the length and breadth of the country, walk where countless generations have walked before. Lives that were rich and fully lived, though often beset by hardship, have left little, if any, trace; but perhaps with the help of this brief history and some small effort of imagination we can at least see some of the ghosts of the past, rather in the way that the evocative montage of the Panting funeral reproduced here restores the presence of the people who mourned the soldier's passing, though we, for our part, should *celebrate ALL our predecessors* as we recall a world we have otherwise lost.

Chapter 1

Guarlford's Beginnings

Earliest Times

The story of Guarlford begins when, in Neolithic times, the nearby River Severn was first used as a trade route through the wet lowlands to the east of the Malvern Hills. Rivers such as the Severn provided a way of penetrating the barriers of marsh and woodland for an ancient people who have left little trace of their presence in the area other than a few scattered flint remains, such as a flint axe of Scandinavian origin found at Colwall on the other side of the hills. However, writing in the *Malvern News* in December 1963, 'Coriander' observes that Guarlford "…may be the newest parish in the district, but it is also one of the oldest inhabited places. The Anglo-Saxon tribe of the Hwicce who came up the Severn cleared land between the Rhydd and Poolbrook and had a settlement at the foot of the hills. Before them, some authorities believe ancient Celtic chiefs had a dwelling where Guarlford Court now stands and earlier still there were people who fortified Dripshill during the Iron Age. Their earthworks can be found in the woods that now cover the hill." Guarlford, then, has a history as long as almost any settlement in Britain, though it is still to this day a small village and one with limited documentary and other records.

Guarlford lies just beyond the shadow of the Malvern Hills, a little over a mile and a half from Barnards Green to the west and nearly two and a half miles from the foot of the Hills themselves. The dominant geological feature of the Hills, the Malvern Chase which runs down to the Severn at the Rhydd, and the proximity of the Priory Church have together had a shaping influence on Guarlford's story; and the history of the village cannot be recounted without reference to this physical and ecclesiastical landscape. It was the shape of the landscape around Guarlford, which determined the ancient salt way, the links from the Severn at the Rhydd and Clevelode crossings along what is now Rectory Lane to Wood Street and then to Wyche Cutting on the main salt route from Droitwich to South Wales. In July 2004, a hedgerow survey undertaken by Guarlford W.I. indicated that, according to Hooper's Rule, hedges along the boundary of Wood Street are in the region of eight hundred years old; and, in particular, a wild service tree in the hedgerow provides further evidence of great age, since the service tree (Sorbus torminalis) is perhaps lowland England's most reliable 'indicator species' of an ancient woodland or hedgerow habitat. (It should be acknowledged that Hooper's Rule is, of course, a theory and must therefore be treated with some caution.) The present Rectory Lane in Guarlford is part of this prehistoric and then Roman route from the river to the Wyche.

Hooper's Rule and the Wild Service Tree

Max Hooper was an ecologist working for the Institute of Terrestrial Ecology in the 1960s who suggested a strong correlation between the age of a hedge and the number of woody species found in it. 'Hooper's Rule' states that in thirty yards (27.4 metres) of hedge every species represents one century of age. Therefore, a hedge with eight species in thirty yards would be 800 years old.

The wild service tree resembles a maple in leaf shape and autumn colouring, but its leaves are alternate and are also similar in shape to a guelder rose or sycamore. The tree's ascending branches form a conical shape when it is young, but broaden into a spreading, domed head with maturity, growing up to 20 metres. Its bark is dark grey with broken shallow fissures.

The area around Guarlford has yielded evidence of Neolithic (2200-1800 B.C.) movement, and Early, Middle and Late Bronze Age settlement. Iron Age invaders followed, particularly the prominent La Tene culture from about 250 B.C. onwards. There are the defensive banks of an Iron Age hill fort still to be discerned at Dripshill. These earthworks possibly represent the earliest substantial evidence in the local landscape of a settlement which lasted for some time, in this case between 800 B.C. and 42 A.D., the breadth of time meaning that no more precise date can be established on the basis of the available evidence.

There are very few other archaeological remains from these early centuries associated with Guarlford; but some cropmark enclosures have been discovered south-west of present-day Grove House Farm which have been dated within a wide period of time from 2350 B.C. to 409 A.D. Cropmarks provide evidence of the layout of settlements within areas of land under arable cultivation. Some Romano-British coins have been found north-east of the church, dated 43-409 A.D., while some earlier Roman pottery shards were found at Portocks End Farm. Other archaeological finds have been predominantly Medieval, with a few from the Modern period from about 1600 A.D. onwards.

Until about 6,500 years ago, hunter-gatherers moved though the woodland environment of what was to become Worcestershire. Clearance for the growing of crops then began in what is known as the Neolithic period. This Neolithic or New Stone Age gave way to the Early Bronze Age about 4,000 years ago, as more open landscapes and more permanent settlements occurred, as well as hillforts on such vantage points as the Malverns. Gradually, from the Late Iron Age of about 2,100 years ago onwards, more tangible archaeological evidence, such as metal coins and pottery remains, help to identify settlements and the way of life associated with them. In the Romano-British period of the first- to the fifth-century A.D., Roman rule brought with it a culture that left more material evidence of its presence, together with traces on the landscape of small farms, tracks and roads, as well as a few nucleated settlements. Overall, the record is relatively sparse in the county, and there are, in particular, little more than a few hints of our Guarlford predecessors during these long centuries. It is the Anglo-Saxon tribe of the Hwicce, coming after the Romans and creating a settlement between the Rhydd and Poolbrook, who begin the history of continuous occupation of the tract of land between the river and the Malvern Hills where today's Guarlford is situated.

Perhaps the clearest way in which the imprint of permanent settlement is put upon a landscape is through naming it, as, for example, the field which became Guarlford's neighbouring village of Madresfield. The origin of Guarlford as a name is less easy to trace, although one of two fords (the first at the bottom of Wood Street and the other by the present War Memorial) must account for part of its derivation. Perhaps a pre-Roman tribal leader known as Gaerla stayed long enough here to leave his permanent mark unknowingly on the Worcestershire landscape – the name Guarlford. Of Gaerla himself there is no record. The site of Guarlford Court might even be the more precise spot where his tribe made their home, and it is worth noting its close proximity to the ford by the Memorial. Joan Bradshaw has noted that the spelling of the village name changes through the centuries before it became the spelling we know today:

1275	Garford	Lay Subsidy Rolls
1333	Gerleford	Lay Subsidy Rolls
1535	Garleford	Valor Ecclesiasticus
1820	Galvert	Map of Worcestershire
1830	Galfords	Ordnance Survey

Of course, it is not particularly remarkable that the spelling of the place name varies so much, given also that the standardisation of English spelling as a whole did not occur until the eighteenth-century. Perhaps the most curious detail and a somewhat baffling addition is the letter which gives strangers especially the most difficulty today, the intrusive 'u'. In 1981, the Guarlford Parish Council consulted appropriate authorities to try to establish the more precise origin of the village name as we have it today, but without success.

Medieval Lost Village

It is the neighbouring settlement of Baldenhall that first gives clear definition to this corner of Worcestershire. The name seems to emerge from the hall or house of the 'balg-dun', or bare hill, thus echoing the Celtic 'moel-bryn', today's Malvern, the Saxon settlers appearing to follow their predecessors in paying a kind of tribute to the physical feature which so dominates the immediate surrounding area. There are, though, other theories about the origin of 'Baldenhall': one is that it derives from the Anglo-Saxon god, Baldur, another that it comes from 'Bealda's rycg', a tract of land mentioned in a tenth-century charter. For several centuries, the manor of Baldenhall, as it became, and 'Balden' recur as names in the documentary records of the Medieval period and even on into the sixteenth-century. Moreover, as Brian Smith records, as late as 1836, Barnards Green House was referred to as Balders Green. 'Coriander' says in the article already quoted, "Coming down to historical times Sherrard's Green, Hall Green, Barnard's Green and Guarlford probably mark the bounds of the lost Manor of Baldenhall..."; and he goes on to say, "Edward the Confessor gave the Priory of Great Malvern a 'Virgate of land' in Baldenhall, and it is mentioned in the *Domesday Survey* (1086) '2 Villeons at Baldenhall render to the Manor of Hanley 2 ounces of silver pennies' ". In 1192, a Walter de Baldenhall was mentioned in tax rolls as Lord of the Manor. Then, in Elizabeth I's reign, Baldenhall was still an important place; the court for the manor of Malvern was held here, and as late as 1596 Malvern appears as "part of the vill of Baldenhall belonging to The Priory". Thus, the stretch of land so familiar to us today between Poolbrook Common and the long, straight road that continues until the church corner was the manor of Baldenhall, the extent of the manor having shrunk to this with the growth of Great Malvern. After the dissolution of the monasteries, with the sale of ecclesiastical estates to a variety of persons, it was lost as an entity and Baldenhall almost disappears from official records, though in deeds of 1732 and 1771 the lane from Woodbridge Farm led "northwards to Baldenhall green". When, in 1866, Guarlford became an ecclesiastical parish in its own right, its boundaries extended westwards to include most of the area which was once Baldenhall village. The only direct trace now of Baldenhall as a name is the small area called Hall Green. Smith says, Hall Green "...was the real centre of both manor and hamlet, and even today numerous tracks and paths cross the fields and strips of waste around which a few timber-framed cottages stand." As a kind of aside to the direct line of the name's descent, a new estate was developed in the 1990s, a little west of Hall Green on what had been a Post Office telephones depot, and it was given the name of Baldenhall.

Baldenhall, then, is a deserted Medieval village, its place taken today by Barnard's Green (with a boundary at first lower down the Guarlford straight than at present) by Hall Green, and by Guarlford. The most significant feature, other than the scattering

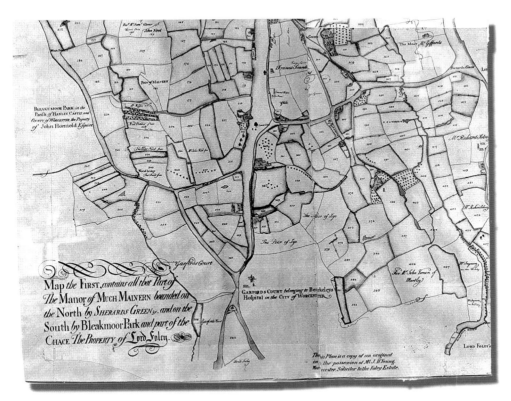

Figure 1.1 Copy of a map dated 1744 showing part of the Manor of Much Malvern.

of cottages, was the small church dedicated to St. Leonard, the first recorded mention of which occurs in 1217, although it would have been constructed some time earlier. It survived until about 1560 when, according to Smith, it was demolished by Gowen Nycolls who was renting the churchyard. The chapel, of which no physical trace remains today, stood where now there is a house in Hall Green called Guarlford Lodge.

Baldenhall appears to have been one of an estimated 2,000 lost or deserted villages that have been recorded, most of them in the Midland counties and eastern England. These were settlements which once existed, but which were subsequently deserted by human populations for a variety of reasons, including the Black Death of the fourteenth-century. Enclosures were the most significant single cause of villages being deserted, a process which continued intermittently from as early as the twelfth- and thirteenth-centuries with the Cistercian enclosures, through the dismantling of the feudal system in Tudor and Elizabethan times, to the setting up of large estates in the eighteenth-century and on until the middle of the nineteenth-century.

Guarlford has a number of ponds, but the remains of those around Hall Green probably indicate the sources of clay for wattle and daub used in the construction of the Medieval village's cottages. The most prominent of these was known as the Fladder, a pond which was just across the road from Friars Elm (also known as 'Old Elm'), a tree which was another landmark on the present-day 'Guarlford straight' until the removal of protective railings in the last war and its subsequent disappearance after surviving since the early sixteenth century. Of the cottages, Joan Bradshaw says in her study, *An Account of the Origins of Baldenhall and Guarlford,* "Within living memory seventeen of these were scattered around the Green but now no traces remain, most of them being mainly replaced by modern houses, the rest completely gone." In the vicinity of Jessamine Cottage, too, there stood a tithe barn, recorded as being used for distribution of bread to the poor on into the eighteenth-century.

Priory and Chase

The Medieval history of what was to become Guarlford is inextricably bound up with the history of Malvern Priory and Malvern Chase, while Church and State themselves, of course, were bound together much more closely during this period than they were to be in subsequent modern history. In his *History of Malvern,* Brian Smith states, "At the Norman Conquest only one dwelling was recorded at Baldenhall, and it was during the twelfth-century that the priory cleared and colonized the lands that had been given by the abbey of Westminster." He goes on to say, "…many local place names, like Guarlford, Sherrard's Green and Poolbrook, which first appear in thirteenth-century records, were probably current a full century earlier."(p.84). Agricultural expansion meant that by the end of the thirteenth-century Malvern Priory ownership included 360 acres of arable land in what is now Guarlford, along with the Priory's other large holdings in the district. The landscape of Guarlford still bears some marks of Medieval farming, including ridge and furrow systems south of Grange Farm and south-east of Cherry Orchard Farm. As well as farming, woodland craftsmen such as potters, brickmakers, tanners, glovers and charcoal burners carried on their occupations in the vicinity of the Priory.

The dissolution of the monasteries by Henry VIII, the first Act to set this process in motion being passed in 1536, brought about the sale of ecclesiastical estates including those belonging to Malvern Priory. Guarlford's most significant and substantial surviving building from the Medieval period is Guarlford Court, and of course, as has been suggested, the site was occupied much earlier. The Court was a grange of Malvern Priory and was specifically named as Priory estate in 1291. It is not known whether Richard Cave, who was in possession of this demesne manor at the dissolution, was tenant or bailiff, but the property was valued at £9.1.0 (£9.05) per annum. The Court was surrounded by a large fish pond or moat, part of which remains as a prominent feature of the property to this day; it seems likely that it was more fish pond than moat, since such ponds were a common feature of Medieval monastic buildings and granges. One of the consequences of the dissolution was that new landlords such as those who acquired the Court sought to curtail peasant farmers' rights to stock grazing on fields which had been largely enclosed in the Tudor period - a process which continued on into the seventeenth-century. This led to protracted disputes and some violence. The history of the Court and its changes of ownership is a long one and might provide material for a separate account, but in outline it is the story of a house that grew organically over the years and played quite a shaping part in the village's history. It is recorded that in 1609, when the then owner Richard Wheeler died, the house contained a hall, five bedrooms, a study, a parlour, kitchen, buttery and little buttery, dairy and cider houses, brewhouse and stables. There was also a dovecote – not to be confused with the pigeon house which was built in the eighteenth-century. The Court's estates, reaching as far as the Severn, embraced Great and Little Heriots, Earlsmore, Easthall, Dripshill, Rednall, and Troughridge, the last of which still has Medieval ridge and furrow traces as well as being the location of the mysterious death of a stranger found killed here in 1576.

Figure 1.2 Guarlford Court, c.1930.

One of the most interesting features of Guarlford Court and a direct link with the Priory is the use of decorative tiles, some of which were found under the floor during renovations some years ago. It is another sign of the importance and relative wealth of the Court's Medieval owners that tiles were used for decoration and would probably have shared this function with other contemporary expressions of wealth and status such as wall hangings, paintings and coats of arms, which have not of course survived. The tiles are of the traditional two-colour design, glazed, and with brown and yellow colour variation of the kind to be clearly seen in the Priory's extensive display. As the Sites and Monuments Officer (Records), Hilary White, of the County Archaeology Service in Worcester wrote to Mrs Toby Bruce-Morgan of Guarlford Court, in a letter of 1992, quoted in Joan Bradshaw's notes, "…it is likely that the Guarlford Court tiles, with their characteristic designs mixing royal, religious and architectural features, were left over from the mid-fifteenth century manufacture for the Priory buildings."

Between the Priory and Guarlford, land which had been part of one large estate cultivated by tenant and yeoman farmers underwent a great change in the sixteenth century, the dissolution bringing about a transition from leasehold to copyholding as established

Figure 1.3 A Malvern Priory Tile, c.1480.

families became more prominent in their identification with particular tracts of land. Descendants of John le Baxter, whose name occurs in the early fourteenth century, are amongst these; and the Baxters had land holdings in Guarlford, amongst other places, after the dissolution. Another Guarlford name, which occurs in sixteenth century records, is that of John Badger who, rather unusually for the time, had a large flock of twenty-two sheep and forty-six lambs. Most of his neighbours would have had cattle and some swine, together with perhaps some crops such as wheat and mancorn (usually a mixture of rye and wheat). A large part of the local countryside remained uncultivated at this time. The Chase provided some common land for grazing. Brian Smith says, however, that "…by mid-Tudor times arable land and meadows in Guarlford and Baldenhall were enclosed and held severally," but "…during the late autumn after harvest they were thrown open to common pasture, and other lands and riverside near Dripshill were common from harvest time until Candlemas in February, a valuable privilege for the peasant farmer wanting to keep his stock through the winter."(p.142). However, John Badger of Guarlford opposed these rights in Edward VI's reign, 1547-1553; this lessee of Guarlford manor died a year after the king, leaving livestock and grain worth £20.0.0. Enclosure continued, as did disafforestation, in the seventeenth century, the Malvern landscape steadily evolving to what we see today. Cottage plots, though, were claimed by poorer commoners along the Guarlford Road, for example; the royal Chase not being sufficiently strong or interested to assert itself or counter these. Of course, in the seventeenth-century, too, the English Civil War came very close to Guarlford - evidence of which perhaps is the canon ball found in the garden of Yew Tree Cottage in Chance Lane – and both the Rhydd and Madresfield were touched by the conflict as it moved to and fro across Worcestershire. However, Guarlford itself does not appear to have been affected directly, though perhaps some of the inhabitants of the village were amongst those who took advantage of the instability caused by the war to try to destroy enclosures and regain commoners' rights.

A Landscape of Farms, 1775-1914

It was during the eighteenth and, more especially, the nineteenth-century that the landscape in and around Guarlford took on the shape that we still largely know and recognise today. Fields and farms were defined, and certain local farming families became prominent owners, some names continuing on into this twenty-first century. Farms and farming are, of course, at the heart of Guarlford's history, and the next chapter will explore this much more fully, but two developments might be made an exception at this point: the assignment of land to John Lane in 1775 and the impact on Guarlford life of the large Foley Estate. The *Indenture* still in the possession of the Lane family represents a significant step in the progress towards the pattern of farms and their ownership that we know today, well over two centuries later, albeit the document itself is couched in somewhat opaque legal language. The purchase was from "Christopher Whiting of the parish of Hanley Castle in the County of Worcester Yeoman of the one part and John Lane of the parish of Great Malvern in the said County husbandman of the other part Witnesseth that the said Christopher Whiting in Consideration of the Sum of One hundred and seventy Pounds of lawful money of Great Britain…" purchased "…one parcel of arable Land or Orcharding containing by Estimation about four Acres be the same more or less Also all that piece or Parcel of Meadow Ground containing by Estimation about one Acre and half be the same more or less the whole being called or known by the name of Great Woodbridge having a Lane leading from a certain Green called Baldenhall Green towards Blackmore park on the East or Easterly part thereof and a small Brook on the South part thereof…" Other land included in the sale were one acre "now in Tillage" and about half an acre, now pasture, "known by the name of little Woodbridge…". The land thus assigned remained in the possession of the Lane family until the late twentieth century.

> ### Marie Hall and Ralph Vaughan-Williams
>
> *There are few if any pieces of music more evocative of the English countryside and its beauty than 'The Lark Ascending' by Vaughan-Williams. The work was dedicated to Marie Hall who became an internationally famous violinist after living for a few years of her childhood in the 1880s in a small cottage on the Rhydd Road now part of a larger house called 'Maywood'. Having played her violin for pennies in Church Street, Gt. Malvern, as a young girl, she later became a pupil of both Elgar and the eminent Czech violinist, Jan Kubelik. 'The Lark Ascending' was performed by Marie in 1921 with Adrian Boult and the British Symphony Orchestra.*

A particular feature of Woodbridge Farm, which crosses four centuries, is that it has what is believed to be a sixteenth-century water meadows system. The water level in the Pool Brook was deliberately raised by a 'stank', a construction akin to a dam; a series of furrows would then carry water across the land to be irrigated. Edwin Lane, the last member of the Lane family to own the farm, operated the system in the past, and remembers that some original old sluices were still visible in the twentieth century in fields along the Guarlford Road, with another at the back of the farmhouse. Such irrigation systems are believed to be relatively uncommon in this part of the country but more numerous in East Anglia. Woodbridge Farm was, of course, only one of a number of farms in the district, which were well established by 1800. New House Farm, for instance was built by the Foleys in the 1700s; and there was also Dripshill Farm, built as the Home Farm to Dripshill House in the 1750s. It is important to note here that the dominant feature of land ownership in Guarlford and the surrounding area in the nineteenth century and early twentieth century was the pervasive presence of three very large estates: the Foleys' Malvern Estate, Earl Beauchamp's Madresfield Estate and the Hornyold Blackmore Estate; these estates had taken over, in effect, the dominance in earlier centuries of the Royal Chase and of the Priory.

The Eve of War and Change

A revealing surviving document from the early twentieth century is Madresfield Agricultural Club's *Quarterly* of January 1914. The president at the time was Earl Beauchamp, whose address to the 22nd Annual Meeting is recorded in the *Quarterly*. His evidently commanding role gives perhaps one small insight into the old order in the British countryside at the end of the nineteenth century and the beginning of the twentieth, and, not least, the deference with which an Earl was treated. Looked at from another perspective and with the benefit of hindsight, we can now see that – on the eve of the First World War – an upheaval was imminent which would set in train events that would irrevocably re-shape both society and the landscape itself over the next fifty years. There is, too, a certain poignancy in the fact that this same *Quarterly* has a fascinating article, "A Visit to the South of Germany", by A. Slater, a Madresfield member of the English Arboricultural Society who was one of a ninety strong party which made an extensive tour of Germany in September, 1913, less than a year before the outbreak of the First World War. It is an enthusiastic report, praising German hospitality and acknowledging the assistance given in making arrangements for the visit by the Society's President, Sir William Schlish, "who, although a German born gentleman, has rendered many great services to this country... and is now the Professor of Forestry at Oxford University".

What is most striking perhaps about this *Madresfield Quarterly* of 1914 is the breadth and depth of local agricultural life which it records in Madresfield and the wider area, including Guarlford. It is an invaluable document detailing committee proceedings and competition results, as well as the weather in 1913 and its effect on the farming year and crops produced. A Guarlford farmer, Mr Stephen George Medcalf, was one of the leading figures in the Club. Born in 1862, " Mr Medcalf has held, and still holds, many public appointments...", as it says in a profile of him in the *Quarterly*. There is also an impressive portrait photograph of Mr Medcalf on a front page facing a list of the 1914 Club officers. The *Quarterly* vividly reflects a richly-textured and intricately-structured world of farming and associated activity, the culmination of centuries of steady evolution. At the same time, it can be seen now as a kind of peak moment that was to be followed by two successive World Wars and a gradual lessening through the twentieth century in farming's diversity, richness and pre-eminent importance in Guarlford life.

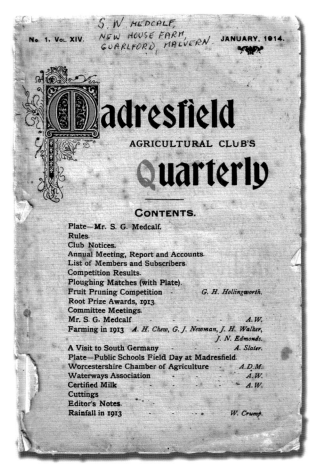

Figure 1.4 Cover of the Madresfield Quarterly.

Guarlford's history should be seen in the wider context of rural history: whatever the variations of farming, rural life, and the landscape itself across England, there was much common ground; and, as George Ewart Evans argues in *Ask the Fellows who Cut the Hay*, country people in the middle of the last century still belonged to a tradition that extended back in an unbroken line at least to the early Middle Ages. Notwithstanding progressive changes in farming and improvements in farming methods over the centuries, those who worked on the land as late as the 1940s and into the 1950s would have shared a great deal of the experience and outlook of their predecessors over many earlier centuries – a kind of common language. It is notable, of course, that the culture to which Evans refers was transmitted orally for most of this long period of time. Thus it seems appropriate that much of the work for this book, even though undertaken some fifty years after the great changes in agriculture hastened by the Second World War, has been based on memory and the oral recollection of older residents, not on written records. The long oral tradition itself lost ground gradually as universal education and literacy developed in the nineteenth and twentieth centuries; but it was two World Wars and the internal combustion engine, which together disrupted forever the continuity of rural life, a continuity that had been expressed, not least, in folk song and folk lore. The internal combustion engine came to the countryside in the form of the tractor, a powerful workhorse that, unlike the generations of horses that had laboured on farms over the centuries, never tired. Tractors were not at first universally popular as they took over the work of horses, and there were farm workers in this parish, too, whose attachment to their horses perhaps betokened a deeper attachment, a relationship to the land and a tradition of husbandry stretching back to the Middle Ages, if not earlier. So many other changes have also contributed to the decline and virtual loss of a once coherent, complete and largely self-contained rural way of life in the last fifty years, including the infinitely greater mobility that most people now enjoy, a mobility which would have been unimaginable to our not-so-distant ancestors. The high watermark of English and, more especially, of local Madresfield and Guarlford farming and a whole way of life based on it so vividly captured in the *Quarterly* of 1914 was to be followed, as we now know, by some four decades in which the rural tradition and old ways largely ebbed away.

Chapter 2

Farming

Introduction

Farming was the principal activity in Guarlford until recently, playing a vital part in most village residents' lives; and even if few people work on the land today, Guarlford remains a very rural community. Everyone who lives in and around the village is within a stone's throw of farmland, and cannot fail to be aware of the sights, sounds and smells of stock, the noise and bustle of farm machinery, and the cycle of growing crops. Moreover, growing leisure time means that, although few people work on the land, more are able to enjoy walking on the many public footpaths over farmland.

Despite enormous change in the farming industry, Guarlford is fortunate to have farming families who have lived and worked their farms for long years, and in some cases hundreds of years. Their memories are a rich resource, for their farms were central to the lives of so many; the farms, which we know today, were born out of a long and fascinating history. This chapter explores life on the farms, looking at the stock, the crops that were grown, the farming methods and the people involved; it reflects some of the hardships and joys of rural life over the last two hundred years.

It starts by taking a look at farming before living memory, and at the many events, which led to a changing landscape over the centuries to create our farms and our countryside as they are today. This background to farming is provided in a table in Appendix 1,showing the main historical events to affect farming, set beside change or events locally. These events shaped the countryside, together with the distinctive culture of country people whose values and a sense of community derived from hardship. Developments in agriculture in Guarlford need to be seen in a wider national and, indeed, international context in order to be more fully understood; Appendix 1 provides such a context by outlining the chronology of change.

The 1840 – 1841 Tithe Maps

The area that is now Guarlford parish was covered by the tithe maps of Malvern and Madresfield, out of which parishes Guarlford was created. These tithe maps and apportionments show who farmed the land in 1840-41, all the field names, the land use in each field at that time and field sizes.

FARM OWNERS AND TENANTS FROM THE 1840-1841 TITHE MAPS			
FARM	TENANT	LANDOWNER	No.
Cherry Orchard	Walter Haynes	Richard Benbow	7
Dripshill	Robert Hart	Richard Greenaway (Dripshill Estate)	17
Fowler's	W and T Fowler	Beauchamp Estate	14
Grove House	George Hill	Foley Estate	6
	George Hill	Beauchamp Estate	
Guarlford Court	John Bullock	Foley Estate	8
	John Bullock	Berkeleys hospital	
	John Bullock	Poor of Leigh	
Heriots	James Bullock	Archibold Cameron	9
Little Clevelode	In hand	Beauchamp Estate	18
Little Heriots	In hand	John Allen	16
Mill	William Bullock	Foley Estate	1
Moat Court	William Taylor	Francis Gifford Dineley	2
New House	Thomas Need	Foley Estate	5
Rhydd	Henry Lakin	Richard Greenaway (Dripshill Estate)	13
Portocks End	Thomas Cowles	Beauchamp Estate	15
Priestfield	William Haynes	Richard Greenaway (Dripshill Estate)	12
Rose	Samuel Roe	Foley Estate	3
	In hand	Samuel Roe	
White House	John Blake	Richard Greenaway (Dripshill Estate)	11
Whiteacres	James Matthews	Beauchamp Estate	10
Woodbridge	George Lane	Foley Estate	4
	In hand	George Lane	

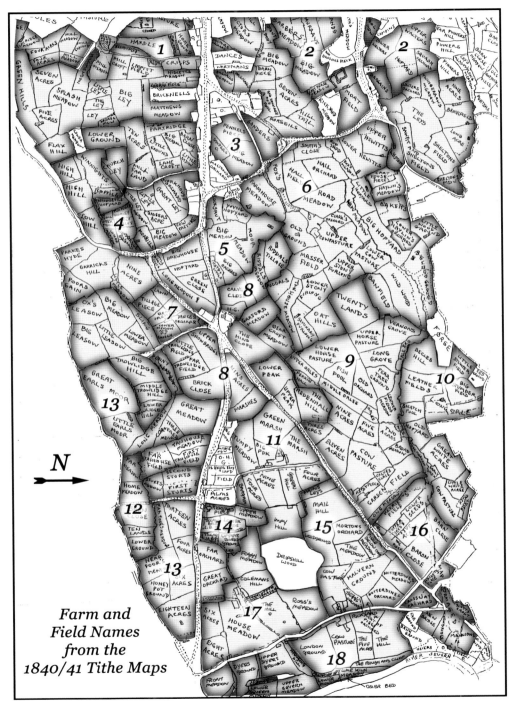

Figure 2.1 Extract from the Great Malvern and Madresfield Tithe Maps.

Old Maps: Historic Documents

Old maps provide an interesting insight into the past, showing old place names, field patterns, houses, farmsteads and some other features such as marl-pits and ponds. Marl-pits are a recurring feature on this area's old maps, and many remain today. These hollows were formed when marl, which is the local sub-soil, was excavated and spread on the land. Marl was a soil conditioner, which reduced soil acidity, and added nutrients. Stephen Friar, in *The Sutton Companion to Local History*, says "The practice of spreading marl and manure on fields is undoubtedly of prehistoric origin. Marl, a mixture of clay and lime, is known to have been used by the Romans to improve the fertility of acid soil and Saxon charters refer both to lampytts (loam-pits) and to marl-pits." (p.268)

During the reign of Edward VI (1547-1553), Guarlford Court was involved in litigation, when a peasant farmer opposed ongoing enclosure and the removal of his rights to graze some of the land in autumn. Joan Bradshaw refers to some transcribed notes from Star Chamber Proceedings at the time and to fields referred to as Reddenhyle, Harryett, Dryppshalle, Oxlesowe, Cowlesow, Yerlesmore, and Trowricg Meadow. One hundred years later, in the tithe apportionment, these field names persist: Redenhall Hill, Harriet's field, Dripshill, Ox's Leasow, Earls Moor and Trowlidge. Today many farmers still refer to their fields by very old names or similar names, which derived from them. As Flora Thompson says in her classic account of a village childhood, *Lark Rise*, "The field names gave the clue to the fields' history." (p.42)

It seems beyond coincidence that Robert Blake farmed in Blakes Lane (White House Farm in 1841), and Samuel Roe farmed at what became known as Rose Farm. In 1840, the tithe map and apportionment show that William Fowler farmed the land we now know as Fowler's Farm. The field at Grove House Farm called Vernon's Grove belonged to the Reverend John Vernon in the late 1700s, and Workhouse Orchard reminds us of the nearby workhouse which was at one time near the Chance Lane and Guarlford Road junction. Heriot's Farm is likely to have derived from the field name on the Malvern tithe map, Harriet's field. Many other old field names relate to the field use, such as 'Young Orchard', or provide a description of the field, such as a field size, 'Twenty Lands', its poor drainage, 'Marshes', or its trees, 'Orles' (alder trees). 'Tanhouse Meadow' and 'Clark's Meadow' relate to neighbouring property or occupants. But the origins of many field names remain a mystery, and many have changed along with tenants or ownership. Many names on the Foley Estate map of 1744 are not spelt as we spell them now: Sherards Green, Maddersfield, Tythe, Lye (Leigh), Bleakmore (Blackmore), Horniold (Hornyold), and Garford (Guarlford) itself. Place and field names change on maps through history, even after standardization of spelling in the eighteenth century.

Modern Ordnance Survey maps show the parish's public rights of way. Nearly every farm has a footpath or bridleway leading from the farm to the church or the public house, or paths to cottages where farm workers lived. Paths sometimes end abruptly, in the middle of nowhere, indicating the site of a former cottage. Where the path crosses a field, rather than following boundaries, it suggests that the field it crosses was a grass field. The public footpaths are a legacy from farming people who trod those paths, often to and from work six days a week, for many years; and they are integral to the history of this village as they are to so many others.

The Common Land

A strong characteristic of the Guarlford landscape is its common land, a visible consequence of its history, thanks to Kings, their sport and hunting laws, and, more recently, the protection afforded by the Malvern Hills Acts. Not so long ago, this common land, too, was farmed, and provided the opportunity for more people to farm livestock in a small way. Many of the local cottages, as well as farms, still have an allocation of common rights, although these rights are now largely unused. Older members of the community can remember when the commons in and around Guarlford were heavily over-grazed, such was the demand for grazing. Now the commons make little or no contribution to food production and have become a part of the local distinctiveness of the area; they are managed as an important public amenity, landscape feature, and reminder of the past. Food production is now generally limited to the farms of the parish, although many of them are less dependent on food production for a living than ever before. A look back over the centuries shows that life on these farms since the land was enclosed has never been far from set-backs and struggles, influenced by wars, economic instability, labour shortages, competition from abroad and surpluses. Farming has employed fewer and fewer people over the years, and average farm size has grown, especially in the last forty years.

Farms in the Parish

The tithe map and apportionments show the size of farms in the Guarlford area in the early 1840s. It is difficult to identify some of the original farms of that time, especially smallholdings that have long-since merged with their neighbours, and their farmhouses have disappeared; but this detailed record provides an interesting comparison with farm size today. In 1841, there were around twenty-five farms above the size of ten acres, all apparently managing to make a living off the land, although many incorporated a degree of direct selling of their produce. Today, there are eight main farms, and incorporation into neighbouring farms or diversification to other land uses account for the remainder.

Many farms shown on the tithe map were still there one hundred years later at the time of the Second World War, and were still employing very many people. Now the number of people fully employed on the land could almost be counted on two hands.

Cherry Orchard

Records show that in 1744 Cherry Orchard belonged to the Trustees of Berkeley Hospital, and was farmed by the Bullock family, along with Guarlford Court Farm. By 1841,

Figure 2.2 Cherry Orchard, early in the 20th century.

Cherry Orchard comprised twenty-six acres of orchard and pasture, and belonged to Richard Benbow. He had a tenant called Walter Haynes. Cherry Orchard has a ditch running parallel to Rectory Lane within the hedged boundary of the holding, which was said to have been dug by Lady Foley in order to make a distinct boundary between her neighbour's land and her own. Like many other houses in the village, Cherry Orchard was added to as the family prospered. The original Cherry Orchard Farm was a small timber-framed cottage built in the early eighteenth-century. A new house was built of brick adjacent to the cottage, with access from the original cottage through the first floor only. Further prosperity permitted the building of the new part with the present Regency front.

Penny Meadow

Land near Penny Meadow was developed to reduce the dependency of farm employees on their employers and lent its name to Penny Close, which was developed in the 1950s. Initially only two farm workers moved into the new houses: Bill Sims and Arthur Beauchamp. The remainder provided low cost housing by Upton-upon-Severn Rural District Council.

At the turn of the twentieth-century, Mr Robathan farmed Cherry Orchard. Cartloads of cherries were taken to the station for despatch to London and Birmingham markets. Before World War Two, a farmer was thrown from his horse and killed. During the 1930s depression, another farmer committed suicide in the barn. One of these disturbed spirits continued to haunt Cherry Orchard until laid to rest by the Reverend Hartley Brown in 1978. Mr George Price, whose wife was called Rose, owned the farm just after the Second World War; his grandson was born at Cherry Orchard and still lives locally. Mr Bill Watkins bought the farm from Mr Price in 1950, and he subsequently sold the house and five acres to Lucie Bartleet, Dr Peter Mayner's mother.

Clevelode Farm

Bill Sims worked at Clevelode Farm for fifty-five years and his memories of his working life were recorded in an article in *The Grapevine*, No.137, December 1993. The article records that Bill was born at Paddock Cottage, one of the two-bedroomed thatched cottages, which stood where Ricolet

Figure 2.3 Dick Bullock, who worked for Mr Robathan at Cherry Orchard, taking Cherries to Market.

now stands, opposite what is now A J Gammond's yard. Bill and his three sisters went to Guarlford School. His father, William Sims, worked at Home Farm, Madresfield, along with at least twelve other men, before leaving to work on the forestry side of the Madresfield Estate in 1915. In 1920, Bill left school, aged fourteen, and went to work for the estate at Clevelode Farm. In 1938, Bill married Vi Bullock and moved to the home of Vi's parents, Guarlford Stores. Vi continued to manage the shop until some time after the Second World War.

Mr Humphries was Bailiff and lived in the farmhouse when Bill started work at Whiteacres. The farm was a mixed farm, with Dairy Shorthorn cows, which Bill milked, as well as sheep and pigs. Bill took the morning's milk to the railway station in Malvern by horse and float to travel by train to Birmingham. He also took the milk to the Tuberculosis Hospital in West Malvern: the milk was the first in the area to be classified as 'Grade A', which meant it was TB-free.

After working under Mr Humphries for fourteen years, Bill worked for nearly two years under Bailiff Eric Duncan, who worked for Hugh Lygon; and then, after Hugh Lygon's untimely death, for the first tenant, Sir William Wiggin. Lady Wiggin continued the farm after her husband's death, when the farm passed to Jerry Wiggin until he gave up the tenancy in 1981, and Bill Sims retired. The next tenant was 'Velcourt' and the farm was run by Mr and Mrs Anderson. The farm was then amalgamated with Falconer's Farm, tenanted by Mr Jim Nugent. The Clevelode Farm and Whiteacres Farm tenancies were taken, along with Falconers Farm, by Simon Micklethwait when Jim Nugent died in 1988.

Dripshill Farm

This farm was built as the Home Farm to Dripshill House in the 1750s. It was owned by Sir Charles Trubshaw Withers, and then, by 1840, by Robert Blayney, who was his son-in-law. Malvern tithe awards tell us that Blayney let 137 acres to Henry Lakin, thirty-two acres to Robert Hart, and fifty-nine acres at White House Farm to John Blake. Edward Corbett wrote in his regular column for the *Worcester Herald* in the 1920s, "I found the Blayneys still at Dripshill in mid-Victorian times. They had continued to be of the class with whom we have so often come in touch, hereditary landowners with professional occupations and holding local public appointments. They seem to have sold Dripshill towards the close of the last century (1800s); and it is now held by Commander F J Ratcliff, R.N."

> ### Local Families
>
> *Bernard Attwood's brother, John Attwood, lived at Kennel Cottage in Sink Farm Lane. He was the round rick builder and thatcher: his skills were employed on many local farms. His daughter Muriel married Alan Webb, who farmed Portocks End Farm. Muriel's niece, Irene Attwood, married Philip Cooke, whose father farmed Whiteacres Farm.*

We know that Dripshill House and Dripshill Farm were owned for a time by the Madresfield Estate. H W Whatley purchased Dripshill House for £2,100 in the Madresfield Estate sale of 1919. Gerald Radcliffe was the owner until around 1925, when he sold to Commander Francis James Ratcliff. The next owner, Major Monty Smyth, also owned Dripshill Farm. His foreman lived in the farmhouse, and the farm had a dairy herd of Jersey cows.

Mr Jimmy Hunt bought Dripshill Farm from the Madresfield Estate in the 1919 sale for £2,400. Mrs Hunt was recorded as the tenant at that time and the farm had eighty-six acres of land. By the 1940s, Bernard Attwood and his sister farmed Dripshill Farm. Bernard Attwood was regarded as a very good farmer, with fine working horses. Edward Jenkins, who has worked all his adult life on farms in the parish (born 1927), remembers that Bernard never altered his clocks in spring and autumn, a practice which was not unknown amongst old-fashioned countrymen. Rod Vivian was their cowman.

Major Smyth gave Dripshill Farm to his daughter, who sold the farm to Arthur Burford and his son, Richard, in 1969. Major Monty Smyth continued to live in Dripshill House for some years after. Richard Burford and his father had a milking herd until the early 1990s; now Richard has a suckler herd and sheep as well as offering Bed and Breakfast.

Falconers Farm and Pixham Farm

During the Second World War, the Nugent brothers, Tom, Jim and Patrick farmed Pixham and Falconers Farms, where eleven men were employed. Each farm had twenty to thirty hand-milked Ayrshires whose milk was cooled and put into churns and taken in the Nugent's own lorry to Bennetts Dairies. They also grew sugar beet and potatoes on land on the Teme at Lower Wick. Tom also worked for Gascoigne's in Worcester, where hops were traded. Hop kilns are among outbuildings at Falconers Farm today, indicating, of course, that the farm once grew hops. Dairy production continued at Falconers Farm until the late 1960s, when the herd was sold and Pat moved to farm at Lower Woodsfield Farm in Jennet Tree Lane. Jim continued to farm Falconers, which was then amalgamated with Clevelode Farm, until his death. In 1988, Simon Micklethwait took the tenancy and extended the farm acreage within and beyond the parish.

Fowler's Farm

At the time of Madresfield Estate sale in 1919, H Y Bladder was tenant of Dripshill Wood. Sale records show that H Bladder was a tenant of a cottage and osier bed at Clevelode. This may or may not have been a relative of Henry Bladder, tenant of Dripshill Wood. Henry Y Bladder had moved from Lower Skilts, near Studley, and became a tenant of Fowler's Farm in the 1800s and then purchased the farm from the Madresfield Estate in 1912.

After the death of Henry Y Bladder, his twin sons, Humphrey and Harry, lived with their mother at Fowler's Farm until Humphrey moved to a bungalow at their other farm, Portocks End. Portocks End was sold in 1994, and Fowler's Farm is home to Humphrey and his son, Daniel, who carry out contracting for other farmers in the neighbourhood.

The Bladders had a pedigree flock of Oxford sheep, which they took to shows, along with horses. They had an excellent Shire stallion, called Dripshill Forest King. In 1935, the groom, Rod Vivian (who later became cowman at Dripshill Farm), would take the stallion around the county each week, calling at Cotheridge, Wichenford, Droitwich, Doverdale, Hampton Lovet, Salwarp, Porters Mill, Claines, Hawford, Hadley and Hallow. Horse and groom would spend each night of the journey on a farm where the stallion visited mares. There was another stallion standing at Fowler's Farm, called Dripshill Bob.

1939   SEASON   1939

Dripshill Forest King
41392

The Property of H. C. BLADDER,
FOWLERS FARM, GUARLFORD, MALVERN

J H Wood, Stud Card Printer, Penistone, Yorks   18339

There was a Shorthorn dairy herd at Fowler's Farm, and at one time there was a milk round; eventually their milk was collected by Tilt's who had a dairy herd and milk round at Hanley castle. For a while, the cows regularly grazed the common near the farm, along

Figure 2.4 Card advertising Dripshill Forest King, stallion at stud at Fowler's Farm, 1939.

with sheep and pigs. Dairy farming continued until 1994.

Grange Farm

Victor Bradshaw bought some land and built the Grange opposite Guarlford Court where later his daughter, Joan Bradshaw, and her friend, Joan Newell, decided to settle and farm in about 1950. Each was caring for ageing parents at that time. They milked largely Ayrshire cows, using buckets and a suction line, gradually increasing the size of the herd to twenty-five cows and followers. They also lambed around fifty ewes and had horses, some of which were at livery. In the 1960s, they bought in and reared around seventy Friesian barley beef calves. The milk was collected by Mr Ford, who had a float and delivery round, and later Mr Tilt picked up the milk for his round. The stand where the churns were picked up stood where the Village Hall sign is now. Grange Farm had thirty acres, with some additional land rented, and Joan and Joan employed Nita Panting. Although the work was hard, the times were happy ones, and the two Joans remember that neighbours were always ready to help each other when it came to jobs such as shearing, which required many hands. In 1973, after the farm buildings had been used for stabling horses for a time, the two Joans opened Grange Farm Nursery and employed, as a young girl, Carol Nicholls who now owns the business.

> **The Vivian Family**
>
> *The Bladders' groom was Rod Vivian. Rod's family lived in the cottage on Blakes Lane near the Plough and Harrow, which they had purchased from Madresfield Estate in 1919.*
>
> *Rod Vivian's grandson, Tom, rebuilt the little cottage and lives there today.*

> **Woodland**
>
> *The tithe awards refer to an arable and pasture field at Grove House Farm, called Wild Wood. The name suggests it had at one time been woodland.*
>
> *The Madresfield Estate purchased the farm, and in 1914 Wild Wood was planted with woodland along with an adjacent field called Banfield, and the wood was called Cabinet. This name commemorates the Earl Beauchamp's appointment to the Cabinet at Westminster. Other woods planted on the Madresfield Estate were similarly named after notable events or occasions associated with the Beauchamp family.*

Grove House Farm

This farm belonged to the Foley Estate in 1841 and was 194 acres in size. The tenant at that time was George Hill, who also farmed forty-two acres on adjacent fields belonging to the Madresfield Estate. The farm had several hopyards, although no old hop kilns exist today; these must have been demolished. When the Foley Estate was sold in 1910, Grove House Farm, with 153 acres, and cottages, was purchased for £4,500 by the Madresfield Estate.

The grandparents of Charlie Williams's wife Doreen had worked at Grove House Farm many years ago, and they spoke of there being a tan house and another house at one time down 'Grove House Lane'. The 1744 map of the Foley Estate shows that Bromley

Green was situated on one of two drives from Chance Lane to Grove House, and there was a small community, or at least several buildings, down that drive. After the Second World War, Mr Wall was tenant, followed by Mr Hubert Bakewell, then his son, Bill, with two of his sons. The Bakewells left in the 1970s, and were followed by Fred and Helena Hawkins. Fred Hawkins farmed Grove House Farm for approximately fifteen years, and was the last dairy farmer on the farm, ceasing milk production in the early 1980s. In 1988, Michael and Helen Simpson took up the tenancy, and continued to extend their acreage by taking on additional land outside the parish.

Guarlford Court Farm

Guarlford Court Farm was specifically named as Priory estate in 1291, and continued as a 'demesne manor' for two and a half centuries. Joan Bradshaw, whose grandfather, Mr A Bradshaw, farmed there, records that before the Second World War, the Worcester Historical Society visited the house, which at one time was moated, and said that the beams in the kitchen were over 600 years old. Joan's research shows that, following the dissolution of the monasteries, it was leased for three years and then sold to William Pinnock in 1544. The following year, William Pinnock sold the farm to Francis Wheeler and his wife Ellen, and the farm passed down their family for a further 100 years.

Another reference to Guarlford Court in local archives occurs in an indenture in 1648, when Anthony Barnes makes provision for his wife Kathryn of the "Manor House and the appurtenances called or known by the name of Guarlford Court with the Dovehouse, Courtyarde, Backsides, gardens, orchards, houses, edifices and buildings thereto belonginge" and land of about 140 acres. According to Joan Bradshaw's research, a few years later the Court and demesne lands were the property of the Berkeleys of Spetchley, for when Robert Berkeley built his almshouses in the Foregate at Worcester this farm became part of the endowment of the Charity. In 1841, John Bullock was the tenant, farming 121 acres at Guarlford Court, and a further thirty-seven acres owned by the Poor of Leigh, a charity, and the Foley Estate. Over about 150 years, the Guarlford Court tenancy passed from father to son for several generations of the Bullock family until the farm was sold to the Madresfield Estate.

> **R H Smith**
>
> *Ron Smith came from a farming family at Berry Hill near Droitwich. His father was forced by ill health to take a smaller farm near Leigh Sinton, and soon after died, leaving Ron to support his mother and young sister and brother.*
>
> *After a spell as a farm pupil on a farm in Staffordshire, Ron went to work for Albert Jones in Leigh Sinton, where he managed a herd of pedigree Herefords, and then for the Bennett family, firstly at Lower Wick, and then as manager at Hayswood Farm, Madresfield, before taking his own tenancy at Guarlford Court Farm.*

Joan Bradshaw's grandfather, Absalom Bradshaw, took the tenancy in 1898. Absalom's son, O Victor Bradshaw, had married Florence before the First World War, and they were farming at White House Farm, where Joan and her brother were born. When Absalom retired, Victor Bradshaw moved to Guarlford Court to take on the farm.

Cottages in Clevelode Lane

When Edward Jenkins married Win in 1952, they moved to one of two thatched cottages in Clevelode Lane, near the Homestead. The adjacent cottage was lived in by Mr and Mrs Little. Mr Little worked at Guarlford Court Farm.

Joan Bradshaw remembers that these cottages did not face onto Clevelode Lane, but southward. This suggests that the land they faced had been common land when they were built. The fields, which they overlooked were owned by the Foley estate, surrounded by land in other ownership, suggesting that they were enclosed at a later date than surrounding land.

The cottages were later demolished.

Major Derrington followed Victor Bradshaw as tenant, and he was followed, in turn, by Mr Ron Smith who took on the farm at a rent of £1 per acre in 1939. The farm had become neglected through the harsh times of the 1930s, and was considered to be one of the poorest on the Madresfield Estate. Many a tenant had become bankrupt attempting to make a living from the heavy land. Ron worked hard to get the farm in order, determined to farm on his own, especially as he had just become engaged to Dorrie, whose father had forbidden them to marry until Ron was in a position to provide for her. He could only afford to employ one boy, Edward Yapp, and a retired farm worker, Tom Williams. They were both twenty-eight at the time, but they accepted the conditions. Happily, Ron and Dorrie married in 1941.

A small herd of Dairy Shorthorn cows was purchased, and improvements were made to the farm buildings and the milking parlour. Ron worked long hours to improve the arable and grassland, and within three years the five-bay Dutch barn was full of harvested crops. This was a huge achievement: only one and a half bays were filled in Ron's first year at The Court. The Estate's agent admitted when Ron took on the farm that, so poor was the mowing grass, it would have been possible to catch a mouse in it.

Ron and Dorrie let out the house at Guarlford Court and moved into Guarlford Court Cottage in 1966. Their tenants in the house were Mrs Dix and her companion, Miss Allsop, followed by Mr and Mrs Pettigrew until 1983, when the house was sold to Toby and Margaretha Bruce-Morgan, the present occupants.

During the Second World War, Charlie Williams and Jim Tustin worked for Mr Smith. In 1957, the Madresfield Estate offered Mr Smith the adjacent Heriots Farm, also owned by the Madresfield Estate. Edward Jenkins came to work for Mr Smith in 1959, and he and Win lived at the Heriots Farm until Mr Smith's retirement in 1983, when he gave up the land at the Heriots and the arable land at Guarlford Court Farm, which was added to Grove House Farm and Fred and Helena Hawkins's tenancy.

Mr Smith continued to farm 43 acres of grassland with his daughter, Meriel, and they had beef cattle, and sheep on tack in winter. Meriel farmed the land after her father's death in 1997, finally retiring to nurse her ailing mother in 2003. The land then passed to the tenants of Grove House Farm, Michael and Helen Simpson.

Heriots

The tithe awards show that in 1841 The Heriots was 172 acres in size and owned by Archibold Cameron, Trustee of John Cullis. The tenant at that time was James Bullock. By the Second World War, this farm was part of the Madresfield Estate, and the tenant was Teddy Waters. His son Frank, and daughter Alice, were involved in the business. Alice ran a shop in St Johns, Worcester, called Heriots Farm Dairy, where she sold the farm's dairy produce and home-grown fruit and vegetables. Frank had a milk round. He took a milk float up Clevelode Road, supplying milk from the tap to the many rural cottages as well as to households in Clevelode, Callow End and Powick. The milk float continued to St Johns, to supply the shop. Frank's brother, Tom, was wagoner at New House Farm. When Teddy died, the Madresfield Estate did not permit his sons to take on the tenancy, and Frank moved to Storridge. The two sisters were moved to a cottage at Clevelode. Mr I Castle, who was farm manager at Beauchamp Farm, Callow End, then managed the farm for a few years; but the land was heavy, wet and not drained, and the Madresfield Estate added the land to Mr Ron Smith's tenancy.

Little Heriots

In 1840, Little Heriots was owned and farmed by John H Allen, and at that time the farm comprised forty-three acres. No-one today remembers the holding as a working farm, but it eventually became part of the Madresfield Estate, and was amalgamated with Whiteacres Farm. Locals remember that before and during the Second World War Harry Wellings lived in one of the two cottages, which had probably been part of the farm at one time, and ran his smithy in an old farm building. His neighbour in the cottage next door was Dick Gowan, whom parishioners remember driving a steamroller for Bomfords who laid new roads.

When Harry Wellings died in about 1956, John Gammond's parents purchased his cottage from the Madresfield Estate. John Gammond rented the site of the old smithy and surrounding area from the late 1960s, eventually buying the premises from Madresfield Estate in 1974. A J Gammond Limited, agricultural machinery distributors and drainage contractors, still trade from these premises.

Little Clevelode Farm

Mr Alan Webb bought this farm of sixty-nine acres from the Madresfield Estate in 1919, for £2,375. Later, the land was swapped with Alf Wilkes's parents' farm, Portocks End. The Wilkes family were followed by the Armstrongs, and then, in the 1950s, Mr A F Hall bought the farm. Mr Hall was a director of Chad Valley toys, and lived in Birmingham. Mr Geoff Munslow, an ex-army officer, was the bailiff, and the farm had a good herd of British Friesians known as the 'Guarlford Herd', which were taken successfully to shows. They had excellent, modern machinery and provided a contracting service for local farmers, some of which were still using horses. Edward Jenkins carried out the contracting work, gaining a valuable insight into the new opportunities provided by modern equipment. Mr Hall sold the farm, and the land became a caravan site. The herd was sold to the Wiggins family at Clevelode Farm, and Mr Munslow went to work there.

Figure 2.5 Edward Jenkins and a bull from the Guarlford Herd of Friesians, Little Clevelode Farm, c.1950.

Mill Farm

The tithe awards, 1840s, show that five Bullocks farmed in the parish at that time, although they may not have all been related. William Bullock farmed 265 acres at Mill Farm, a very large farm at that time, and Joseph Bullock farmed fifty-three, both on the Foley Estate. In 1910, the Bullock family purchased Mill Farm, with 279 acres, in the Foley Estate sale. Until that time, Mill Farm was let to Messrs Tilt Brothers. Mr John Bullock and his sons Jim and Nigel, the present owners, have expanded to farm additional land outside the parish.

Moat Court

This farm has a very interesting past and was originally part of the Priory estate, built in the fourteenth century on land cleared by the monks. It was a 'demesne manor', providing food and beer for the Priory; and, having a supply of water, it was more productive than land on the slopes near the Priory. Originally a timber-framed building facing the hills, it was defended by a moat, which is still there today. The moat is fed from water from the hills, which enters Moat Pond at Sherrard's Green. Water from the moat overflows into a small stream, which flows into Whiteacres Brook.

The Moore family purchased Moat Court in 1555, some time after the dissolution of the monasteries, and Malcolm Baxter was the tenant. The Moores sold the land to Rowland Gifford for £272 in 1605. Rowland refurbished the house, giving it a complete skin of hand-made bricks and the Jacobean style staircase, which is still in use, and a dovecote. In the mid seventeenth-century, Rowland Gifford was practising a four-year rotation on his twelve-acre field, Moat Piece, growing rye, barley, oats, vetches and fallow. By 1841, the owner was Francis Plumer Gifford Dineley, whose name suggests he may be a descendant of Rowland Gifford; the farm had a tenant, William Taylor.

Moat Court was purchased by the expanding Foley Estate, and then was sold to the Madresfield Estate in the Foley Estate sale of 1910, when the tenant was George Oliver. The farm was described in the sale particulars: "This is the best mixed farm of a moderate size to be found in the county of Worcester. There is a good road to every field, the road frontage being about one mile in length. It is well shaded and watered, close to good markets and in every way desirable either for occupation or investment". It appears that tenants often left, or had to leave on the sale of land.

Mr Percy Hughes was the tenant in the Second World War, and Edward Jenkins went to work for him shortly after the war. Edward remembers a hay barn on staddle stones. Barns for hay or straw storage were sometimes built upon the mushroom-shaped stones, to keep vermin from damaging the stored crop, a floor of wooden poles making up the base. The house and some land were later sold by the Madresfield Estate, and much of the farmland amalgamated with Grove House Farm.

> ### The Workforce at New House Farm
>
> *Just before the Second World War, New House Farm employed a wagoner, Tommy Waters, a wagoner's boy Harold Clarke, a cowman, Harold's father, Fred Clarke, stockman Bernard Clarke, and Tom Roberts, who looked after the blackcurrant crops (and possibly other fruit crops, as apples and pears were also grown). There were also Edwin Waters and Charlie Roberts, sons of Tom Waters and Tom Roberts, who were on the milk round. Sam Finch carried out hedge work and thatched haystacks, although at peak times, such as hay-making and harvest, all would work together. Later Arthur Beauchamp worked on the farm for fifteen years.*
>
> *Charlie Williams and Jim Tustin, who both worked at Guarlford Court in the Second World War, married Harold and Alice Clarke's daughters, Doreen and Marina.*

New House Farm

New House Farmhouse was built by the Foleys in the 1700s, originally in a similar style to the Foley Estate's neighbouring farmhouses, including Grove House Farm. The house now has a different front, which was an addition made in 1908. The three farm cottages on the roadside near the farm were built in 1891, and bear the date and initials of Emily Foley. They were occupied by the employees' families of Fred Clarke, his son, Harold Clarke, and Tom Roberts. The farm was an amalgamation of several smaller farms, including Lower Elm Farm. Lower Elm Farm is shown on the map of the Foley Estate drawn up in 1744, and stood near the Guarlford road junction with Chance Lane. In 1841, Thomas Need was the tenant, and the farm had 128 acres. Mr Need was followed by Stephen John Medcalf, who arrived in 1884. When the Foley's Malvern Estate was sold in 1910, Stephen Medcalf was able to purchase the farm and eventually pass the farm to his son, Derrick. Derrick was Bill Medcalf's father and Andrew Medcalf's grandfather.

Immediately after the First World War, when unemployment in the towns was very high, Reg Green (born October 1903), father of Rosemary Williams who lives in Penny

Figure 2.6 New House Farm, home of the Medcalf family, c.1910.

Lane, moved to Guarlford from Dudley, and took employment with Mr Medcalf, for whom he delivered milk for twenty-one years.

Charlie Williams recollects that, shortly before the Second World War, New House Farm, then a mixed farm of 147 acres, employed eight men, many of them from the same family. At his time, Charlie remembers that New House Farm produced black currants for 'Ribena', apples and pears, milk, peas, potatoes, eggs and corn.

Portocks End

Portocks End, originally part of the Madresfield Estate, was farmed by Thomas Cowles in 1840. In 1919, the Madresfield Estate sold the farm comprising of fifty-three acres to Mr W W Collins, who was the sitting tenant. By the Second World War, W W Collins had exchanged Portocks End for his neighbour, Mr Alan Webb's farm, Little Clevelode. Two thatched black and white cottages opposite the present Gammond's yard, now demolished, were part of Portocks End Farm, and were occupied by Tom Sims, the cowman, and George Patrick, who worked in Worcester. Bill Sims was wagoner at Portocks End. Bill's father, Jarvey, lived in the cottage in South Wood and rode a three-wheeled bike (as did Harry Wellings, the Madresfield Estate blacksmith). The Bladders bought the farm in the 1970s to increase the size of their holding at Fowler's Farm. Humphrey lived in a bungalow, which he built there, and farmed until the early 1990s. The land is no longer farmed.

Priestfields

In 1841, this smallholding belonged to William Greenaway, and was tenanted by William Haynes. Fred George owned the land at the time of the Second World War, and had milking cows and a float and dairy delivery round. He farmed it into the 1970s, when it was divided to form several smallholdings.

Rose Farm

The tithe awards show that Samuel Roe was the owner-occupier of what is now known as Rose Farm (twenty acres). Mr Roe farmed an additional sixty-two acres on the Foley Estate. The Foley Estate purchased Rose Farm, and when the Foley Estate was sold in 1910, Rose Farm was sold to Andrew Bettridge and later was farmed by Frank Hill, who had a milk round, which delivered around Malvern. The land is now owned by the developer, Martin Wilesmith.

Figure 2.7 Hay rick and elevator at Guarlford Court Farm, c.1950.

Whiteacres Farm, Clevelode

From tithe records, we know that Whiteacres Farm belonged to the Madresfield Estate in 1840, and at that time the farm had eighty-eight acres. In the Second World War, Mr and Mrs Bill Cooke, Heather and Philip lived at Whiteacres. Edward Yapp, whose father worked as forester for the Madresfield Estate before Fred White, worked for a time for Mr Cooke. Philip Cooke had worked for Mr Ron Smith at Guarlford Court Farm as a young man. With specialisation and enlargement of farms, Whiteacres was amalgamated with Falconers Farm, and the farmhouse was sold off – initially to George Ridley. A subsequent owner ran a restaurant business there for a few years, before it reverted to being purely a family home.

White House Farm

White House Farm was owned by Richard Blayney of Dripshill House in 1841, and the tenant was John Blake. The tithe awards indicate that the farm at that time was fifty-nine acres in size. The farm was later bought by the Madresfield Estate.

Figure 2.8 White House Farm, c.1930.

The Madresfield Estate sold White House Farm in 1919 to H G Busk of Bransford, for £2,100. Messrs A and O V G Bradshaw were the tenants at that time (grandfather and father respectively of Joan Bradshaw), and were farming Guarlford Court Farm as well. Mr Busk also ran an agricultural engineering business.

Mr Geoffrey Bott, the present owner, understood that the farm was then run by five different farmers in twelve years, one of whom wrote for *Dairy Farmer* magazine and was an innovator of silage-making. In 1927, it was a fruit dealer from Manchester who finally sold the farm to Mr and Mrs Billy Bott, Geoff Bott's parents. Mr Bott senior was involved in much public work, and was a trustee of the orphanage in St Johns, Worcester, as well as a keen member of the Free Church, where he played the organ. He had dairy cows and, like most farms, White House had pigs, sheep and crops. Mrs

Figure 2.9 A farm implement bearing the name of Mr Busk's agricultural business.

Bott was a headmistress at a secondary school in Malvern. Mr and Mrs Billy Bott retired to Weston-super-Mare.

Woodbridge Farm

Figure 2.10 Water-colour of Woodbridge Farm from Cherry Orchard in 1903 by J.E.D.

Edwin Lane and his sister, Margaret Omar, have documents which show that in 1762 their ancestor, John Lane, was tenant to "...the said Thomas Need". John Lane then bought the property in 1775, as outlined in Chapter 1, 'Guarlford's Beginnings'. (p.7)

The Work Force at Woodbridge

Ernie Clarke started work on the farm when he left school just before the Second World War. Sid Lane and Bill Creese also helped at busy times.

Ernie fought in the Second World War, after which he returned to work at Woodbridge for a few years, before leaving to work on the railways.

The tithe awards record that Woodbridge Farm was owned by George Lane in 1841. This may be the George Lane who died in 1846, and was one of the first parishioners to be buried in the new churchyard at Guarlford. His name appears on the first page of the new church register. George Lane was an ancestor of the present owner, Edwin.

Edwin Lane's father owned a greengrocer's shop in Holyrood Terrace on the Promenade in Malvern; and the farm grew vegetables for the shop. The Lanes also grew wheat for sale, as well as barley for their own cattle feed, and had sheep together with a Shorthorn milking herd, and reared their own calves. Edwin milked until the 1970s. Milk went to the Co-op and was collected by Tilt's. Edwin Lane says that their first tractor was a Fordson, which was a pre-war import from the USA (See Chapter 1, p.7, for description of 'stanks' at Woodbridge Farm.)

In 1999 Edwin Lane sold 122 acres to Chris Burton, but retains eight acres.

Farming: Livestock and Crops

Tractors and Horses

Until tractors replaced horses on farms, the methods and tools of the farmer had remained little changed for 200 years. Even when tractors were introduced, they merely did the work of the horse at first, albeit with less effort and at a faster pace. During the Second World War, fuel was hard to come by, so horses were still commonly used. Before the war, there was little corn grown in the parish. When the demand for corn increased, there was still a limit to the amount of corn which could be grown: ploughing was very slow and heavy work for horses. Farmers had to take care of their horses and, unlike tractors, they tired. In summer, hot weather would also limit the amount of work which a farmer could ask of a horse, so mowing for hay would often be carried out early or late in the day.

Figure 2.11 Edward Jenkins driving an early Massey Harris Tractor.

The War Agricultural Executive Committees ('War Ag') were set up by the Ministry of Agriculture during the Second World War to encourage increased agricultural production locally and thus counter food shortages. They ensured that farmers ploughed grassland and increased arable acreage, while they also provided contracting services at cost. Locally, the 'War Ag' had depots at Hanley Swan and Deblins Green, which provided modern Fordson tractors, with rubber tyres or spade luggs; and they were much preferred to the more usual tractors on small farms which ran on tracks, such as the Bristol tractor, which were not allowed on roads. John Gammond, Alf Wilkes, Mr Rees from the Old Hills, and Gene Cubberley worked for the 'War Ag'. After the war, when the 'War Ag' finished, there was a need for contractors. Many farmers were still reliant on horses to draw farm implements. Edward Jenkins's friend, Edward Yapp, worked for Alf Wilkes just after the war. Mr Wilkes had been boss at the 'War Ag' and had a yard at Hanley Swan, and took on Edward Jenkins, who remembers that the charge for baling in the 1950s was nine old pennies per bale. These bales were heavier and denser but the same size as modern small bales, and were tied by wire rather than twine.

Hay Making

Figure 2.12 Mr Ron Smith pushes up hay with tractor and sweep.

The process of haymaking was important, as it enabled farmers to preserve surplus grass grown through spring and summer to feed to stock in winter when grass barely grows. Before the Second World War, and even during the war, the grass was mown by horse-drawn mower. The hay was spread out with a swathe turner and turned until it was dry. It was then put into rows called 'wallies' with a side rake. When it was dry, the hay was pushed up by a 'sweep', which was on front of a tractor. The loose hay was then lifted or pitched onto the stack in the field or on a wagon to be drawn to the stack yard. Humphrey Bladder remembers that they had a monkey pole and a gib, and a horse was used to draw the hay up high onto the stack or the wagon. A petrol-driven elevator was often used to take hay to the top of the stack. An iron horse was fitted to the shafts of wagons, which were designed to be horse-drawn, and this connected the wagon to a tractor. When machinery became tractor-drawn, the same machines were used, but adapted. Horses, of course, always pulled the implement, but tractors were able to pull and push.

Haystacks were then thatched in order to encourage rain to run off them. A hay knife was used to cut out a block of hay called a 'keetch', which would be thrown out to feed stock in winter.

Silage Making

Although very much more silage is made than hay nowadays, it appears that the farmers of Guarlford knew all about silage's merits and were producing it soon after the Second World War. Nowadays, it is preferred not only for its higher feed value than hay, but also because the process of making silage is less vulnerable to the weather and is less labour intensive. Systems have evolved so that it is easier to store because it can now be bagged in the field. It is cut earlier in the growing season than hay, and is collected up to be compacted in the 'clamp', where it is stored in bulk, or compacted by machine in the bag while in the field when it is merely wilted, rather than sun-dried like hay. Edward Jenkins recalls how he was making silage at Little Clevelode

Farm in the 1950s, as were Joan Newell and Joan Bradshaw at Grange Farm, often from a crop of lucerne. Edward tells how the key to producing silage of good quality was to cut the grass when it was young, in May, and to ensure that every layer of grass was spread out evenly on the clamp before being compacted by the tractor wheels. The process of spreading it out could only be carried out effectively by hand. Edward used to spread molasses between the layers before compacting it. When the clamp was full, it was sealed with a layer of lime to exclude air, to ensure good fermentation. Nowadays, the clamps are sealed by a cover of black plastic, weighed down with tyres. It is essential to exclude air, which would cause the grass to rot.

Figure 2.13 Hay rick at Guarlford Court Farm, c.1950.

Harvest

Until 1965, August Bank Holiday was on the first Monday in August, and this date signalled that the corn would be ready to harvest. The process was started by cutting the headland by hand using a 'hook and crook'; the corn was gathered up into sheaves, and each was secured by winding a few long stems of corn around the sheaf and securing it with a knot. These sheaves were set aside on the edge of the field, allowing the reaper-binder access around the field to the rest of the crop. The reaper-binder cut the corn and tied it automatically into sheaves. Oats were a tall crop sometimes growing six foot high with long straw, wheat was medium height, and barley shorter. The binder had to be adjusted to tie the string centrally around the sheaves; the binders were horse-drawn before and during the Second World War, and in later years were drawn by tractors. Then, the sheaves were stacked in rows and left to finish ripening and to dry out. More oats were grown than barley or wheat, and the general rule was that the church bells should ring three times on three consecutive Sundays between reaping the oats and bringing in the sheaves. Wheat and barley could be collected within a week to ten days. The sheaves were then pitched by hand onto the wagon and taken to the farmyard, where they were built into stacks and thatched, or stored in barns.

When oats were stored in barns or stacks, sacking was used as a chimney in the centre of the sheaves, to prevent them heating. The labour-intensive harvest might take many weeks; and, with no means of drying corn, was even more weather-dependant than it is now. Humphrey Bladder remembers that it was not unusual for farmers to

Figure 2.14 Charlie Williams giving a demonstration of a horse drawn binder at work.

be reaping and binding still after the beginning of the pheasant-shooting season, which starts on 1st October. During the winter, the corn was threshed. Before the arrival of the mechanical threshing machine, which was around 1850, this was carried out in threshing barns, which had huge doors on opposite sides of the barn. The wind would blow through the barn and separate the heavier grain from the chaff. Threshing machines were sometimes driven by steam power, but Edward Jenkins remembers that in Guarlford, by the Second World War, they were driven by a tractor, usually a Standard Fordson, with a pulley. This process took place throughout the winter, and was carried out locally by a contractor who travelled from farm to farm. The local contractor who visited White House Farm, Fowler's Farm, Portocks End Farm and Priestfield Farm was Tilt's from Hanley Swan. J C Bakers contracted for Guarlford Court Farm during the war instead of the 'War Ag'. The string on the sheaves was cut and the whole sheaf of corn was allowed to fall into a drum. The threshing took place, and grain, tailings etc fell into different bags according to the weight. Grain was then stored in hessian sacks, hired from a local company, Godsall Brown. The straw passed on to a stationary baler, and the bales were held by wire rather than string. Edward Jenkins remembers the Land Army girls with huge needles threading the wire into the bale, to be pulled out on the other side and tied by another girl. The threshing was very labour-intensive, requiring about eleven people to do the job, and Land Army

Figure 2.15 Steam-driven threshing machine and assembled workforce.

girls and prisoners of war formed a valuable part of this labour force. Sacks of grain were then lifted up to granaries, often above stables or cowsheds, where much of the corn would be used. This system of harvesting left broken ears of corn and shed grain on the ground. It was an annual activity of the wives and children of the farm workers and their mothers to spend long days in August after harvest gathering these 'gleanings'. Most families would make good use of the corn they collected, possibly to feed a pig or hens. It may be that some wives ground wheat to make flour.

The first combine harvesters were trailer combines and had very narrow five-foot cutters. These were power-driven by a tractor, which towed the combine harvester. The grain dropped into bags, which were tied and dropped on the ground when they were full and were picked up by another two men with a trailer. Each sack weighed two hundredweight (cwt). Self-propelled combine harvesters were subsequently developed; they cut a wider swath, but for a while still dropped the grain into bags on a platform on the side. The grain harvested by a modern combine comes out of a chute straight into a trailer.

The corn was sold to corn merchants, who would come and collect the corn. Weaver from Castlemorton, Bibbys, Holthams, and Needhams were all local merchants, who would send a traveller round to the farms to quote a price for the corn. These same businesses would supply seed corn, too. It would be usual to 'spring tine' the stubble, after harvest, and then leave the weeds to germinate before ploughing and sowing with the next crop. This was one of the methods of reducing weeds in the crop; growing break crops, and leaving fallows were other methods. Farmyard manure was the main fertiliser used during and just after the Second World War, and low inputs producing low yields by modern standards of one to two cwt per acre were usual. Nowadays, three or more cwt per acre are usual. Weeding was usually by hand, especially charlock and later in the year wild oats. Manure used to be taken from the muck 'bury' (muck-heap) into the field and tipped out into small heaps over the field. This would be on stubble before cultivation, or on grassland in winter. The muck would then have to be spread by hand with a fork.

Dairy

Reg Green was born in 1903 and he worked at New House Farm after the First World War. He records in a memoir written for his family, *I Got on My Bike*, how his job entailed working seven days a week, starting at six a.m., milking by hand four or five cows: "This was before the days of stringent regulations regarding the production of milk. The milk was drawn from the cow by hand, put through a cotton-wool strainer, then straight into the churns and was then ready for retailing to the customer. Housewives often used to refuse to have the milk unless it was still warm from the cow; in that way they knew that it really was fresh". (p.22) Reg would be out on the road by 7.30 a.m. to sell milk to housewives, "Ladling it out of carrying-cans into the housewives' jugs or basins, in half-pints, pints, or quarts".

Edward Jenkins's earliest experience of farm work came later, during the Second World War. He had learnt his farming skills in the orphanage in St Johns, which had a small farm with enough cows for their own use; and when he was fifteen years of age Mr Billy Bott, who was a governor of the orphanage, found him employment at White House Farm. The farm offered none of the comforts of the orphanage: there was no electricity or running water at White House Farm during the war. Hurricane lamps were used in the milking parlour. In the dairy, sterilising took place by placing equipment over steam, which came out of a hole in the metal lid on copper boilers. Edward also recalls how wells were frequently used to keep food such as milk cool. Milk deliveries were daily, often seven days a week, since no-one had refrigeration.

Milking was carried out by hand during the Second World War, and six to eight cows were usual. But, in the years after the war, most dairy farmers installed electric pump or engine-driven 'suction lines'; and then twenty cows would have been a good-sized herd. Sometimes these were portable 'bails', and milking took place out in the field. More often a permanent suction pipe ran along the wall in the cattle shed, above the cows, which were tied up. A bucket, lid with pulsator and 'cluster' (four cups to fit onto teats) were carried from cow to cow as each was milked. The bucket was connected to the suction line above the cow, then the cluster was fitted to the cow, and milk was drawn into the bucket. After which the milk was carried to the cooler and into churns.

Edward Jenkins remembers the milk-cooling process at White House Farm during the Second World War. There was a 200 gallon water tank on the third floor of the farmhouse, serving the bathroom and kitchen, which was filled by a hand rotary pump from the well. The fresh milk was poured into a tank above the 'plate cooler', and water passed through the cooler pipes, over which the milk flowed, thereby reducing its temperature. Then the milk passed through a cotton strainer, and into churns, the water returning to the well for recycling.

Before and during the Second World War, much of the milk produced on farms around Guarlford found a direct market in Malvern and Worcester. There were milk rounds from Medcalf's of New House Farm, Webb's of Portocks Farm, Freddie George of Priestfields, Bladders from Fowler's Farm and Frank Hill of Rose Farm. Edward Jenkins remembers that the milk from White House Farm was taken to George Smith, the butcher, in Barnard's Green Road, during the Second World War. Humphrey Bladder remembers butter being made regularly on Fowler's Farm by his mother. This would have been sent out on the float for sale. They had a milk round up to the time of the Second World War, after which the milk was collected in churns by Tilts. All milk, which was not delivered directly to households or institutions by the farmer was put outside the farm in churns on a stand and picked up by Tilt's lorry from Hanley Swan. Farmers remember Tilt's collecting the milk initially in churns and later by tanker lorry. Joan Newell sold milk from a milk float for a time, starting from Tilt's premises in town at 5.00 a.m. by grooming the pony and tacking it up before setting off with a large churn of milk with a brass tap at the front of the float. Milk from the churn filled a bucket into which a pint or half-pint measure was dipped to then pour the milk into housewives' jugs. There was also a gill measure for cream. Joan had two rounds each day, finishing at 2.00 p.m. Gradually, as farmers specialised in milking cows, specialist dairy processors set up and grew. Eventually, milk producers were obliged to install bulk tanks to hold the day's milk, and bulk tanker lorries began to collect the milk. Humphrey remembers that the milk was treated and bottled at Tilts, whose farm and dairy premises were at Broadacres, where the incinerator was built at Hanley Swan. Eventually, the Co-op bought them out, but for some time the milk continued to be bottled and distributed from Hanley Swan. Bulk tanks installed on the farm to refrigerate and hold the milk until collection vastly improved the cooling and storage of milk and standard of hygiene. Milking parlours contributed further to the efficiency, providing pipes through which milk flowed from glass jars beside the cow to the bulk tank via the plate cooler. Milk no longer had to be carried in buckets and churns, making the milking process faster and easier, and enabling more cows to be milked in less time. This allowed farmers to enlarge further their herds.

Most of the local farmers had Shorthorn cows, and Edward Jenkins remembers that when he worked for Mr Bott in the Second World War, if a cow required serving, she would be driven down the road to the Shorthorn bull at Portocks End. This was long before the days of artificial insemination. The cows were kept in the yards in winter rather than out in the fields. The yard usually had cover, as well as an open area where they were fed silage or hay. Silage would be cut out of the clamp with a knife and be brought in on the back of the tractor. Cows would be tied in their stall to be milked and be fed concentrate feed, such as rolled oats and barley, while being milked. Many farmers grew enough corn to feed their stock, and a day would be set aside regularly for grinding corn to be fed to the animals. Oats and barley were rolled or ground to make the corn more digestible and the grinder was powered by a tractor's pulley, the tractor standing outside the barn. Another feed was cow cake bought in slabs, which were crushed on the farm before feeding to the animals. Later, Edward remembers Oldacres coming to Mr Hall's Little Clevelode Farm, with a mobile 'miller and mixer' which rolled, ground and mixed the various feed ingredients, and these had the much larger capacity required as herds grew larger.

Sheep, Pigs, and Poultry

In recent years – between 1977 and 1991 – Mr T Geoffrey Boaz of Rhydd Farm made a significant national contribution to the re-establishment of the Merino sheep breed and to the promotion of fine wool in Great Britain. Geoffrey and his wife, Margaret, moved to Rhydd Farm, where Geoff's parents and youngest sister, 'Bobbie', lived, in 1976, when Geoff retired from the Department of Agriculture at the University of Leeds. During the 1980s, Geoff became a recognised Merino breeder. The holding at the Rhydd had thirteen acres, enough land to support a flock of fifty Merino sheep. Geoff's publication on his work with the breed, *The Merino Story*, tells how he

became "...determined to accept the challenge to prove that Merinos could be kept satisfactorily in England and make a contribution to fine wool supplies." (p.3) At the same time, he sought conformation – the particular form and adaptation - for meat production. Merinos in New Zealand and Australia are purely wool-producing, with poor suitability for meat, while in England sheep breeders have been more concerned with the production of meat. When crossed with native British breeds to improve fleece quality and quantity, the progeny still graded satisfactorily for meat. Geoff's fleeces won many Championships, including the local Championship of the Golden Fleece

Figure 2.16 Geoffrey Boaz's 'Rhydd Green Benjamin' Merino ram.

Competition at the Three Counties Show for three consecutive years, and Championships at the Royal Show, as well as the 'ultimate fleece' competition at the Smithfield Show.

A more general earlier Guarlford memory of sheep farming was a requirement during the Second World War that sheep should be 'dipped' to rid them of parasites. Edward Jenkins recalls that a policeman watched over the process and timed each sheep in the dip. There was a sheep dip at White House Farm, and many farmers would drive their sheep there for their annual submersion. There was another in a building at Cherry Orchard.

Most farmers had a few of all sorts of livestock: working horses, dairy cows, beef cattle, sheep, pigs and poultry. Pigs would make use of scraps and any waste milk, or milk produced just after the cow calved. Fat stock would be taken to market in a lorry driven by Bill Evans, who had a smallholding at Poolbrook. A sow and piglets, or calves, or sheep would be taken to Worcester market by horse and dray, which had side rails and compartments. Bacon pigs at Fowler's Farm were a cross between Large Black sows and Large White boars. Piglets were 'sheeted': white with mottling. When fat, they were sent to a bacon factory. The Bladders had two pigs a year for the house. These supplied a year's bacon and ham. The butcher, Harry Brindley, killed them on the farm. Then the hair was burnt off the carcases; and they were cleaned and cut into two 'flitches' before being hung up in the cart shed for two days. After this, they were laid on a slab in an outhouse, and salt was rubbed into them. This salt came from Brickell's in a huge bar, which had to be grated to produce salt in a powder. The flitches were then left to cure for three weeks. The salt was washed off next, and the flitches were covered in a flour paste to seal them. Humphrey Bladder said that the meat would finally hang in the kitchen and keep for twelve months, and it was lovely.

Most farms had poultry. These would most usually be free-range, in wired-in runs out in the fields, or kept in a farm building and running around the yard. One of the daily chores was to wash the eggs and put them into trays, which would be collected once a week by the Egg Marketing Board.

Hops and Orchards

Hops and orchards have for a long time been distinctive features of the local landscape. Now no hopyards remain in this parish, and the orchards of Guarlford are largely relics of a time when they contributed important income to the farmer and employment for the locals at harvest time. Some houses in Bamford Close still have old apple and perry pear trees in their gardens that are a reminder of the Cherry Orchard land on which they were built some thirty-five years ago. As far as hop growing was concerned, the high point in Great Britain was 1870, when 29,000 hectares of hops spread across fifty-three counties. Hops have been a very high value and profitable crop until recently. Acreage has fallen to just 1,280 hectares in fewer than ten counties, and very few are now grown in Worcestershire. Those that remain are in the Teme valley. Production has dropped by 40% nationally over the last six years. A global over-supply of hops is cited as one of the main causes of the drop in land area, with America and Germany predominant now. Low prices and more effective use of the hop by brewers are other contributory factors.

However, Guarlford's hop-producers left the industry before long-term decline set in. When prices of 'permanent' crops such as hops fluctuate, farmers have to ride the storms, as the costly infrastructure – in this case of hopyards and hop kilns – ensures a long-term commitment to the crop. Hops were grown at North End Farm, Madresfield, until the 1980s; but survival of the enterprise would have been dependent on considerable expertise, and, as with other crops at that time and since, on specialisation. The time for a hop grower to consider whether or not to continue his commitment to hop-growing would be when facing the prospect of major capital expenditure on his hopyard or kilns. Also, hopyards, like dairy herds, are often handed down to the next generation, but the interest and commitment does not necessarily pass on with it; and this factor may have also have

Figure 2.17 Local hop-pickers, Mrs Panting second from the right.

contributed to loss of hopyards in the parish. The tithe map of 1841 shows field names indicating hopyards at Moat Court, Grove House Farm, New House Farm and Whiteacres Farm. Other farms known to have had hopyards are Woodbridge and Guarlford Court.

Reg Green's memoirs, *I Got on My Bike*, (p.13) record his childhood memories of "…wandering round the meadows, apple scrumping or riding on the farm wagons taking the hops to the kilns for drying." Hop picking took place in September and lasted a month or so, and was a time of very hard work for his mother, who was one of the mainly local hop-picking workforce. Reg says, "The hops were picked from the bines into cribs made of sacking and were measured at intervals by the 'busheler', who came round with a large basket and entered into his book the amount picked by each picker. The highest price I remember being paid was 6d (2p) per bushel, but even at that low price a good picker could earn quite a considerable amount during a month's picking." He continues, "I was often allowed into the hop-kiln and was fascinated to see the hops being dried – a process which went on night and day – the hop dryer being at work all the time, not taking his clothes off or getting any real rest for weeks on end until the whole drying was completed. Sulphur was burned in the drying process to give the hops flavour and this could be quite overpowering at times. The hops when quite dry were then pressed into large sacks known as 'pockets' and sent off to the hop warehouses, the nearest being at Worcester."

Phyl Bayliss lived at Hall Green, and spent three years in the Land Army, cycling to Charlie Lewis's farm at Braces Leigh, between Malvern and Worcester. The farm was a typical mixed farm, producing hops, beef cattle, sheep, pigs and chickens. Phyllis remembers going round with the busheler, booking the weights as they were checked.

She recalls picking the hops by hand and some years she worked in the kiln all the time, where they dried the hops. She says, "The cap on the roof brought in a wind to draw the sulphur up. I used to have to bag the hops up when they were dried; a long 'hop-pocket' fitted into a ring and dropped down through the upper floor to below. In the morning I had to stamp the farmer's name on and number all the pockets. We used to do twenty to thirty a day, and you used to have to push the hops in with a sort of spoon, weigh them and sew them up, then drop them down through the floor."

"We were OK for food", Phyl remembers, "But it was a hard life, long days, especially when we had double summer time. Sometimes we'd go on to 11 o'clock; we started at 7 a.m." While working on the farm, Phyl began to suffer from asthma, no doubt aggravated by the sulphur, which was later recognised as a health hazard, and its use was banned in hop kilns. The Madresfield Agricultural Club Quarterly published in January 1914, reports that the Club organised hop-drying classes. In the President's report, Lord Beauchamp "…regretted that more pupils did not take up hop drying – there had been a complaint about the night work and sulphur fumes." Lord Beauchamp went on to report that in 1913 "The hop crop, the most important in the district, had proved very light owing to the persistent blight, coupled with the drought … under these circumstances high prices were anticipated, but from various causes these have not been realised, and except in a few favoured instances, there will be little remuneration for the growers for many months of unceasing toil and anxiety."

The last hops in the parish were grown in 'Young Hopyard' at New House Farm, around 1920. The hopyard's name suggests that it was the last to be planted on the farm. Although their original roofs and cowl tops have gone, the hop kilns at New House Farm are still recognisable. Joan Bradshaw was told by Mr Cole, who had the blacksmith's shop near New House Farm, that he witnessed the collapse of the wire work in the nearby hopyard, when the crop was at its full height and weight in summer. Great effort was made to try to haul the frame of wires back up with a steam traction engine. Joan believes that the rescue was unsuccessful, and it marked the end of hop-growing in Guarlford.

Growing fruit was an important activity in the parish, and the fruit harvesting involved many people. The tithe maps of the 1840s show orchards on virtually every holding. These would have been grazed orchards with standard trees: pears, plums, apples and cherries. At one time, locally produced beer and cider were a part of the wages on farms, a formality passed in the Truck Laws, which allowed payment in kind, and the cider-making culture continued locally into the twentieth-century. Joan remembers that most farms had a cider house and produced cider from their own fruit, and the millstone and the shaft and harness for the horse, which pulled the millstone round, crushing the apples in the big circular stone trough, known as the 'chase', at Guarlford Court. Edward Jenkins remembers the chase and the screw-press at White House Farm. While he worked there during the Second World War he removed the millstone and mill chase to the garden, where, like many others elsewhere, it made an attractive feature.

Chapter 3

Family Life

Families at Work

Guarlford in the Nineteenth Century

Since the Second World War the parish of Guarlford has changed considerably from its character in the first half of the twentieth century and the latter part of the nineteenth, not only in the physical appearance of fields and buildings but, most significantly, in the way that families in the village live their lives. In her autobiographical account of an Oxfordshire village childhood, *Lark Rise*, Flora Thompson describes her Cotswold family in the 1880s as being part of 'the besieged generation':

"The hamlet was indeed in a state of siege, and its chief assailant was Want. Yet, like other citizens during a long, but not too desperate siege, its inhabitants had become accustomed to their hard conditions and were able to snatch at any passing pleasure". (p.97)

This seems to have been true of many country villages, including Guarlford, at that time and even into the twentieth century. Victorian and Edwardian England may have been experiencing a time of industrial wealth and imperial expansion benefiting some sections of society, but the families of some farm labourers had a very different experience. Indeed, Mr Charlie Williams tells of his own grandfather having to move in secret to Shipton Moyne from a harsh employer in the Cotswolds in the late 1880s. Even then Charlie's father (born in 1879) could not go to school but had to work in the fields, scaring the birds off the corn for a penny a day. The family eventually came to Worcestershire.

The working and social life of Guarlford in the nineteenth century was very much influenced by the agricultural and rural nature of the environment. The farm labourer was typically poor and often lived in a tied house, a situation which naturally influenced his attitude to his employer. In 1845, John Noake, 'The Rambler', visited the new church in Guarlford, describing in his book, *The Rambler in Worcestershire*, how he found a congregation of "about seventy people, chiefly of the poorer classes" (p.320); and a *Malvern Advertiser* report in 1877 about the dedication of the new church organ describes the parish as having been a "wretched, poor district", though slowly improving.

Figure3.1 Myra Panting knitting socks for soldiers in 1918.

Mrs Panting, who lived in a small cottage on the Clevelode Road, was born in 1830 and in his memoirs, *I Got On My Bike*, her grandson, Mr Reg Green, (father of Mrs Rosemary Williams) described life in villages before the First World War: "The old saying 'God bless the Squire and his relations, and keep us in our proper stations' was lived up to in the country in my grandparents' time. I well remember my grandmother telling me that it was woe betide any villager who did not doff a cap or make a curtsey to 'Her Ladyship' when she passed by." (p.3) He goes on to say, "My Grandfather was a farm worker all his life and the most he ever earned was eighteen shillings (90p) a week. His last employment was on the Madresfield Estate, the ancestral home of the Lygon family. For many years before he died he was crippled with gout and was only able to get about on two sticks. At that time all they had to live on was 'parish pay', a mere pittance." (pp.2-3) The Parish Records state that, in 1891, twenty adults in Guarlford were receiving parochial relief.

> **The Vote**
>
> *In 1867 the vote was extended to almost all workingmen except agricultural day labourers; in 1884 rural male householders over twenty-one received the vote. So generally the male farm labourer could vote, but not his wealthy lady employer until 1918 at the earliest!*

The parish of Guarlford lies at what was the junction of three great Estates: the Foley Malvern Estate, Earl Beauchamp's Madresfield Estate and the Hornyold Blackmore Estate, all of which influenced the parish. There was no 'Lord of the Manor', although the Earls Beauchamp and their ladies were particularly involved in local projects and the Madresfield Show was an important local event.

Surviving On The Land

In the first part of the twentieth century, farm labourers and others may not have had much spare cash from their earnings, but they used all resources available to support their families as best they could. Guarlford was a great hop-growing area, and village women often shared the work, as, for example, at New House Farm. Hop picking was also a way of having a 'holiday' – for the children, if not their mothers!

During Reg Green's childhood before the First World War, before he moved to Malvern, the only holidays his family had were their visits from Dudley to his grandparents in Clevelode, when they helped with the hop harvest. He paints a happy picture of children who were expected to spend some of the time picking at the crib, but as often as not having a good time – wandering round the meadows, apple scrumping or riding on the farm wagons taking the hops to the kilns for drying. He goes on to say in *I Got On My Bike,* "How we all enjoyed the meals in the hopyard! Bacon and sausages etc. cooked over a wood fire tasted so good. I also remember the fish-man who hawked his fish, which he carried in a large basket, and how good the kippers tasted. Then at the end of the day – after so long in the open air – how we relished a substantial evening meal of pig-meat or bacon with fresh vegetables straight from the garden." (p.14) And thirty years later, for Mr John Little and his sister, Mrs Mary Thomas, their 'holiday' as children in Clevelode was hop-picking, once a year at Gabb's, a hop farmer at Callow End: "We had to cycle there and take a picnic. There were a lot of nice gypsies. Many people stayed overnight in sheds (a kind of barrack system), but we were close enough to come home."

Food from the hedgerows was also used to supplement the diet of the labourers' families. Reg Green describes taking back to Dudley on the train "tin trunks filled with apples", plus jars of jam made by his mother from locally picked blackberries and apples. His parents used to get walnuts (locally called 'bannuts') from a huge tree by the Severn. He remembers, "These were gathered green, salted down and then pickled in vinegar. I hated them." His father had a friend, a Mr Crowshore, who was a gamekeeper at South Wood, Guarlford. They frequently visited his house in the wood and could generally reckon on being given a rabbit or two. Mrs Panting also kept bees in round straw skeps in the garden and sometimes while the family were staying Reg would be sent over the fields to Madresfield Court to ask for a basin of dripping or a can of skimmed milk. All kinds of 'natural' supplies were used: "Our holiday at Guarlford sometimes coincided with the visit of Aunty Harriet and Uncle George. They had a herbalist shop in London and we helped to collect herbs in hessian sacks. We picked betony, scabious and agrimony and we were paid sixpence a sack – it took us ages to collect a sackful! My Aunty made a green ointment with them – it was a very effective 'cure-all' for all sorts of complaints, including boils and ringworm." (pp.14-16)

A regular occupation for Reg's grandmother at Michaelmas and Christmas was plucking poultry for the local farmers, work which went on for two or three days at a time. This meant that there was always a good supply of goose-down for the making of feather beds, which was popular in those days. As a boy Reg "found it rather wonderful to snuggle into a feather-bed made of goose-down – not very healthy perhaps, but always snug and warm!" (p.12)

Sale of the Foley Estate

At the end of the first decade of the twentieth century, a significant change came about in the village when, in September 1910, the vast Foley Estate (1,363 acres of the Malvern area) was sold, including land and property in Guarlford. Some farms and land were absorbed into the neighbouring Madresfield Estate; tenant farmers, such as Mr Stephen George Medcalf at New House Farm, became the owners of their own land and people with the necessary means were able to purchase cottages for themselves or to let. For example, the black and white cottages, Jessamine Cottage and Lashford Cottage, which stood beside the barn opposite the 'Green Dragon' were sold to Mr J Tomkins of Barnard's Green, for £235; the father of Mr Mark Young, the blacksmith, later rented one of these. This breaking up of the Foley estate meant that ownership devolved to a greater number of new landowners and homeowners, although the situation of the farm labourer did not change significantly for some time.

Employment

In the decades between the two World Wars, the landscape and life of the parish were very different from what they are in 2005. It is from this between-the-wars period that the most vivid memories come.

Graham Road, and it used to go to the top of The Link and back. She had to run all the way down by the theatre, into the 'County Hotel' and drop the washing, then back to pick the bus up." Sam Beard's grandmother worked at Madresfield, now the big black and white house of 'The Madresfield Club', and laundered on her own account, as well as in Poolbrook, and finished up as vestry laundress to Revd Newson. According to Charlie Williams, if a woman lost her husband, "…she had ten bob (50p) a week and half a crown (12p) for a child" financial aid. She might also lose their tied cottage and have to pay 'five bob' to rent a house.

The Domestic Scene

Before the First World War, Reg Green's grandmother and other housewives did all the cooking for the family in a large iron pot suspended on a chain over the fire in an ancient range, most of the fuel being wood, and this method continued for a long time. Vegetables from a large garden and an allotment were put into the pot in nets, together with the boiled puddings, bacon and so on. For the Clevelode people, the allotments were near a piece of ground past the crossroads on the left called the 'Bowling Green', just a rough patch of grass. John Little recalls that in the decade before World War Two their particular family allotment had mostly fruit trees and potatoes.

Many families kept chickens, and in the sty a pig which was the essential main source of meat for most of the year. Reg Green loved the smell and taste of the small potatoes which were boiled in the copper out in the washhouse for pig feed. Miss Joan Bradshaw, born in Guarlford over eighty years ago, describes how on the pig-killing day a Mr Allen rode over from Hanley Swan on his tricycle to attend to the business, which resulted in the family, friends and near neighbours having

Figure 3.5 Back: Rosina Beard and her mother. Front L-R: Samuel T Beard, Jack Beard and Lizzie Beard, c.1900.

a feast of pig meat and homemade faggots. After salting, the rest of the carcase was wrapped in muslin and hung from the rafters to keep the family in home-cured bacon for the year.

It was, therefore, very important that the pigs were raised successfully. In an edition of *The Grapevine* in the summer of 1988, there is a story of how Mrs Phyllis Willis (nee Morris) "saved the family bacon" at Brickyard Cottage at the Rhydd in the twenties. The two pigs had eaten some red lead left behind by workmen. Mrs Willis fed a bowl of empty peapods to the pigs. One ate the peapods, vomited and lived. The other did not.

Mary Thomas, whose family lived in Clevelode in the thirties and forties, says that the diet of the time depended very much on bacon products and eggs. Many villagers had commoners' rights and kept poultry and occasionally sheep on the common in front of the houses. Mary recalls, "We were almost self-sufficient in those days and there were four of us children, which fortunately wasn't such a large family. We kept our own chickens and we used to keep and kill our own pigs. There were two downstairs rooms in our house, one room and a little back place. We used to hang sides of bacon there." John, Mary's brother, says: "The pigs were killed in the back yard and there were hooks from the ceiling to hang the two sides on them. My Grandmother Sims (wife of Jarvey Sims, who was the woodman in South Wood) salted them – she wouldn't let anyone else do it." Salting was an essential way to preserve the pork; refrigeration was unknown in most domestic kitchens, except for the 'meat safe', often placed against an outside north facing wall to keep things cool.

> ### The Pig
>
> *Nothing about a pig was wasted: the 'caul', a lacy membrane surrounding the stomach and intestine, was used for wrapping faggots for cooking, and pork scratchings were made from the pig's skin. The rind was rendered down in a low oven to produce pork dripping and the remaining rind was placed back in the oven on a high temperature to make pork scratchings. Sometimes the 'leaf' was used. The 'leaf' is the layer of fat round the kidneys. It was boiled and the top skimmed off, which, after oven baking, also produced crispy pork scratchings. Villagers also tell how the pig's bladder would be used as an inflated football.*

According to Mr Rob Gilroy and his Aunt Lil, who was a member of a large family that also lived in Clevelode, the sides of bacon in their household were covered in a lime and water wash as a preservative. Rob has his own memories of visits to his grandparents in Clevelode in the 1950s and life then seemed very much as it had been before the Second World War: "Like most people around them, they were self-sufficient in most fruit and veg, and bottled much of their produce for the winter. They kept chickens and also fattened a pig to about four hundred pounds for their own use. In addition, they raised pigs for market; most of these were purchased by Walls for bacon. The target weight was 'eight score', one hundred and sixty pounds. A butcher came to kill the family pig, and he split the carcass into two. It was then painted with lime and water wash to preserve it. When you wanted a joint, you cut it off, painted the exposed remains, and then cleaned the joint. With age, the fat turned a very nasty yellow. We also used to have eels, which we caught in the Severn. They weren't killed, but kept in a damp sack to keep fresh. We usually had them for breakfast, when Gran would stick a fork in the body just behind the head, run a knife round the trunk, pull the skin off and throw the eel into a large frying pan, still wriggling."

Mr Gilroy continues: "Gran gave us sausages on Saturday night as a treat, or, if the Littles' relations were also home on holiday, we might all get together for fish and chips. One person went to Barnard's Green to collect the food, which was always cold by the time he had cycled back. We all enjoyed it nevertheless." And then there were rabbits. John Little used to keep a lot of rabbits: "I used to take them up to Barnard's Green to the 'Rabbit Club'. Going to Barnard's Green was like going to the big city!"

Mrs Lil Gilroy, who was born Lil Morris in 1907, described what the whole Morris family in Clevelode would drink, including the many children: "We drank cider, which we would have in little cups made of horn, not glass." Rob Gilroy says that the main part of his grandfather's diet seemed to be cider, which he made himself in fifty-six gallon barrels (hogs), having purchased the apples and had them pressed. Grandfather Morris also made wine and he never drank tea or coffee, just cider for breakfast, lunch and dinner. Mr and Mrs Morris distrusted cows' milk as "…there had been TB epidemics in the early years of the century, and the Littles and the Morrises, who had not drunk cows' milk, were the only family locally not to have lost any children", according to Rob Gilroy and his aunt.

Joan Bradshaw draws a vivid picture of life in the village during the two decades immediately before the Second World War: "Some of the older villagers can recall the hard life of the farm-workers, who endured intense cold and wet, no hot water except that heated in a kettle over the open range or in a boiler in the scullery on washing days. Others remember the chilblains; every winter every child dreaded chilblains, practically unheard of today, painful swollen toes and fingers, and even sometimes ears and noses. And having to go to bed by candlelight and breaking ice to wash in the mornings. So much has changed in the way we live and in our homes. It is tempting to think of the past as rosier than it was, the unhurried pace and the softness of lamplight, and to forget the constant work needed to keep old cottages clean and warm." Mary Thomas recalls that in their cottage in Clevelode, the upstairs rooms were covered in lino with rugs by the beds, so a broom, dustpan & brush, plus a soft mop, were used. Downstairs were quarry tiles, which were brushed and then scrubbed (on hands and knees) with water and a scrubbing brush – more hard work.

For some time cooking continued to be done on coal or wood burning ranges; the ranges needed much stoking and cleaning with blacklead but created warm cosy rooms in winter. According to Mary Thomas, the blacklead "…was put on with a flat brush with a handle across the top, so that you could push your hand in. You worked at it until it shone! The chimney sweep was Tippus Allen." When the modern oil cooking stoves appeared on the scene they were a godsend to those who could afford them, and meant that the dust-making ranges did not have to be used in summertime. Many meals were cooked in the farmhouses on these two or four burner 'Valor' or 'Florence' stoves, which had a removable tin oven for baking. The paraffin sold at Mrs Bullock's 'General Store', for example, was essential for the hurricane lamps and others used in the cottages and farm buildings.

Figure 3.6 Earth closet at Woodbridge Farm.

In some of the larger houses an indoor WC (water closet) was installed, but the water had to be pumped by hand - "Twenty strokes to flush the loo" - so generally people still trekked out to the 'little house in the garden'. Alf Young said, "Up until 1938, there were no toilets to these houses (on Guarlford Road, near Hall Green), just an earth closet right at the top of the garden and it was always next to the pigsty. These earth closets were over just a pit with a cover. Two or three times a year my father or the man next door would take it in turns: they'd dig a trench in the garden the night before and the next morning would get up about five o'clock, with some Woodbine cigarettes and empty all that – the pit – into the trench. Then put a bag of lime in it. Most of the houses like ours were built in the 1800s in Lady Foley's time."

Mrs Margaret Llewelyn (nee Woolley), who lived in the original School House, said, "The range in the kitchen/living room provided a fire which warmed only those nearest to it, an oven and a space on top for stews and so on. This was also our only way to get hot water for cooking and washing. Water had to be pumped up from the well below the wash-house several slippery steps away from the back door. On Saturday nights we took turns to wash in a hip-bath before the fire. I was lucky – being the youngest – I went in first! After World War Two, we had a zinc bath, which hung outside the back door when not in use. By this time the old range had been removed and my brother Pete had built a brick fire-place."

Since the 1960s the domestic scene in Guarlford has changed considerably. Advances in technology have brought central heating and new equipment. The loss of the village shops and gardens too small for growing many vegetables make necessities of refrigerators and freezers rather than luxuries; and in the twenty-first century women working outside the home all day need time- and labour-saving devices.

> **Lady of the Manor**
>
> *On the red-brick cottages, next to 'Rosemeade' on Guarlford Road, now part of New House Farm, can be seen a plaque with EF and 1891 on it, EF standing for Lady Emily Foley, who was 'lady of the manor' at that time.*

Seasons of the Year

In general, though, and in spite of the hard life described, memories of Guarlford's past are happy ones. No-one seemed to mind the cold if it was dry. Hurrying home to 'toast and dripping' in front of the fire in the old iron range, John Little also remembers the range with a toasting fork to hand and how a glass of cider would be warmed by a poker made red-hot. In the first half of the twentieth century when the snow and ice came everyone had fun apparently, like tobogganing down Ox Hill, or - something that would not be encouraged today - sliding on the ice on the pool on the corner by Guarlford Nursery. There was more water in the ponds then and winters were harder. Many recall that more snow fell and lasted longer so that, as Margaret Llewelyn (nee Woolley) remembers, children could "build satisfactory snowmen and indulge in snowball fights, after being wrapped up in a thick woollen scarf which was crossed at the front and pinned at the back, before being allowed out to play". When the pond in front of Guarlford Court was frozen hard one year some of the grown-ups skated there either by moonlight or by hurricane lamps hung on the railings. Alf Young remembered enough ice for one of the people nearby to skate on 'The Fladder' (the pond on the common near the postbox at the junction of Hall Green and the Guarlford Road).

Of course, as Joan Bradshaw says, it was not so much fun for the people who had to look after animals; every drop of water had to be pumped by hand from deep wells, or the ice broken, once the pump was thawed out. Mrs Clarke, who lived in a house where the bungalows opposite the church are now, used to go early to the school and stoke up the huge iron tortoise stoves to reduce the chill on winter mornings and on damp days to hang the pupils' wet coats on the guards round the stoves to dry. Memories, too, of the harsh winters, such as that of 1947, are still vivid, as when, for example, Joan Newell had to fetch fuel for the farm machinery in two jerry cans attached to her horse.

Floods were not uncommon, especially in Clevelode; quite a few residents had canoes for such times and were always ready to move themselves and their belongings upstairs. Mrs Lil Gilroy remembers walking to school from Clevelode during the First World War and that her mother would rake one or two pieces of hot coals from the fire and shake them into the family's boots to dry them out afterwards. At Brickyard Cottage at the Rhydd, floodwater would come up to the front steps of the house, and in winter, if the water froze, swans would waddle and slide up to the door to be fed.

Then there was fog, as Alf Young recalled, "I've seen the 'Sentinels', quarry steam wagons, in November-time, coming back with the fireman walking in front of them because the fog was so thick." The noisiest vehicles on the roads were these steam wagons from the quarries on the hills. At dusk they resembled the dragons from fairy tales, with the flying sparks from their fireboxes and the hissing and rumbling.

People remember the pre-1914-18 War summers as long and sunny, and a much earlier reference in the Guarlford School Log Book, on August 22nd 1906, reports that the thermometer in 'the room' registered 82 degrees and as (so it says) the temperature in the sun outside was 118 degrees the Headmaster did not take drill.

Families at Play

Children at Play

Spare money was not plentiful for many families in the village, and so the entertainment was often 'home-made' but none the worse for that it seems, as is seen by the way that the progress of the year brought its own homemade pastimes. According to Joan Bradshaw, and as many will recall from the twenties and thirties, there were seasons for children's games in those days.

Apart from the obvious one of conkers in autumn, it was a mystery how these games and their timing evolved: suddenly everyone was skipping, with a supply of skipping ropes with bright coloured handles appearing in the village shops for the lucky ones; the others made do with bits of old rope, begged from the farms perhaps. At another time, ropes were discarded and hoops made their appearance; every cottage seemed to have an old iron hoop hanging in the garden shed, until later the shops stocked light cane ones. But most exciting were the brightly-coloured whipping tops, made of wood, making such a pretty show in the shop window. The whips could be bought, too, for about three pence (1p), but most children made their own. The roads were very much quieter then, and the occasional motor vehicle could be heard coming a long way off, in plenty of time for the children to remove themselves and their hoops or whipping tops to safety.

> ### Mr Kenneth Woolley
>
> *Mr Kenneth Woolley, son of the Guarlford Headmaster, also remembered the freedom of childhood - and the scrapes they got into! He was friendly with Johnny Jones, the son of the carpenter living in one of the red brick cottages on the road to Old Hills. They used to 'pinch' plums from the Robathan orchard and always thought that they could escape easily, as the son of the owner had a damaged foot. Kenneth and Johnny were in the orchard in Penny Lane one day when they heard him coming: no time to escape, so they climbed a tree and the next thing they knew was that a shotgun barrel was being aimed up through the tree and they were ordered to come down. Mr R. marched them back to School House, where the two boys were handed over to father for summary punishment.*

Alf Young said that they used to play tops all the way down to school in Guarlford along the road from Hall Green. Guarlford was a very safe and happy place for children to grow up, safe to wander and later cycle around their small world.

Adults at Play

From the nineteenth century onwards, Church events and socialising between the various farming families provided the adults with their recreation. The photograph shows a Whist Drive on the Rectory lawn in about 1920. Note the suits of the gentlemen, although it must have been summer time.

Figure 3.7 A Whist Drive on the Rectory lawn, c.1920.

After the First World War there were, of course, the theatre and cinema in Great Malvern to be enjoyed. Mr Woolley arranged educational visits to these for his pupils in the 1920s and 1930s, but events arranged by the people themselves living in the village and surrounding area were still the most popular. For hard-pressed farmers and workers, the Agricultural Shows were a welcome break and opportunity to show off their skills. In the parish there were traditionally Social Evenings on Shrove Tuesday (no social occasions in Lent) and the week before Christmas – tickets threepence - where local talent held sway.

Joan Bradshaw describes how everyone who could do anything at all to entertain did his best:

"Old Dick Bullock, Mr Medcalf's pigman sang 'Termut hoeing', vigorously 'hoeing' with a broom until everyone was choking with the dust raised and Mrs Newson tactfully removed the offending tool. The Rector, Revd Newson, sang 'Widdecombe Fair', helped by realistic 'skirling and groans' from the audience; Mr Cole, the wheelwright from Chance Lane, who for many years walked up to Malvern Priory twice a day on Sundays to sing in the choir, sang 'Asleep in the Deep' in so deep a bass that he almost finished up in the cellar! Frank Jarrett, butcher from Hanley Swan in daytime, dance bandleader in the evenings, accompanied himself with 'I do like an egg for my tea'. Then came 'Riding on a Camel in the Desert' by the local saddler, while Major Derrington (of Guarlford Court Farm) gave 'The Old Rustic Bridge by the Mill'. Items were interspersed with dances to Frank Jarrett's Band, those taught in Mrs Newson's dancing classes being the most popular – The Lancers, Military Two-Step, Valetta, Polka and St. Bernard's Waltz among them. One year, Mrs Newson and Francis Hyde of Clevelode, in costume, danced the stately Gavotte."

Mrs Pamela Fairhurst tells of the Poultry Whist Drive: "Each village round and about held one, and cut-throat affairs they were, everyone keen to win their Christmas Dinner. Competitors came from far and wide - at least from Madresfield, Hanley and Callow End."

Figure 3.8 The 1969 Harvest Supper.
L-R: Mrs V Roberts, Mrs Sims, Miss J Bradshaw and Mrs D W Medcalf.

Edwin Lane of Woodbridge Farm and his sister Margaret recalled that, when they were teenagers in the 1950s, they used to go down to the Village Hall for dances: "The Marjorie Chater School of Dancing used to run the ballroom dancing classes down in Guarlford Village Hall – boys at one end doing one step with an instructor and the girls at the other end. Take your partners, which was quite embarrassing. We had Modern and Old Time Dancing classes and they were great fun. There was a young lad called David Harrison from Hanley Swan, a superb dancer and demonstrator, who used to come with Mrs Johnson, the teacher."

More Entertainment

In the 1920s, where Guarlford Nursery and Penny Close are now, was an orchard of cider fruit and perry pears, large old trees, and the Village Sports Day was held there. There were races for the schoolchildren, tug-of-war teams for the men, and Mrs Betteridge from the Hills brought her donkeys to give rides. Phyl Bayliss remembers her father taking her for a ride on one of these donkeys up on the Malvern Hills when she was about six years old in 1922. Mrs Ackerman of 'Tan House' did a very popular line in homemade ice cream, a rare treat in those days. There were bowls and various sideshows, and Joan Bradshaw believes that the Men's Club did most of the organising. Cdr Ratcliff, R.N. of Dripshill, who seems to have taken on the duties of the 'Squire', was well in evidence and gave the prizes; he was President of the Men's Club and took a great interest in village affairs. Later the venue moved to a field near 'The Green Dragon', but it was never revived after the Second World War.

There was also a 'Guarlford Marathon' (admittedly only three and a half miles and not twenty-six) before and just after the Second World War, which was a very popular event with the young men of the parish. Mrs Kath Lockley's father, Bill Sims, won the prize a couple of times; Mrs Mary Jones's husband, Archie, well known in the village, won it in the 1930's; and Derrick Bladder in 1951. The marathon was a handicap race, run on Derby Day each June. The course went from 'The Homestead' (then the home of Captain Chester) down the lane to Clevelode, on to the

Figure 3.9 The Guarlford Marathon, c.1930. Included above are Bill Sims, Frank Jarrett, Tom Sims and Archie Jones.

Rhydd, then back along Rhydd Road to Guarlford Village. One year the 'handicap' was even greater for Ken Woolley (who won the race in 1948), when Captain Chester's stopwatch stopped!

Mr Keith Chester remembers listening to the gramophone (HMV,with horn) and singing around the piano, as well as playing bridge, with neighbours. In 1936 the BBC began broadcasting some television programmes from Alexandra Palace in London; but the development of television broadcasting to the whole population as it is today was held back by the advent of the Second World War. The wireless, however, had been popular since the 1920s, and some of the older residents particularly found it useful as a form of entertainment, as did Rob Gilroy's grandfather, Bill Morris, who was born in Castlemorton in 1880 but spent his married life in Guarlford. He had never learned to read or write properly, having had to leave school at the age of seven

Leslie Halward

Leslie Halward had worked as a toolmaker, labourer and plasterer and began to write stories for magazines in the 1930s, later for the BBC. In an article on October 13th 1950 about his eighth play for the BBC, the Malvern Gazette described him as "well-known to radio listeners for his human domestic and back-street comedies". (Leslie Halward died in 1976 and his ashes are buried in Guarlford Churchyard.)

to work with his father when his mother died. Derrick Bladder recalls the wireless sets found in most homes: "There was a big battery – a dry battery – and then the accumulator. Someone came from Callow End every Friday, took the old one away, recharged it and brought it back the next week. And we used to make crystal sets." Accumulators had to be treated with respect, as they were made of heavy glass and contained sulphuric acid. John Little says that when he was a youngster during the Second World War batteries could be recharged at 'Ranfords' in Barnard's Green (which stood where 'Somerfield' is now) and 'Woodwards' at the end of Chance Lane.

Figure 3.10 Leslie Halward by Catherine Moody

Derrick remembers his mother listening to radio plays and stories by Leslie Halward, who was born in 1906 in Selly Oak, but eventually lived at the Heriots with his wife Gwen and children Kay and Anthony. The Woolley family at School House also found the radio a good source of entertainment: "We had a radio and rejoiced in ITMA ('It's That Man Again'), 'Take It From Here, 'Monday Night At Eight' and 'Dick Barton, Special Agent'. Any other spare time was devoted to reading or listening to music on a wind-up gramophone." Now in the twenty-first century, with the invention of the DVD player, together with television sets and video-recorders, the residents of Guarlford do not have to leave their own homes to see a film – and can have 'all round sound' included!

Derrick Bladder is one of four brothers, brought up in the village, and remembers how he learned to swim in about 1930: "I learned to swim in the pool 'across the Tanhouse', opposite the Plough and Harrow. The three fields there were called the Tanhouses and in the left hand side against Mr Bott's side there was a big pool. In the old days they used to dig out all these narrow pools around here to get the 'marl' for fertilizer; the pools would fill with water and were for the cattle. My grandfather cleaned them out every so often, but they couldn't clean the whole pool, just the two ends where it wasn't too deep." (Marl is a soil consisting of clay and carbonate of lime, a valuable fertilizer.) When Derrick was older, he used to go swimming in the river under the cliffs at Clevelode and also occasionally hire a punt from the Little family. He said, "Four or five of us lads, for threepence (1p) – a lot of money in those days - for two or three hours. One rowing boat, for two people, was a shilling (5p) and the other was one and sixpence (7.5p) an hour. We used to go out in those occasionally, when we had visitors. All you had to worry about in those days were the old barges and steamer-boats pulling barges of coal and all sorts going up and down regularly – you hardly saw any pleasure boats. The trouble was when they came down there was a tidal wave behind them which would wash our fishing tackle away!"

At the beginning of the century children would be able to swim in Penny Meadow when it was flooded for irrigation. Then Keith Chester of 'The Homestead' has memories of cycling or riding around the countryside, swimming in the Severn at Clevelode, and shooting with a .22 rifle and a shotgun, when he was home from boarding school. There were also many Sports Teams and Societies in the Parish in the first half of the twentieth century, and the Guarlford Men's Club was very busy.

Christmas

Christmas was definitely a time for families and neighbours to relax together. In a 1988 *Grapevine*, Phyllis Willis described Christmas in her late teens at Brickyard Cottage, near Dripshill House, where the Morris family lived from 1923 until 1928, when her father worked for Mr Gerald Radcliffe: "Every Christmas morning she and her sister, Cassie, would get up before their father at 6 am and sing 'Christians awake, salute the happy morn' outside his bedroom. Christmas was celebrated in fine style, with pork pies and a goose and a barrel of beer donated by Mr Radcliffe. Mrs Emma Morris knew how to make orange wine, and many a happy party was held in the cottage with neighbours such as Mr and Mrs Insley from Dripshill Lodge and Mr and Mrs Roland Hayes from Clevelode."

Mr Keith Chester remembers very good and jolly Christmas parties with the Medcalfs, neighbours at New House Farm, which were always held only after Christmas; and Ken Woolley described the "hard-working genuine country gentleman, Mr Medcalf's cowman, Mr Fred Clarke, and his wife, whose four sturdy sons, Harold, Bernard (known as Tom), Ernie and Rusty, would sing carols at the School House with voices of angels".

Margaret Llewelyn, born in Guarlford in 1929, was the youngest child of Mr Woolley, the school Headmaster and she recalls: "Christmas in the School House was a lovely time when I was young. Mother had made a cake and puddings beforehand and on Christmas Eve Ken and I decorated the kitchen and the sitting room, known just as 'the room', with holly and mistletoe while she made pastry for the mince pies. We had a tree, which was hung with baubles and tinsel. No early decorations and flashing lights for us. Next morning there was the pleasure of finding a pillowcase full of goodies from Santa Claus – nothing expensive and much of it homemade. Mother cooked a wonderful Christmas dinner, which we enjoyed on our return from Morning Service. The rest of the day was spent in the 'room' with its roaring fire (only ever lit at Christmas), playing games and eating yet more Christmas treats".

Royal Events

George V's Jubilee was celebrated in 1935. Commander Ratcliff organised a tea and races for all the children at Dripshill House. He certainly knew how to entertain children. Derrick Bladder says, "He showed us how to throw boomerangs. Of course, when we boys got home we tried to make one, but it didn't come back." Alf Young remembered that Cdr Ratcliff had a swimming pool, a big place. The children were given tea, a mug and an orange. "There were tractor rides and all that sort of thing. In the wood behind he had a watchtower, in Dripshill, a crow's nest on the top of a tree." According to Ken Woolley, the chains from the school swing, which usually hung from a beautiful silver birch tree in the girls' playground, were transferred to Dripshill for the day.

Another Royal event was when the Duchess of York (later Queen Elizabeth the Queen Mother) was due to travel through the parish in 1934 to Malvern Girls' College to open the York Wing, and local children (one of whom was Sam Beard, a member of a Guarlford

family of long standing) used bean sticks, binder twine, a few small Union Jacks, and oddments of coloured cloth to make a triumphal archway on the Guarlford Road near the Plough & Harrow. When the great moment arrived and the Westminster green and brass-embellished car drew near, the Duchess was seen to make a hand signal to the driver. The car slowed considerably, the children waved, so did the Royal party, and cheers were loud and long.

Figure 3.11 The Parish's Golden Jubilee Picnic, Tuesday 4th June 2002 at Cherry Orchard.

The Tan House

There was another shop, next to the 'Plough and Harrow' at the 'Tan House'. Derrick Bladder remembers it run by "old Granny Thomas and Mrs Ackerman"; and Alf

Young recalled that, when he was a boy in the 1920s and '30s, they used to put all the 'merchandise' out on the tables in the front room. Mrs Pamela Fairhurst (nee Newson) said that Granny Thomas "…had a cupboard in her front room full of the most marvellous sweeties: sherbet dabs, sweetie cigarettes, gobstoppers, wonderful ice-cream cones full of 'goo' and covered with chocolate – most costing a halfpenny and some even a farthing." The children would also go "down the main road to Mrs Coupar Bladder, who did teas at her cottage and

Figure 4.2 Mrs Thomas and her daughters outside the Tan House.

on the common, and who sold wonderful fizzy pop, something not allowed at home". Pamela also remembered that for some weeks in the summer a few pennies would buy a newspaper screw of cherries from Robathan at the Cherry Orchard and "I've never tasted such gorgeous cherries since." Mrs Thelma Collett told Joan Bradshaw that her grandmother Mrs Thomas, who was Jane Ann Till, born in 1847, kept her little shop in the 1920s and '30s, selling sweets together with tobacco, and toys in season. There is a photograph of the old lady by the gate, over which stands an archway sign advertising this.

Mrs Collett believed that the property had belonged to her family for hundreds of years. As its name implies, the 'Tan House' was originally a tannery, and the names Barber and Taylor are mentioned as Mrs Collett's tanner ancestors. George Till and Mary Ann Barber are reputedly linked on an 1841 tithe map with the "Blacksmith's shop and approximately two acres." It is reported that, upon the death of Mr George Till, his daughter, Mrs Thomas, and her mother ran a sort of finishing school for the local young ladies in the front room of the 'Tan House' in the 1870s.

Malcolm Russell

For many people the name of 'Tan House' is inextricably linked with Malcolm Russell. Malcolm came to Malvern to teach at the Chase High School in the early 1970s. He left the teaching profession in 1982, and, in 1984, decided that he would use his Honours degree in Botany from Durham University to take up plant cultivation. Miss Pauline

Figure 4.3 Malcolm Russell with Sue Edwards.

Jones says that Malcolm began by selling his bedding plants to friends and villagers: "I remember Mary, his mother, telling me at Parish Singers' practice that I should buy Malcolm's 'lovely pansies', which was my first contact with 'Tan House Plants'. As the years passed, the nursery gradually developed. Friends gave him old sheds and greenhouses and helped him construct a series of ramshackle shelters, which were still leakily and shakily in existence at his death and are still there some years later. At first Malcolm just tried growing everything, including shrubs and roses, though he abandoned the latter because, with so many new varieties coming on the market each year, he could never stock enough to satisfy customers' needs. Cuttings and divisions of plants were Malcolm's speciality and the secret of his low prices."

In the early years, Malcolm had one full-time helper, Ken Pountain, who, with his wife Joyce, rented one of Bill Medcalf's cottages on Guarlford Road. Later, Malcolm employed many young people, some of them from Cliffey House seeking 'job-experience'; and some pupils from the Chase High School came as 'weekend workers'. Sarah Green, daughter of Revd John and Margaret Green, having spent three years doing two days a week at 'Tan House', went on to Pershore College to gain a qualification in horticulture. Apart from local customers, Malcolm's growing collection of unusual herbaceous perennials, his knowledge of the needs of the plants he sold, and his extremely reasonable prices were attracting an ever-increasing number of customers from further afield. Ten years after he started up, he was able to say in 1994 that for the first time at the end of the year he was in profit.

By 1995, when Pauline Jones joined the business, it had expanded considerably: "Malcolm took a stand at the 'Malvern Spring Show' each year and won a Silver Medal for his display of bedding plants. The certificate and a sun-faded photograph of the display were hung proudly in the old glass lean-to on the cottage, which Mary called 'her' shop, where also resided the old 'open-all-hours'-type till, a load of clutter, and Malcolm's carboys of damson or sloe gin. Malcolm was also one of the first traders at the 'Malvern Friday Market', trundling up every week in one of his ancient and dilapidated vans with a tenuous hold on his even more dilapidated trailer, which frequently spilled out trays of bedding plants on to the road as it bumped and rattled its way up to the car-park where the 'Waitrose' supermarket now stands."

Malcolm's mother, Mrs Mary Bruce, a popular and familiar figure in the village, became ill in 1997, and, with Pauline working alone in the nursery by that time, Malcolm needed extra help. Pauline Jones recalls that "this led to the advent of Sue Edwards, who, with her knowledge of nursery skill, her boundless energy, enthusiasm and efficiency, proved to be the 'making' of 'Tan House Plants', turning it round from being Malcolm's therapeutic hobby, as it was at its inception, into a proper business."

Sadly, Malcolm died from cancer in 2001 and is buried close to the entrance of the church, St. Mary's, where he was a Layreader for many years.

Grange Farm Nursery

This was at one time a farm whose buildings had been used for cattle and horses. The nursery was started in 1973 by Miss Joan Bradshaw and Miss Joan Newell and the original buildings were used "in order to preserve some of the agricultural atmosphere". In 1975, Carol Nicholls began working at the nursery on Saturdays and, after attending Pershore College of Horticulture, bought the nursery in 1980. It is now a specialist plant nursery and has on a number of occasions won Royal Horticultural Society Medals at the 'Malvern Spring Garden Show'. The nursery provides quite a focal point in the village and is a bustling place in spring and summer especially, when gardening enthusiasts from a wide area come for new plants. Unlike Malcolm's nursery, Carol's is supplied by outside sources such as the Dutch wholesalers whose large trailer vehicles can often be seen backed into the nursery for unloading. Guarlford is fortunate to have one thriving business drawing visitors to it still, other than those providing hospitality, a nursery which has a family atmosphere, unlike the many 'garden centres' to be found in and around Worcester and elsewhere. Grange Farm's achievements over the years include a number of awards from the Royal Horticultural Society and, most recently, recognition by a national newspaper, the *Daily Telegraph*.

Barbers and Bosworths

Between the Wars there was another plantsman near Hall Green: Sam Beard and Alf Young both recalled Mr Bosworth's plant nursery in a cottage on the corner of Mill Lane. Sam describes Alf Bosworth's stepped display of begonias against the walls of his cottage as "a splendid sight", and Charlie Williams says that there were several greenhouses

Figure 4.4 Bluebell Hall, formerly Bosworth's Cottage.

where "you could get a bouquet, wreath, bedding out plants, lettuce, tomatoes". Alf Bosworth's was the left-hand one of two semi-detached thatched cottages, very old and now all one, 'Bluebell Hall'; the nursery garden covered the area now occupied by a modern house. The other cottage housed 'Barber's General Store'. Mrs Barber was a widow and had a shop that sold sweets, cigarettes and Carrs' biscuits. Mr Young said that it was running in his school days in the 1930s, and 'Barbers' and 'Bullocks' were not really in competition. Some time after the First World War Mrs Barber's son returned home and built the wooden extension to provide extra living space. There is a story that this was used as a sort of tea-room at one time.

Within a hundred yards of the 'Bosworth's Nursery', at 'The Oaks', near Mill Farm, was 'Marsden's Nursery'. Both thrived, although 'Marsden's' was a bigger concern, employing eight men and women and supplying shops in Malvern and even Birmingham.

Hayes of Clevelode

Finally, Mr Derrick Bladder remembers that, as boys in the 1920s and '30s, he and his brothers would go to see "Mrs Hayes and old Pop Hayes (Clifford's grandparents) down at Clevelode where they had a little store up on the bank", where people could buy cigarettes and sweets. John Little says that in his time the shop was in the middle (run by Mrs Hayes' sister, Nancy Wilks), with Clifford Hayes's parents at one end and his aunt at the other. John Little also recalls Mrs Vivian at 'Honeypots' and a Mr Togue who delivered newspapers.

The little shops and general stores supplied some vital provisions for the villagers, who also had a certain amount of self-sufficiency with their own farms, gardens, allotments and animals. Other necessities were delivered first by horse and cart and then later by motor van.

Milk Deliveries

There were a number of competing milk rounds, one prominent local delivery being provided by Medcalfs of New House Farm, described by Reg Green in his autobiography. Another was that from Fowler's Farm. Early every morning, seven days a week, the milk floats would trot up the road from Guarlford to Malvern. Derrick Bladder was one of those who delivered the milk from Fowler's Farm with his father in the 1930s: "We milked twice a day, morning and night, and we made our own butter, too." If people ran out of milk the dairymen would make a special delivery, as Derrick says "to keep the custom – because there were a lot of people delivering milk round here then." There was no refrigerator in every home as is the case today, so customers would like the 'afternoon milk' for freshness. Derrick describes how he worked for Fred George of Honeypots Farm after his 'demob' from the RAF Regiment in 1946: "You would do your hand-milking and walk across the yard with the buckets open, full of milk; they'd take it into the cooling house and put it through the water cooler. The winter of 1946-47 was a terrible year for frost and snow, and at the Old Hollow (on the Hills) people tunnelled underneath the snow to get through. Fred George had a little van by then, and we made a toboggan, which I put on the roof, so we could pull the churn down Moorlands Road in Great Malvern, to ladle the milk into customers' own jugs. They were delighted to see us!"

Other Tradesmen

Mrs Phyl Bayliss said that all the tradesmen came round with horses and carts – the coalman, milk, butcher, baker. The old bakery stood on the corner of Chance Lane and the lane to Grove House Farm; it has now been demolished and rebuilt as part of a modern house, though it is still known as 'The Old Bakery'. It was the home of Mr Nicholls, the last baker to use a stick oven and one of the first to use a motor van for his daily bread round; a curved brick lean-to on one end of the cottage contained the oven. Later the baker was a Mr Derrett. Another baker and grocer from Malvern also delivered regularly in a horse-drawn van – "the horse knew all the customers and would move on and stop at each place on his own". 'Brickells' of Callow End delivered bread to Guarlford until the 1980s.

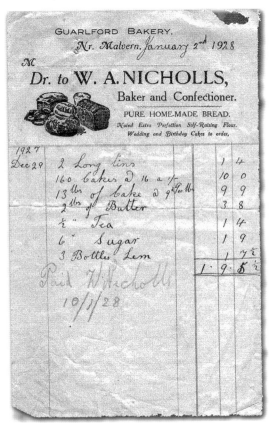

Derrick Bladder also remembers the tradesmen: "In those days you had the grocer who delivered; we used to have 'Howell and Stevens' from Link Top. He used to come round and take the order; then the next week he delivered it, collected his money and took the next order. The same with the fish man on the Friday and the butcher, 'Preece's' from Upton, at that time." One fishmonger was called Mr Thorne, and Frank Jarret, in 'a spotless white coat and blue striped apron', used to

Figure 4.5 Baker's bill for a church event, dated 10th January 1928.

drive the butcher's horse and cart. He also played the piano for some of the 'dos' at the village hall.

Another of the first motor vehicles to deliver in the district was a truck, which came from 'Fords', a hardware shop in Barnard's Green, now 'Dobsons'. Hung about with buckets and brooms, it had a tank with a cap on the back from which farmers and people using a lot of the essential oil could fill their containers. And Margaret Omar tells of later "Mr Tout, who had a place in Quest Hills Road, who used to come round

with a lorry; we'd buy paraffin and sweets from him – all sorts of things." Mrs Margaret Hunaban remembers that he called on Tuesdays and "Mr Turberfield used to deliver the *Worcester Journal* on his three-wheeled trike every Saturday evening."

Members of the Little family from Clevelode fished for eels, as well as salmon. There were three ways of catching eels. One method was with funnel-shaped baskets called 'putchins'. These were baited with lob worms gathered during the night by

Figure 4.6 Tradesman with horse and cart.

members of the family. The 'putchins' were weighted so that they lay on the riverbed and were attached to cork floats on the surface of the water. A ten-shilling licence from the River Authority enabled twenty 'putchins' to be operated all the year round. Another way of catching eels was by means of a net. This method could only be used in October and November, as the eels came downstream heading for the sea. The third way, employed in summer months, was by means of a nightline. This was a line stretched across the river from which were suspended twenty baited hooks, and not only would large eels be caught in this way but also pike, which, in the opinion of Mr Little, were "nicer fish to eat than even salmon". The Littles built up quite a trade for eels in the locality. Having skinned and cleaned them, they would then cycle round Callow End, Hanley Castle and Barnard's Green selling them. A medium-sized eel would sell for ninepence a pound and a large eel, which had a very rich taste, for a shilling. People used to look upon eels as a great delicacy and the arrival of the Littles' eels was greeted with great enthusiasm.

Barnard's Green and Great Malvern

There were, of course, shops and department stores in Barnard's Green and Great Malvern. When she left Guarlford School at the age of fourteen in 1930, Phyl Bayliss was apprenticed to the dressmakers at 'Kendalls' in Great Malvern (where the 'Halifax Building Society' is now) for five shillings a week. She later worked at 'Warwick House', a department store since converted into flats: "It was lovely working at 'Warwick House', altering beautiful clothes; the workroom was on the floor over the clock and stretched to the other side overlooking the valley. Before I worked at 'Warwick House' all the shop assistants lived in; the shop was open from 8.30 am to 6 pm, with a half day on Saturday. There were twenty-four of us in the workroom at 'Warwick House'; I cycled to work from Hall Green."

The Lanes of Woodbridge Farm had a 'high class florist and fruiterer's shop' in Great Malvern, in Holyrood Terrace on the promenade beyond 'Brays'. At one time they used to grow vegetables and flowers in Sherrard's Green, and Mr Lane would go round the farms with a horse and cart to buy eggs, butter and dressed chickens to sell in the shop. Villagers remember with nostalgia "the lovely shops" that used to be in Great Malvern, of which only 'Brays' now remains. However, for the essentials of daily living during the first half of the twentieth century, people did not need to go beyond the boundaries of the parish.

Basket-Making at Clevelode

At the beginning of the twentieth century, the tiny hamlet of Clevelode in Guarlford parish was a thriving centre of basket-making. Three families earned part or all of their living from making baskets from the osiers that grew along the banks of the River Severn. The three families were the Hayes, the Hydes, and the Littles.

According to an article published in *The Grapevine* in 1989, Mr Harry Hayes came from the Birmingham area to Clevelode at the end of the nineteenth century and brought with him the art of weaving baskets from osiers. He made his home at 122 Clevelode. His son, Thomas, appears to have earned his living first as a male nurse at the Powick Asylum and only later as a basket-maker. He lived at the Rhydd and then at 'Hilltop Cottage', Clevelode. Thomas specialised in fine work and Thomas's son, Roland, who spent all his life as a basket-maker at Clevelode, could turn his hand to making almost anything from osiers. The Hyde family consisted of three sisters, Nora, Frances, and Mrs Willis, and a brother, Fred. Nora lived at 123 Clevelode, Frances at 'The Orchard' and Mrs Willis at 'The Honeypots'.

Figure 4.7 Mr F W Hyde and the basket workshop at Clevelode, 1934.

Fred was formerly landlord of the 'Green Dragon' pub. Two of the Little brothers also tried basket-making for a while, but the main occupation of this family was fishing.

The osiers used were grown in several 'beds' along the riverside. There were 'beds' at the Claypits, Upton-upon-Severn (where 'Upton Marina' is now sited), at Beauchamp Court, Callow End, and three acres at Clevelode itself, on land belonging to Clevelode Farm. One villager remembers that before the Second World War the field below 'The Homestead' on the Clevelode Road was an extensive osier bed, where her mother and a friend earned sixpence a bundle for cutting them.

The osier beds were specially planted by the basket-makers. If an osier stick was simply stuck into the ground, it would straightway root and begin growing. The osiers were planted in straight rows and had to be tended during the year so that they were not choked by weeds. Then, in February or March, they were cut and the bundles transported to sheds at Clevelode. If short 'withies' were required, one-year-old osiers were cut, but if longer 'withies' were needed, two or three–year-old osiers were used.

According to a *Grapevine* account, Clifford Hayes, son of Roland the last basket-maker in the family, vividly remembered, as a boy, travelling down the river in a punt laden with osiers. So heavy were the bundles that the top of the punt was only three inches above the water line. Once the osiers had been cut, they were pulled through a V-shaped prong, which stripped away the outer skin before the osiers were boiled, producing a white 'withy', particularly useful for making linen or bread baskets. If the osiers were boiled and then skinned, a buff-coloured 'withy' was produced, suitable for making shopping baskets. Finally, the osiers could be left unskinned if they were to be used for rougher work such as fencing hurdles or pot hampers.

> **Osier Tanks**
>
> *These large flat tanks had brick ducts, which allowed hot air produced by a fire to circulate underneath and round the tanks. The osiers were pressed down tightly below the water level in the tank and boiled for a whole day. They then remained in the tank for a further day to ensure they were really supple.*

John Little, born in 1930, remembers cutting osiers on the river bank near Pixham when "Jack Meek would cut and skin the 'withies' and boil them. We'd also boil the pitch and melt it to paint it on to the flat bottoms of the punts. We made baskets of different sizes for fruit picking – sieves, half pot, pot." John Little can recall how the fruit baskets would be loaded directly on to the railway lorries, with newspaper tied with string over the top of the baskets to keep in the fruit being transported to the sidings at Malvern Link Station.

The basket-makers did not lack customers. They made a wide variety of baskets: pot and half-pot hampers for the fruit growers, 'putchins' for eel fishing, 'kypes' (which were one-handled baskets used to deliver coal), as well as specialist orders for customers and hurdles for fencing from as little as eighteen inches high to nine feet. Anything over six feet tall had to be made outside the workshops, otherwise there were problems when it came to moving it. Roland Hayes used to supply coal merchants, the wholesale fruit markets at Evesham, Littleton and Badsey, and, toward the end of his working life, many small craft shops. One of the more unusual commissions Mr Hayes received was to make a series of hurdles to decorate the ceiling of a public house. He also made baskets for shopping, bicycles, clothes, logs etc. for many local people. Phyl Bayliss has fond memories of the Hayes family, as they made a cradle for her brother John; it went all round the family, including use for Phyl's own children, and is still in use today in Bridlington.

The life of a basket-maker was hard. The *Grapevine* account describes how Mr Hayes often used to work twelve hours a day and his hands were covered with calluses from bending the 'withies' to the desired shape. It was evidently possible to make a living from basket-making (albeit augmented by fruit picking and hiring out rowing boats), but it was described as "very much a hand-to-mouth existence". It is said that Roland Hayes had no desire to see his son carry on the trade, and when he retired in 1972 at the age of sixty-five, basket-making at Clevelode finally ceased.

Blacksmiths

In 1809, mention is made of a 'Burston', "blacksmith of Barnard's Green" – Barnard's Green was at that time the long common running down to Guarlford. 'Rosemeade', the white house on the edge of the common just above New House Farm, is on the site of an earlier smithy, and the garden running on to the common is where the smith was allowed to tether the horses. In 1841, this was worked by John Reynolds. There are in existence bills of his, charging one penny a foot for remoulds and a halfpenny for frost-nailing. The smithy was owned by George Lane of Woodbridge Farm just along the lane opposite. In addition, the 'Tan House' premises were once listed as a 'Blacksmith's Shop'.

As has been shown, this was a society very dependent on the horse, and between the two World Wars there were three blacksmiths working in Guarlford. Mr Mark Young, father to Alf and his brothers, operated near the Old Elm, which stood on the common near where the horse trough - moved from Barnard's Green - now stands. He was kept busy on icy winter mornings

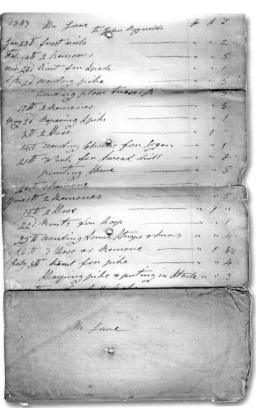

Figure 4.8 Bill from Mr Lane's blacksmith, 1857.

Young's Smithy
No. 2 on Map

Cole's Smithy
No. 9 on Map

Lashford and Jessamine
Cottages
Near No. 7 on Map

Figure 4.9 The Smithies and Lashford and Jessamine Cottages.

frost-nailing the horses and ponies who pulled the milk-floats, so that they could negotiate the steep Malvern streets. Unlike regular horseshoe nails, frost-nails are not flat but have a peaked top. In 1912 the R.S.P.C.A. and the Roads Association had offered £100 to "anyone inventing a horse-shoe which would give a safer, surer grip on roads now tarred for motor traffic". Mark Young's shop still remains next to 74 Guarlford Road, and you can see the old timbers fixed with wooden pegs. The thatched barn alongside has however been replaced by a modern house. Alf Young said that there were, by the two pear trees on the common at the end of Chance Lane, several cottages, in one of which his family lived for three years from 1923. In addition, his grandfather occupied 'Lashford Cottage', one of two cottages beside the old barn further down the common and came there in the first instance to run the blacksmith's shop owned by Mr Raymond Cole. Sometimes Alf used to go and help the wheelwright to turn a bandsaw to cut the 'felloes' out for the wheel. (A 'felloe' is the rim of a wheel supported by spokes.) However, one day Alf's grandfather was shoeing a horse which pushed him against the wall and broke his shoulder; he couldn't work and lost his job. Mark Young had been asked by Mr Bullock of Mill Farm to consider opening a smithy nearby and, when his father recovered, the two men did so, moving to the smithy on Guarlford Road about 1926-27.

Mr Cole was a wheelwright who lived in the first house on the right in Chance Lane and built carts and wagons for farmers and tradesmen. He owned a wheelwright's shop on the edge of the common and opposite, a smithy where he employed blacksmiths, including Alf's grandfather. The blacksmiths shod horses but also fitted the carts and wagons with their iron furnishings and fixed the iron tyres on the wheels. Sam Beard remembers the finished vehicles painted in bright colours standing outside to be admired by passers-by until collected by their owners. In the blacksmith's yard was a large round iron platform on which the wheels were shod with iron bands. Men with large pincers carried the band red-hot from the forge and dropped it over the wheel in place on the platform; buckets of water were quickly thrown over it, and the smith, in clouds of steam, hammered it all round until it cooled and fitted tightly, ready for many years' hard work on road or land. This process held a great fascination for children peering through the palings of the gate, always closed for safety on such occasions. So there was a hive of industry at the end of Chance Lane in the first part of the twentieth century, with farm machinery to be repaired and horses to be shod. The wheelwright premises were later taken over by 'Woodwards Coaches', known to many still living in the village today, and then by 'Miles Transport'.

Charlie Williams of Sherrard's Green recalls how, as a child of six, he saw how the smithies and wheelwrights were affected by the Depression of the 1930s, when Mr Ray Cole said that only the milk ponies were being shod and people were economising by not having harness and carts repaired.

According to Joan Bradshaw's notes, another forge, at 'Little Heriots', was in a very old

---

A J Gammond Ltd

The firm was founded by John Gammond who was born in Madresfield and spent his early years in Whitbourne. John's parents bought Little Heriots, and when John was demobbed after the Second World War he joined the Ministry of Agriculture Drainage Department. This was disbanded in 1964. John then formed Gammond & McKay with a colleague and rented some land around the site of the old smithy next to his parent's home at Little Heriots. In 1974 John bought out Mr McKay, and John's two sons subsequently joined him in the business, A J Gammond Ltd - Civil Engineers, Agricultural Machine Suppliers, and specialist pipe manufacturers serving major contractors and utility companies.

building in an orchard, covered now by Mr J Gammond's premises. Harry Wellings was the blacksmith, a wonderful character whose bills were written in the most immaculate copperplate writing. He had a wealth of stories and would tell of the times he used to walk into Worcester on a Saturday evening after work to fetch the weekly household shopping. Harry was also the Madresfield Estate blacksmith and cycled to Madresfield twice a week, very early, to get the forge going in the shop with the horseshoe entrance at Home Farm, (which incidentally has the date 1924 set into it.) His bicycle was specially made with a very strong frame to carry pieces of iron strapped to the frame when necessary, and his primary task as a young man was to shoe Lord Beauchamp's show horses, a famous stud of Shire horses, all greys. The highlight of Harry's life occurred each year when he accompanied them to the annual 'Shire Horse Show' at Islington, London, at the beginning of the twentieth century. They travelled in special horseboxes attached to a passenger train from Malvern Link Station. Harry worked until the 1940s and died in 1959.

Salmon Fishing at Clevelode

Angling is the most popular sport in Britain today, and the banks of the River Severn still provide many a haunt for an angler. In the early years of the twentieth century, the Little family made their living at Clevelode by salmon fishing; and the late Mr Walter Little gave Joan Bradshaw a graphic account of how he, his father, and brother worked. The main fish that were caught were salmon returning from the sea to their spawning grounds in North Wales.

The salmon-fishing season started on February 1st and continued until the end of August. Later the season was reduced to the end of May. So eager were those who fished in the river to catch the first salmon of the season that the Littles would begin work at midnight on February 1st. The weather conditions at this time of year can easily be imagined, and Mr Walter Little remembered the numbed fingers and the flapping of arms to keep warm.

Salmon Fishing

The salmon were caught in a large hemp net, eighty yards long and twenty-four feet deep with a six-inch mesh which allowed small salmon and other fish to escape. The net had four-inch cubes of cork along one side and lead weights along the other. A person stood on one of the banks and held the end of the long net against the bank. The other fishermen then paid out the net across the river, using a flat-bottomed punt with paddles. Once the net was stretched completely across the river, with the lead weights resting upon the riverbed, the net was allowed to float 100 yards downstream. The men in the punt would then begin a circular movement across the river to rejoin their colleague on the other bank. Any salmon swimming upstream were, therefore, encircled in the net. As the net was gradually drawn in, the trapped salmon went into a special pocket in the net called a 'cod'. When this was reached, the salmon were pulled into the boat and tapped on the nose with a small truncheon, which stunned and then killed them

The best time for salmon fishing was when the wind was in the southwest and the warm rain had been falling. The salmon came up the river in shoals, with the tides. Those who fished lower down the river had the first chance of catching the salmon, but, even so, those at Clevelode managed to catch enough to support a family of fifteen.

The heaviest fish Walter Little ever caught weighed thirty-eight pounds and his father once caught a forty-pound salmon. When caught, the fish were washed and then sold whole. Much of the catch went to Billingsgate fish market in London, having been taken by donkey-cart to Great Malvern station and put on a passenger train. Frequently a telegram would be received at Clevelode on the same day that the fish had been despatched, relating the sale price. Phyl Bayliss remembers, "They used sometimes to bring the salmon up on the front of their bikes to 'Fishy' Davis in Great Malvern – that was opposite 'Kendalls', (on the corner at the traffic lights). It was lovely to see that shop at Christmas, all lit up, all the poultry and so on." 'Fishy' Davis was W H Davis of 'The Exchange', who used to buy two or three salmon a week, and many of the people in Guarlford have memories of Miss Annie Little cycling through the village, on her way to the fishmonger, with the tail of a large salmon sticking out of her cycle basket! The closed season was spent making the new nets for the next season. All the family were involved with the 'knitting'.

Salmon fishing came to an end in 1929 when the River Authority decided to ban all netting above Tewkesbury, claiming that the salmon population was declining because not enough fish were getting through to spawn in the gravel beds of the upper reaches of the river. So the water bailiffs came and took away the nets. The Little family received just forty pounds in compensation for the loss of its livelihood.

Mr G E Beard, who lived at 'The Noggin' at Little Clevelode, was another salmon fisherman. He was the father of George, who was verger and sexton of St Mary's Church at Guarlford for many years and died in 1963, aged ninety, grandfather of Sam Beard who has contributed many memories to this history.

Beer Deliveries

When Charlie Williams's father worked for 'Arnold Perett's Brewery' of Tewkesbury, he used to come along the A38 from Tewkesbury at about five o'clock in the morning with two horses pulling the dray, into Upton and then up to Guarlford. One day when he'd just finished at the 'Green Dragon', he started off up the road and met a circus. It is not known if the elephant smelled the beer or not, but the animal put its trunk up in the air and bellowed. Away went the horses and the dray and Mr Williams with them. There was no Barnard's Green roundabout in those days, so they didn't stop until they reached Great Malvern!

Public Houses

Public houses have long played a significant part in the social and recreational life of English villages and, while generally undistinguished architecturally, they are often buildings which have an interesting history and important place in the rural landscape.

The two existing public houses in Guarlford were and are an integral and popular part of village life, the 'Plough and Harrow' and the 'Green Dragon'. To this day, a small group described as 'the village elders' meets regularly on a Saturday morning at the 'Plough and Harrow', in effect perhaps carrying on a long tradition in so doing.

There is a tradition that two cottages at Hall Green, now replaced by 'The Paddocks', were an old cider house hundreds of years ago. One resident of the village recalls that the wooden beams in the cottages were of very hard oak and were reputed to have come from broken-up warships; wood from these was brought up-river along the Severn.

> ### The Acker or 'The Guarlford Axe'
>
> *In the 'Plough & Harow' you will find a notice about 'The Guarlford Axe'. Shortly before the First World War, George Beard, a Plough & Harrow regular, asked Harry Welling, blacksmith to the Madresfield Estate, at Clevelode Smithy - later A J Gammond Ltd - to make him an axe. It was in use until 1984, the old file beaten into its edge helping to retain its sharp edge.*

The Plough and Harrow

Figure 4.10 The Plough and Harrow.

Sam Beard describes the 'Plough and Harrow' in the 1920s and '30s. He thinks, that the premises were at one time used for storing and distributing coal and a building to the front of the pub was a dray house and stable: "The locals gathered here on a regular basis; work on the farms was discussed; far-fetched tales were told and some rude ones. There was no bar as such in the pub, but the landlord positioned himself by the doorway leading into the inner area, kept a watchful eye on the white mugs with the golden band around and refilled them as required. So, in the smoke-laden atmosphere, the parish business went on. From time to time the clean sawdust in the cast iron, black-leaded spittoons erupted as one or another cleared the way for another draught from the pint mug. 'Time' at the 'Plough' was strictly observed and the men would set off in search of the next meal - on Sunday usually a roast - but not without the occasional prank, such as the dairy man who found his milk float with the shafts put through a five-barred gate, and the pony harnessed therein."

Rob Gilroy also describes how his grandfather, Bill Morris of Clevelode, used to go to the 'Plough and Harrow' and would play cards for money, as well as a game where pennies were flicked into a tin, the winner taking the kitty. Evidently, it was not unknown for poaching expeditions to be planned there, sadly necessary with so many children to feed in many families.

Mr Derrick Bladder says that the Revd Newson always maintained that the two most important places in the village were the church and the pub. The Bishop used to have a walkabout in the summer and the Rector would bring him into the 'Plough' and say, "This where I meet most of my flock." Revd Newson also said at Confirmation classes, "If you want a drink, you should go into the pub and buy a drink, like I do, and not round the back door (off licence) with a black bag!" According to Derrick, the 'Plough and Harrow' was licensed only as a beer and cider house before the Second World War. After the War, Dick and Pam Capstick renovated the pub and obtained a full licence; Derrick was the first person to have a glass of whisky when the licensee got his new 'Spirits Licence'.

With various licensees, among them Dennis Atkins the jockey, the pub underwent changes in the last two decades of the twentieth century, culminating in a major refurbishment of the restaurant. In the autumn of 2004, the licence was taken over by the brewers, 'Wadworths', with Juliet Tyndall and Michael Weir as the licensees.

The Green Dragon

The 'Green Dragon' is mentioned in a Directory for 1855, where Joseph M Sheen is noted as 'beer retailer', and in 1860 when William Hall was in residence.

Phyl Bayliss can remember the 'Green Dragon' being pulled down and then re-built as she used to walk along the Guarlford Road on her way to school in about 1923. It was a black and white house and thatched at one time, like many other cottages along the Guarlford 'Straight' that have long since disappeared. Alf Young said that his uncle was an apprentice bricklayer for Mr Wilesmith the builder, and he thought that the firm rebuilt the 'Green Dragon'. While this was happening, the business of the pub continued in a hut that was

Figure 4.11 The Green Dragon.

erected alongside in what is now the beer-garden. Later, this was used as a changing room for football matches and a meeting place for some village functions, such as those of the British Legion.

In 2004, the 'Green Dragon' underwent another physical transformation with the addition of an attractive restaurant, where Mark and Sue Jones serve meals to locals and many visitors.

Other Businesses

Figure 4.12 E Gillett Burton's removal van outside Laburnum House in the 1930s. Mr Gillett Burton is on the left and Mr Archibald Jones on the right.

The businesses in the parish also included a furniture remover, E Gillett Burton of 'Laburnum House', Guarlford Road, who offered 'removals of every description' and 'warehousing'. The heading on a letter sent to Mr Archie Jones in August, 1934, shows the 'Telegram address' as "Burton, Guarlford, Malvern" and the telephone number as just "645" – the days of the local exchanges, of course. In July 1934 Mr Burton accepted a "directorship in Messrs Wm Winwoods of Worcester" who were taking over his business, including all his vans, and he was to continue running the business on their behalf in Guarlford. According to Charlie Williams this kind of removal "was only for the rich folk – the country folk had to go on a horse and cart". When some members of the Little family moved from Clevelode to the newly built Penny Close about 1949, John Little says: "We had a tractor and trailer to move the furniture. I was working for Geoff Munslow, the bailiff at Little Clevelode Farm."

There was also a horse cab proprietor, 'Tucky' Friar, who lived in two old railway carriages near Hall Green, and a petrol pump run by Coupar Bladder, Derrick's father, on the road to the Rhydd. Edwin Lane remembers that "we used to stop and buy petrol there; it was an old hand pump" which Mr Bladder would come out and wind up. Alf Young said that 'Woodwards Coaches' also sold petrol – 'ROP' – which stands for 'Russian Oil Products', costing elevenpence halfpenny (under 5p) a gallon when 'Shell' was one shilling and fivepence or one and sixpence (7.5p) a gallon. Finally, there was a sawyer and coffin maker near the village crossroads. Beside the present bus-shelter there are still traces of his sawpit, where tree-trunks were laid across the top and two men, one in the pit and one above, on either side of a crosscut saw, laboriously sawed it into planks.

At the moment few residents actually work within the village, but with the increase in using computers to 'work from home', this may change – what effect will that have on community life?

Services

Transport

As the residents of Guarlford at the beginning of the twenty-first century drive swiftly and comfortably to Worcester and beyond, it is sometimes hard to realize that it is only just over 100 years ago when, for most country dwellers, the only means of transport would have been their own two feet. John Noake, 'The Rambler', describes his walks around the county in the 1840s, among them one from Powick to view the new chapel at 'Barnard's Green', which was actually Guarlford. Of course, the wealthier families had their horses, traps and carriages, and Shire horses and carts were used on the farms. In the early years of the twentieth century, Tom and Polly Birch lived in 'Maywood', the house associated with Marie Hall; they kept a pony in the field behind and ran a carrier or taxi service to Malvern. Between the two World Wars, for the children one of the highlights of the year was the 'Sunday School Outing'; it was often a trip by horse-drawn wagons loaned by a farmer to the Old Hills at Callow End for a picnic.

The Bicycle

The development of the modern bicycle in the 1880s, especially with pneumatic tyres invented by J B Dunlop in 1888, liberated many, especially women. People were now not restricted to their immediate neighbourhood for work and pleasure, and the women's clothes changed, too – they no longer wore bustles and voluminous skirts, as can be seen in photographs of the time.

Reg Green entitled his memoirs *I Got On My Bike*: he cycled to Clevelode from Dudley to find a job after the First World War. There are still vivid memories of the tricycles ridden by George 'Jarvey' Sims of South Wood and by Mr Cole of Chance Lane, the latter into the 1980s.

After leaving Guarlford School in the 1930s, Phyl Bayliss cycled from Hall Green to work in Great Malvern; then, as a Land Girl in the First World War, she had to travel firstly to the 'Guinness Hop Farm' at Braces Leigh and later to work as a switchboard operator at the American Hospital Camp at Blackmore. One day her bike disappeared from the racks, and the commanding officer had to find her some transport night and day, because she worked at all sorts of hours. So Phyl was collected from Hall Green in an American Command car or a 'jeep' from the Transport Corps, until her cycle eventually reappeared. Where it had been remained a mystery.

Ken Woolley can still remember cycling to Hanley Grammar School on his 'Hercules' bicycle from the late 1930s. Margaret Omar, who went to Worcester Girls' Grammar School in 1945, used her bicycle to reach Great Malvern station from Woodbridge Farm: "I used to cycle up to 'Olivers Garage' along Court Road near Charlie Spencer's butcher's shop. It's only recently that they knocked the old cottage down and built two new houses opposite 'Hunts'. I would leave my bike there for sixpence a week and walk up to the station. If I'd left it at the station, it would have been a shilling a week." It seems to have been customary to 'park' one's bicycle in this way, when going to the cinema or the theatre, too, as several residents recall.

Motorbikes

Motorbikes used to be very popular. In his early days at Guarlford, Revd Frederick Newson rode a 'Red Indian' motorbike and sidecar. Reg Green bought his first motorbike in the 1920s when his family moved to Barnard's Green and he was still working as a milkman for Mr Medcalf at New House Farm: "A large BSA model with belt-drive which I bought from my brother for fifteen pounds. I later exchanged it for a brand new BSA model, which I bought from 'Ranfords' in Barnard's Green and that cost me forty-five pounds. How proud I was of that bike." 'Ranfords' stood where the 'Somerfield' supermarket is now, and there was another garage, 'Preeces', where the chemist and fish and chip shop are now a little further along.

Buses and Coaches

In the early 1930s, Mr George Woodward took over the wheelwright's shop on the common at the end of Chance Lane and started bus services to Great Malvern, Hanley and Upton, as well as coach excursions further afield, to such places as Stratford-upon-Avon, Barry Island and Weston-super-Mare. He had two motor vehicles: a red bus which plied several times a week between Malvern and Upton, and a large yellow conveyance known as a 'char-a-banc', which seated about twenty people on rows of wooden bench seats and had a canvas hood that rolled back for fine days. Joan Bradshaw says that it took two strong people to extend the cover if it rained, so if any shower looked likely to be short, Mr Woodward just pulled under a tree to shelter. One year the 'Yellow Peril', as many called it, took the Guarlford children on an outing a little further afield, to the Hollybush – "an hilarious journey, with all the Sunday School, teachers and helpers packed in, the more adventurous boys perched on the folded hood at the back, with others holding on to their ankles to keep them from being swept away as the party tore along at quite twenty-five miles an hour!"

When Edwin Lane went to Hanley Castle Grammar School in the 1940s, he also travelled by Mr Woodward's bus: "One, which was more modern, picked up pupils from Malvern Link and the other from Barnard's Green. I used to wait for it by the barn wall at Guarlford Court. The bus would cruise down the road at a very gentle pace, and at the first hint of the engine starting to cough everyone would start cheering. Mr Woodward used to get so excited when one or two of the senior lads from the school managed to keep up with the bus, cycling behind it out of the wind. If we slowed down too much, they used to pass us." Alan Tummey says that the Woodward's bus was still running well after the War, when he went to school in Hanley Castle. Mr Woodward's firm was eventually sold to a Mr Miles, who ran a contract transport firm. When he expanded his business elsewhere after the Second World War, the land was restored to the Malvern Hills Conservators.

Another bus service was what people perhaps oddly called the 'Bristol Blue', although it was actually green! It used to run from Cheltenham to Great Malvern and back again, about four times a day. At one time there seems to have been a 'Midland Red' service, too. Villagers could catch the bus to Barnard's Green, have time to shop, and then pick up a bus on its return journey. However, 'Woodwards Coaches' and others did not travel as far as Clevelode and people living there had to walk to Guarlford to pick up the bus, or cycle or, most often, walk. All these bus services to Guarlford eventually ceased. Then, in the 1980s, a free bus took shoppers to the 'Spook Friday Market' in Great Malvern; and services subsidised by the County Council were set up towards the end of the twentieth century. In 2005, inhabitants of Clevelode can use the number 363 and 364 buses, which run fairly frequently from Upton to Worcester via the Rhydd and Old Hills, while for Guarlfordians there is just one 'Flexilink' bus to Great Malvern and back on Friday mornings.

Motor Cars

There were obviously some cars for the rich from the turn of the twentieth century and they did cause comment. From Parish Council records of 1899 we learn: "The Clerk was desired to write to the Superintendent of Police calling attention to the dangers to persons using the roads from the excessive speed at which motor cars were driven". Poor visibility at the corner in the centre of the village came up again and again, and a cart-shed at Guarlford Court, right on the roadside, was blamed. Nothing much was apparently done about it, as the cart-shed was still on the roadside in the 1930s.

Figure 4.13 Mr Bladder's petrol pump.

There is a report in the parish magazine of a party on Ascension Day in 1909, when the schoolchildren, at the kind invitation of Mrs Lattey, assembled at Cherry Orchard to have tea with Jim, her two-year-old boy. The children were "regaled with a sumptuous tea, afterwards being taken for rides in the motor-car", which must have been a great treat.

The motorcar that many residents of the time have remembered was that bought by Mr Bladder of Fowler's Farm. After winning many show prizes for his Shire horses, Mr Bladder was one of the first car owners in the village, adding also a 'Model T Ford' for milk and other dairy produce deliveries. A garage and petrol pump followed, both still standing.

John Little and his sister, Mary Thomas, remember that well into the twentieth century cars were still only for the well-off and many people, including the doctor and nurse, used bicycles. The Littles had a pony and trap, which took vegetables etc. to Upton. The Revd Frederick Newson moved from a pony and trap to a car. Parishioners remember that towards the end of his life Revd Newson's driving did become somewhat "erratic". He thought nothing of leaving his car in the middle of the road if he saw someone to whom he wished to speak, or if he wanted to go shopping. However, Revd Newson regularly used his car to transport people to and from hospital; indeed, his car was a type of parish transport system available to all who required it. People still remember his kindness and how he would stop to offer lifts to any parishioner walking or waiting for a bus.

Evidently, at one time a black and yellow circular 'AA' enamelled plate was fixed high on the Guarlford Court dray shed recording that London was 114 miles distant - not that many Guarlfordians headed off for London. Regular users of the road were the steam wagons called 'Sentinels', with their trailers, from Malvern's quarries. On return journeys they would halt near the 'Plough and Harrow' pub, clear their fires of clinker, and top up with water for the next day's journey.

Figure 4.14 Mr Gillett Burton's taxi, driven by Mr Archibald Jones, outside Laburnum House in the 1930s.

Lengthsmen

Towards the end of the nineteenth century, the rural road network was divided into 'lengths'; these were usually of four or five miles, and a lengthsman was in charge of each section. The roads in the Guarlford area were well tended by lengthsmen up until the Second World War. For example, Tommy Clark used to look after Clevelode Road, Blakes Lane, Cherry Orchard Lane (now Rectory Lane) and Honeypots; George Beard had the Rhydd Road to Pike Bridge and a 'Jimmy P.' tended the road from Barnard's Green House to Mr Medcalf's cottages just past Chance Lane. Their tasks were to sweep the roads and keep the ditches and drains free, trim the vegetation and the edges of the grass verges, as well as filling in potholes. Alf Young recalled that the Guarlford Road was 'immaculate' and a lot of water was then allowed to drain off the road into the 'Fladder' pool, the remains of which can be seen on the common at the junction of Hall Green and Guarlford Road. In 2003, the pool was dredged by the Malvern Hills Conservators; the original shape and size of the pool was much larger and can still be discerned. In one of his articles describing the flora and fauna of Worcestershire, Edwin Lees, a Victorian who co-founded the Worcestershire Naturalists Club in 1847, described the 'Fladder Pool' "round which the herb pennyroyal grows wild". Within living memory this was a delightful village pond, with clean water, good for the ducks and geese, which shared the common with sheep and cattle and took their time crossing in front of the occasional traffic.

Trains

In the 1930s, Edward Corbett, known as 'The Stroller', imitated John Noake 'The Rambler' of a century earlier and wrote a series about Worcestershire villages. Of Guarlford he says: "Communications are excellent. Great Malvern, Malvern Wells and Malvern Link railway stations are all within a mile or two, and the Severn affords facilities for water transport. Motor 'buses run to Malvern, Worcester and Upton." Until 1952, the railway line from Great Malvern across to Upton, Tewkesbury and Ashchurch was still open and some children from the village travelled by train every school day to Tewkesbury High School. The train, which was an old steam engine, was known affectionately as 'The Upton Flyer' – all right going downhill, but very slow coming up the bank near the Three Counties Showground. There was a London, Midland and Scotland (LMS) station near Brickbarns Farm.

The diverse means of transport available to the people of Guarlford in the first half of the twentieth century especially contrasts markedly with the present dominance of the motor car. Though it is unlikely to return, perhaps Guarlfordians would like such an abundance of public transport as that enjoyed by their predecessors.

Communications

Rowland Hill began his national postal delivery system using stamps in 1840. Before that letters were 'franked', and Mr Roger Hall-Jones of Malvern has a letter in his possession dated June 22nd 1857 regarding the appointment of Revd Wathen to the living at Guarlford. Margaret Omar has envelopes addressed to Woodbridge Farm, dated 1877 and 1880, and it is interesting to see that these are addressed to Barnard's Green and not Guarlford. In 1904 a delivery of post on Sunday began and a second post on other days of the week. Letterboxes were first made in 1855. The letterbox in the wall of Guarlford churchyard is Victorian, but its exact age is not known.

In about 1900, telegraph poles were erected on the common, but, according to Joan Bradshaw's notes, it was not until 1911 that there was talk of introducing telephone 'party lines' for "the use of farmers and other country residents". Margaret Omar recalls that when she was a little girl in the 1930s the Lanes' number was 372Y3 and the Chesters, at 'The Homestead', had 372Y4. The 'party line' system worked thus: there were perhaps four houses sharing the one line, and a number of rings by the operator would indicate for which the call was intended.

The public telephone box by the church was not installed until after the Second World War. There is a reference in the Women's Institute (WI) Minutes of March 1946 to the Secretary of Guarlford WI writing to Post Office Telephones about the urgent need for a telephone box to be erected somewhere near the Church; the Parish Council Minutes record that it was finally installed in 1955. So, before that, people often went to the Rectory and asked the Newsons to send vital messages on their telephone.

Now, of course, in 2005, the widespread availability of computers and mobile phones makes worldwide personal communication a reality.

Medical

In 1905, it was announced in the Parish Magazine that the Midwives Act, 1902, had become effective. This Act had been passed "to secure the better training of midwives and to regulate their practice" and meant that only midwives who were properly qualified and duly registered would be allowed to attend maternity cases. Failure to be properly certified under the Act would result in a fine of five pounds. Lady Beauchamp had therefore provided a properly qualified and registered nurse, Nurse McLeod, for the parishes of Guarlford, Madresfield and Newland. Not only the mothers but everyone, particularly the elderly and infirm, would be glad to know that help was at hand in emergencies, as few could afford to call a doctor. The prospective nurse was described by the Matron of the Cottage Nurses' Training Home,

Figure 4.15 Mrs Woolley.

where she trained, as "capable, kindly, gentle and quiet, a woman of high character and principle". It would be the duty of the parishioners to maintain her post, and the following fees were charged for the whole time that Nurse McLeod was attending a maternity case:-

For the wives of labourers – five shillings (25p) each case.

For the wives of those earning one pound to thirty shillings (£1.50) a week – seven shillings and sixpence (37p) each case.

For others, by arrangement – ten shillings (50p) each case.

It appears that the parishes failed in their commitment in the first years, so Lady Beauchamp guaranteed Nurse McLeod's salary until further arrangements could be made. Later a 'Nursing Fund' was set up, into which families paid a penny or so a week to qualify for the nurse's services. Lady Beauchamp provided the nurse with an 'Austin Seven Tourer', and everyone knew where and when the next baby was due when this little car was seen parked outside a cottage! In the decades between the Wars Mrs Woolley, wife of the Guarlford School Headmaster, was also called up occasionally on a voluntary basis to deliver a baby or lay out someone who had died in Guarlford, although she actually nursed private patients.

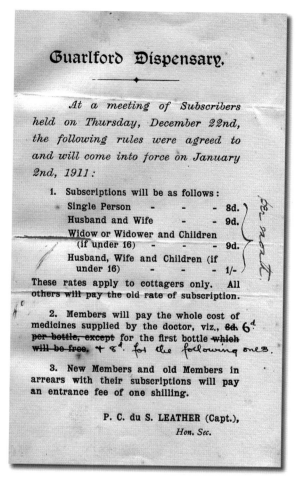

Figure 4.16 Guarlford's Dispensary Rules.

There was a 'Guarlford Dispensary', also set up by the Beauchamps of Madresfield Court. The Parish Magazine of 1910 refers to the 'Boot & Clothing Club' and 'The Dispensary', two parochial benefit societies, which the Rector wished to be supervised by a committee, now that he "is to be absent for so long a period" on his sabbatical to New Zealand. The Dispensary was already in the Rector's debt "to a considerable amount" as the large sum of money needed to enable it to pay its way could not be raised purely from the members' payments. The committee had taken over by Thursday 22nd December 1910 when a committee meeting was held to agree some new rules to come into force on January 2nd 1911. Subscriptions each month were to be:

Single person eightpence, and husband and wife ninepence;

Widow or widower with children (if under sixteen) ninepence;

Husband with wife and children (if under sixteen) one shilling.

These rules applied to 'cottagers' only - "all others will pay the old rate of subscription". At that time, subscriptions had to be paid on the first Monday in each month at the Rectory Room. Dr Baines would then attend, if necessary, for the month of issue only. The cards were not transferable and if subscriptions were not up to date the person concerned would not be entitled to medical attendance. People also had to pay for medicines: "…members will pay the whole cost of medicines supplied by the doctor, viz., sixpence for the first bottle and eightpence for the following ones".

Alf Young remembered that, in the 1920s and '30s, "The doctor used to say, 'If you can't afford to pay for the dispensary, you can't afford me.' He wouldn't come. All I can remember is that I was given the money to take to Mrs Bullock's store at the end of each month for three cards: for the hospital, doctor and the nurse. For the doctor's card you had to take a shilling, sixpence for the nurse's card and threepence for the hospital card. If you'd been ill, Mrs Bullock used to take that card. And I believe that ran up to the War or until the National Health Service came in."

If a man had an accident and could not work, he could lose his job, as happened to Alf Young's grandfather, whose shoulder was broken by a horse he was shoeing at Mr Cole's smithy in the 1920s.

Mrs Margaret Hunaban grew up at 129 Heriots, Clevelode, with her parents, Joseph and Agnes Yapp, who, having lived there since the 1920s, finally bought the cottage in 1933 from the Madresfield Estate (where Mr Yapp was a forestry worker). Mrs Hunaban remembers that the District Nurse and midwife was Nurse Bingham whose husband was Agent on the Madresfield Estate. Nurse Bingham was also the School Nurse into the 1940s and she would travel about on her pushbike. The nurse would do examinations and vaccinations in the Rectory Room, which was put to yet another purpose when the dentist used to visit and patients were treated there. Margaret Omar vividly recalls having a tooth pulled out when the injection hadn't quite numbed her jaw!

The doctors also seem to have travelled quite a distance to visit their patients. Margaret Llewelyn recalls Dr Newton of 'Newton, Brown and Eliot', whose surgery was in Avenue Road, higher up the hill than the present one: "I believe he had been injured in the Great War, as I seem to remember one eye appearing damaged." Mary Thomas remembers Dr Newton also "coming quite regularly on his bike to visit my mother, who had phlebitis and these terrible quinsies (throat abscesses). She'd have them every few months, so he used to have to come and lance them. I can remember him having a car about 1944 when I was about twelve." Dr Eliot of the same practice lived in Yaffle Bank, which he had built for him in Chance Lane. A Dr Devereux and then Dr Stella MacDonald of 'Howard's Lodge' in Avenue Road also visited patients in the village. Mary's brother, John Little, once cut his hand badly and luckily Mr Peake, manager of Clevelode Farm, had a car and took him to the doctor. There were no public telephones locally to call the doctor, so someone would cycle to fetch him if it was urgent, or there was always the telephone at the Rectory.

Mary Thomas was working at Malvern Cottage Hospital at a very significant time: "In 1947 when I was leaving school at the age of fourteen, I went to what was called Prior's Croft, opposite the Winter Gardens for an interview with the two Mr Stockalls, father and son. Malvern Cottage Hospital was then privately owned, and I got a job as a clerk in the hospital. There was only one person there who was trying to start records and we had help from someone from Castle Street in Worcester who showed us what to do. Before that if you went to see a consultant or to a clinic, you just had a piece of paper with your name on top. We started a complete new record system before the National Health Service came in 1948 and in the early days we used to take in accident admissions needing surgery, which was mostly done by Dr Jamieson Meikle of Graham Road." Dr Peter Mayner, who himself underwent surgery there as a child, remembers assisting at operations in the hospital in the late 1960s.

Police

Before the Second World War, there seem to have been plenty of policemen to patrol the village and surrounding area on bicycles. How different from today. 'Neighbourhood Watch' and an occasional passing patrol car now take the place of the more numerous 'bobbies' of the past, though Guarlford does have a 'beat officer' who occasionally attends Parish Council meetings. The policeman from Hall Green between the Wars was Frank Woodings and the Police House stood next to the Tin Tabernacle facing the common. Other policemen, like PC Haynes and PC Snead, would come from the Police House in Pound Bank and Edwin Lane recalls that later the policemen were PC Ainge and PC George Langley. Derrick Bladder remembers that in the 1930s "The lads at our end of the village were quite frightened of Frank Woodings. Frank Worrall came from Hanley and there was another one from Powick. When the gypsies used to park on the Green at Clevelode crossroads, I think they were allowed forty-eight hours and then they had to move. The gypsies used to come and use the willows for making pegs and then came round to sell them, long pegs with a band on the top, split up the middle. These two policemen would go on to the site, kick the cooking pot over, stand back to back and order the gypsies off."

Water

Water is particularly important in an agricultural setting, not only for thirsty humans and their animals, but also for growing crops and driving watermills. Until comparatively recently, the people of Guarlford had water only from wells, pumps, streams and ponds. Edward Corbett, writing in the *Worcester Herald* in the 1920s, describes a legal battle about Guarlford's water supply in the middle of the nineteenth century. A 'Brook', which "until the middle of the last century was a picturesque feature of the Malverns", flowed through Malvern and down the hill towards Guarlford, increasing in size as it went, and eventually it turned 'an overshot wheel' at Mill Lane and another in Guarlford. An 'overshot wheel' is where the water flows over the wheel from above, just as an 'undershot' wheel is driven by water passing from below. 'Overshot wheels' were introduced into the country in the Middle Ages; there is a fine example to be seen to this day in Ambleside, Cumbria. As the population of Great Malvern increased, more water was needed for the town, so the springs of 'The Brook' were tapped and the water was diverted to a reservoir. The Guarlfordians were not happy about this, and John Bullock, of 'The Court', who happened to own the mill, claimed compensation; the case went firstly before a jury "comprised of gentlemen of the county" sitting at the Imperial Hotel, now Malvern Girls' College, and then an appeal was "heard by three eminent Judges, presided over by the celebrated Chief Justice Cockburn". The townspeople had to pay compensation and, according to Edward Corbett, "Malvern … continues to drink dry the stream which a foretime danced and splashed down its hillside and refreshed the low country at its foot. It is a kind of penalty inevitable to the growth of a town."

The people of Guarlford parish used pumps and wells for water until the middle of the twentieth century. Water had to be pumped or wound up for drinking, cooking and all washing – laundry and the weekly bath. John Little remembers, "You had to look in the bucket before you drank it and swish the water round with your hand to see what was in it." Concerns expressed about mains water resulted in a letter being received by Guarlford Women's Institute in May 1947 "from the Clerk to the Upton RDC informing the Institute that a water supply to Guarlford is included in the Council's first instalment of a water supply for the whole area and would no doubt be available during the next twelve months".

Margaret Llewelyn was born in the original School House in 1929: "Because of our proximity to the churchyard all drinking water had to be boiled first. The arrival of the 'Corona' drinks van was a great delight

Figure 4.17 Mr Panting, Clevelode.

and, in our case, almost a necessity. A great advance in our living arrangements was the introduction of mains water into the scullery after the Second World War. Only a cold tap, of course, but what a treat! We also acquired a water heater, which stood next to the sink. This was an enormous help on wash and bath days. No more boiling kettles – hot water actually came out of a tap at the bottom. Washdays were still hard work nevertheless. After washing in soapy water, everything had to be rinsed before being fed through a hand-turned mangle. There was then a long traipse round to the boys' playground, where the clothes line was suspended between trees."

Other Mains Services

Other mains services were slowly acquired. However, in 2005 there is still no mains gas for many residents, although a gas main passes through the village. Solid fuel, wood, oil and LPG provide alternative sources of fuel. Electricity seems to have come down to the village from Great Malvern in 1935 and across the river from Kempsey soon afterwards. Margaret Llewelyn says, "We had central ceiling lighting and one standard lamp in the sitting room. Reading in bed was possible, but I remember the discomfort of having to get out onto cold linoleum to switch out the light", something familiar to many. The introduction of electricity, mains water and drainage must have seemed like absolute luxury to those who had managed without them for so long. Now, in the twenty-first century, not infrequent power cuts show us how much we have come to depend on our electricity supplies especially, not only for essential lighting and heat but also for communication and entertainment. Thus, like the motor car in its widening of horizons, the arrival of electricity opened up a new world of possibilities which, in the twenty-first century, has taken the village dweller away from this small, nearly self-contained place, Guarlford, into a larger electronic world of almost unlimited extent by means of the internet and digital radio and television.

Chapter 5

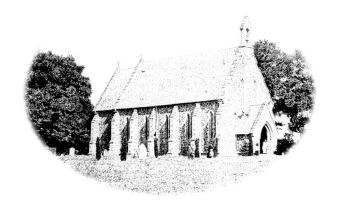

The Church

Early Chapels

Early places of worship in the Guarlford area were centred on the chapelries of Clevelode and Baldenhall. During the twelfth century, the monks of Malvern Priory cleared and colonized lands given by the Abbey at Westminster and eventually built chapels to serve the communities that had grown up on these lands. One such was Clevelode Chapel, which is believed to have been built before 1250. By 1560, it had fallen into disuse, and by 1674 it had been completely demolished. Some large stones from the chapel are still to be found on Chapel Hill, which lies to the north of Clevelode, outside the current parish boundary. Another chapel was St Leonard's, which was at the centre of what was the settlement of Baldenhall (where Hall Green is now). This chapel was certainly there in 1217, and it appears to have been served by the monks from Malvern Priory; but by the end of the thirteenth century it had its own priest who was paid four pounds per annum from the small tithes of Baldenhall. Like the chapel at Clevelode, it fell into disuse and decay and was demolished between 1558 and 1568.

There is also record of a tithe barn by the 'Friars Elm', which was in what is now Hall Green. This barn was used to store produce from the Priory's demesne farms, such as Guarlford Court, and the tithe proceeds from the parish. It was from this barn in 1744 that the overseers of the poor distributed a bread charity. The barn still stood within living memory, but few traces now remain.

The Church of St Mary the Virgin

The Building of the Church

The first stone of a Chapel of Ease at Guarlford was laid by Lady Emily Foley on 19th August, 1843. Finished the following year, it is now a Grade II listed building. It was built by the local firm of George McCann to a design by Thomas Bellamy of London. The structure is of brick with outer cladding in Malvern granite and the cost was about £2000. Many leading residents of Malvern subscribed to its cost, and local farmers and labourers carried materials for its construction without charge. It was served by curates from Malvern Priory. In Pevsner's *Worcestershire*, first published in 1968, part of his comprehensive survey of the buildings of England, the famously severe architectural critic and historian says of St Mary's: "The crazy-paving walling is a surprise. Otherwise the church still represents the Commissioners' type. Nave and chancel, West porch, lancet windows. In the East wall a group of three lancets."

> ### Chapels of Ease
>
> *A Chapel of Ease is a subordinate church in a parish, the purpose of which is to provide a place of worship where the parish church is a considerable distance away. In 1844, the parish church for Guarlford was the Malvern Priory.*

The inscription marking the opening of the church is recorded in the church itself on the west wall above the entrance:

> *This chapel was erected in 1844, it contains one hundred and eighty-four sittings, and in consequence of a Grant from the Incorporated Society for promoting the enlargement, building and repairs of Churches and Chapels. The whole of that number are hereby declared to be free and unappropriated forever.*
>
> *A plan showing the number and situation of the Free Seats is fixed up in the Vestry Room.*
>
> *Vicar: Revd J Wright MA FRS*
>
> *Churchwardens: William Joseph Fancourt and John Archer*

Revd J Wright was the Vicar of Great Malvern Priory. William Joseph Fancourt was a curate at Malvern Priory, and its Vicar almost certainly appointed him to be one of the first churchwardens at Guarlford. Two years later he was appointed incumbent priest.

Figure 5.1 St Mary's Church, c.1906.

In 1866, the Ecclesiastical Parish of Guarlford was formed from land carved out of Great Malvern and Madresfield parishes. St Mary's became its parish church and the incumbent at that time, the Revd John Bateman Wathen MA, became the first Rector. The size of the parish in those days was much larger than it is today. Edward Corbett 'The Stroller', writing in the 1920s, recorded that "Guarlford, a modern parish dating from Victorian times, of which the nucleus was a medieval chapelry, lies south of Madresfield and extends southward to Hanley Castle. It is bounded to the east by the River Severn and to the west by Great Malvern." The present ecclesiastical parish extends westwards as far as Mill Lane.

However, as reported in *The Malvern Advertiser* in October 1877, St Mary's Guarlford in its early years was considered to be "a very delicate and sickly offshoot, for it was planted in the midst of a wretched, poor district with an income of only thirty pounds per year with two acres of glebe land and a residence", compared with the forty pounds income of a typical village parson at that time. This state of affairs continued from 1844 until, in 1867, the sixth Lord Beauchamp generously endowed it with the great tithes of Malvern, worth some three pounds per annum. Since then, what was considered a neglected corner became "as well shepherded as any other part of the county."

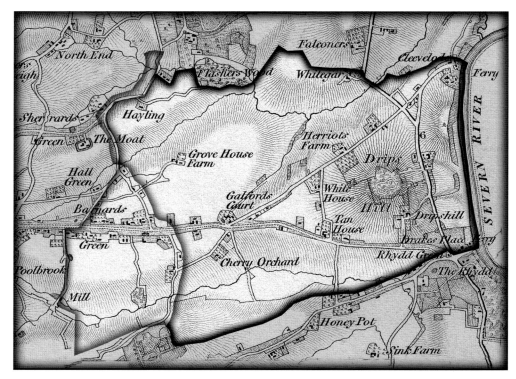

Figure 5.2 The former ecclesiastical parish and the smaller current civil parish.

In 1877, an organ chamber costing several hundred pounds was built entirely at Lord Beauchamp's expense; a new organ was installed, its cost of about £180 completely covered by public subscription. A lady, well-known in the parish but wishing to remain anonymous, defrayed the cost of general renovation and a new chancel rail was purchased with the proceeds of needlework done by a number of girls under the direction of the daughter of Revd Wathen.

By October 1877, all alterations were complete and there was a formal opening service attended by the Bishop of Worcester and influential persons of the surrounding area, including Lord Beauchamp and Lady Foley. A large number of parishioners also attended. About a hundred ladies and gentlemen then attended lunch provided by Mr Drinkwater of Edith House. After the usual loyal toasts, the Rector of Guarlford in his speech expressed his gratification at the way in which over-indulgence in drink after dinner was dying out and at the great efforts in favour of sobriety being made by the 'Church of England Temperance Society'.

In 1906, there were further major renovations under the stewardship of the Revd Hubert Jones, who had succeeded Revd J B Wathen as Rector. The west end of the church had been built with an entrance porch, but no windows, and consequently the church was very dark. Through the munificence of the seventh Lord Beauchamp, the natural light in the church was greatly improved by the installation of a large three-light window in the west wall. This necessitated taking the wall down to porch level before rebuilding it with the new window. The parish magazine of the time records how cold and uncomfortable the church services were while this work was going on, half of the west wall being open to the elements. An improved heating system was later installed as part of the renovations. During these proceedings, the bell turret was found to be unsafe and the bell cracked. The bell turret was removed, and as a 'temporary' measure the bell was hung in the nearby hornbeam tree where it remains to this day. The cost of recasting the bell was estimated to be thirteen pounds, but, interestingly, the date on the bell indicates that it was re-cast twenty years later in 1926.

The Revd Hubert Jones wrote in the parish magazine: "We hope before long to be in a position to build a permanent structure on the church roof wherein the re-cast bell may hang. We should like the turret to be surmounted by a slender little spire, which would just peep above the trees." In the succeeding years various schemes were put forward, including a separate structure, but the money was never forthcoming. As late as the 1920s, Mr Brewer of Grove House Farm had a large timber frame made ready to support the bell in the proposed structure, but the frame eventually disappeared during the Second World War.

In 1906, the handsome oil lamps now hanging in the church were installed. These were converted in 1935, when the church was wired and connected to the electricity supply. In 2003, additional lighting was installed in the chancel and nave in memory of Malcolm Russell, who for many years was a layreader at Guarlford Church.

In the churchyard, opposite the War Memorial, there stood for nearly seventy years a graceful statue of the Madonna and Child. It was given by the Revd Osbourne Jay, late Vicar of Shoreditch, London, known as 'The Boxing Parson'. He founded a Boys' Club in his East End parish and taught boxing. When he retired to Malvern, he considered St. Mary's at Guarlford the most suitable location for the statue, which used to stand in his vicarage garden. Sadly, it was stolen one January night in 1991; also stolen were the nearby churchyard gates. Through a joint project between Stephen Cooper of the Rhydd and his woodwork tutor at Malvern College,

Figure 5.3 The church bell.

a replica pair of gates were made to replace the stolen ones. Stephen Cooper was the Parochial Church Council (PCC) treasurer for several years. The Rectory Lane churchyard gates were donated by the Boaz family; Mr Geoffrey Boaz was also the PCC treasurer for many years.

The oak tree near the Guarlford Road gate was planted in 1994 by Phillip Goodrich, the Bishop of Worcester, to mark the 150th anniversary of the building of the church.

The Church Interior

Figure 5.4 Interior view of St Mary's, 2002.

The interior of the early church must have seemed very austere at first, as the only furnishings were stone altar, pulpit and font, and there was no organ. The spaces between the narrow lancet windows of the nave were filled with scriptural sentences in red, purple and gold. These were described as "gaudy" by John Noakes, 'The Rambler,' writing about his visit to the church in 1845; but they must soon have been painted over, as the earliest photographs show the walls as plain except for the east wall where the Ten Commandments flanked the altar. These were later covered by the oak panelling and reredos, which were the gift of John Henry Stapleton and his wife Sarah Stapleton. This is commemorated on a small brass plaque near the vestry door. John Stapleton was churchwarden for many years and a generous benefactor to the church. He was the grandfather of Joan Hudson, the well-known local nurse and midwife.

The small portable altar immediately in front of the main altar was a gift to the Revd Frederick Newson by his friend the Bishop of Durham.

Inside the church, the first window on the left is in memory of the wife of the first Rector, the Revd John Bateman Wathen. The plaque of Virgin and Child was a wedding gift to Revd and Mrs Newson from the Countess Beauchamp, wife of the Seventh Earl. Next comes a window dedicated to a Charles Andrew, 1899, whose grave is opposite the church door. The third window is a memorial to a Victorian churchwarden, Thomas Need, who died in 1883. He was one of a family who had farmed in the district for about 400 years.

The magnificent carved oak pulpit, which replaced the original stone one, is a memorial to Revd J B Wathen; it was dedicated on 11th December 1906, and was paid for by public subscriptions. The ornate brass lectern is a memorial given by Ann Lees in memory of her sister, Alice Simpson, who died in 1879. A pair of floor-standing brass candlesticks, which matched the lectern, were stolen in the 1990s, along with the Bishop's Chair. The candlesticks were replaced, but sadly the replacements do not match the lectern. The present Bishop's Chair, made by Vanpoules of Surrey, is a near-replica of the stolen one.

Of the three beautiful east windows, the first is to the memory of the sixth Earl Beauchamp, who gave so much to the new church. He died in 1891. The middle window is to Edward Archer, another most generous benefactor and churchwarden, who died in 1892. He was proprietor of the 'Mount Pleasant Hotel', the 'Foley Arms' and adjoining wine shop at that time; and he paid for the re-glazing of some of the windows in the Priory, as well as giving a new bell to commemorate Queen Victoria's Golden Jubilee in 1887. Of John Bell, donor of the third window, little is known except that he was of Peckham Grove, died in 1890, and had lived in the black and white 'Littlewood House', in Poolbrook, where the mother of Dame Barbara Cartland, the novelist, once lived.

The carved oak cover for the font was given by a Mr Taylor who lived at Cherry Orchard in the 1930s. It replaced an ugly tin cover of which he strongly disapproved.

On the west wall above the font is placed a beautiful statue of Virgin and Child in memory of former pupils of South Lea School who died during the First World War. The school had strong links with Guarlford Church, as Revd Newson taught there for many years and was held in great esteem by staff and pupils, some of whom regularly attended Guarlford Church. There are other memorials in the church dedicated to boys and staff of South Lea School.

The church plate was a gift from Charles Morris; he came from London to live with his sister in Malvern and seemed to spend the rest of his life supporting good causes including provision of a water supply in North Malvern. The chalice was remodelled in 1909 by 'Ramsden and Carr'; it had been too top heavy.

Towards the end of the nineteenth century, an Embroidery Guild was formed and the ladies who met on Wednesdays took responsibility for the provision of altar frontals, vestments and banners. The banner of Our Lady, begun in 1909 and renovated a few years ago by Mrs Barbara Hill, still hangs over the pulpit. In the early 1990s, another group of ladies crafted many of the colourful kneelers to be seen in the church today; and, to commemorate 2000 years of Christendom, yet another group of ladies in 1999-2000 made new communion rail kneelers, cushions and additions to the pew kneelers.

New altar frontals were also given in memory of Frederick and Lily Clarke of Guarlford, Mr Ronald Smith, a long serving churchwarden, and Miss Helen Smith, who for many years gave freely of her time to play the organ at services as well as carrying out sacristan and other church duties.

The British Legion

The British Legion was formed on the 1st July 1921 by the amalgamation of four separate ex-service organisations set up following the First World War. The Royal Charter was granted in 1925 and, in 1971, it became the Royal British Legion. It exists to promote the welfare of those who are serving or who have served in the armed forces of the Crown and their dependants.

Part way down the north side of the nave can be seen the Guarlford British Legion Standard. When the British Legion was formed after the First World War, for the welfare and comradeship of ex-servicemen and their dependants, most veterans from Guarlford joined the nearest branch at Hanley Swan, but in 1929 Guarlford set up its own branch under the leadership of Cdr Ratcliff. Each year on Remembrance Sunday, the members would muster at Hall Green and then march to Guarlford Church for the Remembrance ceremony. By the mid 1980s, membership had dwindled, the few remaining members transferred to the Barnard's Green Branch and the Guarlford Branch was closed. In keeping with custom, the standard was laid up in the parish church.

On the wall, near the British Legion Standard, is a plain wooden cross in remembrance of Second Lieutenant J E Eyton-Lloyd of the 10th Squadron Royal Flying Corps, who died in 1917. The basic construction of the cross and the rudimentary metal labels recording his details leads to the assumption that it is the original grave marker. The Royal Air Force and the Commonwealth War Graves Commission both confirm that the officer was Lieutenant John Wathen Eyton-Lloyd, who died in 1917, aged twenty-two, and is buried in Choques Military Cemetery, Pas de Calais. He was the son of Dr and Mrs Eyton-Lloyd of 'Alanwood', Avenue Road, Great Malvern. Why he is remembered in Guarlford Church is not known. One possibility is that he was a former pupil of South Lea School, another is that, with a second name of Wathen, he could have been a godson of Revd Wathen.

On the north wall of the nave, adjacent to the organ, is a list of men who served in the First World War, but it is disproportionately long for the size of the parish and it is likely that the list is of those for whom members of the congregation wanted prayers offered. Many came from surrounding parishes, some were probably ex-pupils from South Lea School, and some seemed to have no connection with the Malvern area. There are also omissions: for instance, the Panting brothers are not mentioned. Included in the list is Hubert Jones, former Rector at Guarlford.

The fine painting of Madonna and Child, in the ornate gilt frame, was a gift from Mr Robert Bartleet of Cherry Orchard in memory of his father the Reverend Canon H H Bartleet, one-time Vicar of Malvern Priory, who lived at Cherry Orchard in his later years.

In 1998, through an anonymous bequest, an inductive loop for those with impaired hearing and a sound amplification system were installed; and, in 2004, the organ received a major overhaul in memory of Mrs Dorrie Smith.

Incumbents

Little is recorded about the early incumbents. John Noakes, in his book, *The Rambler,* briefly refers to Revd W J Fancourt as "a gentleman who is much beloved for his active and zealous pursuit of his Christian duties." He died in 1851 at the age of 42 and is buried near the northeast corner of the church. Two of his infant children died in 1853.

The first Rector, the Revd John Wathen, was incumbent for forty-eight years and was highly regarded by the people of Guarlford. Testimony to this is the beautifully carved pulpit, which is dedicated to his memory and was paid for by public subscription. There has already been mention of the major improvements made to the church in his early years as Rector. When Guarlford Civil Parish was formed in 1894, he also became the first chairman to its parish council. He and Mrs Wathen are buried in the churchyard opposite the porch.

The Revd Hubert Jones was Rector from 1905 to 1913. One of his first acts was to join in a collaborative project with the parishes of Madresfield and

Figure 5.5 St Mary's incumbents.

Newland to produce a monthly combined parish magazine, each parish having separate pages dedicated to its own events and matters. Each issue cost one penny, and initially Guarlford had 100 subscribers. He also enlisted the assistance of 'The Sisters of the Holy Name', Malvern Link who sent Sisters to work at Guarlford where they held mothers' meetings and classes. The extensive alterations to the church building in 1906 have already been mentioned. Incidentally, the running costs of the church at that time were estimated to be fifty pounds per annum, including the wages of the sexton (Mr Tandy), the organist and various organ blowers. In 1910, Hubert Jones took sabbatical leave and travelled on mission to New Zealand. To maintain contact with his parishioners while on his travels, he sent letters from Canada, Hawaii, and various New Zealand locations for publication in the parish magazine. In 1910, this must have been quite a journey.

Figure 5.6 The Revd Hubert Jones.

In 1913, he moved to Hanley Castle, but came back in 1914 for about sixteen months to take services in the absence of Revd Newson on Army Chaplain duties. Later, he also served as an Army Chaplain.

The appointment of the Revd Frederick Newson as Rector in 1913 at the age of thirty was the start of an incumbency, which, apart from October 1914 to February 1916 when he was away performing his duties (some in France) as an Army Chaplain, was to last for over half a century. At the time of writing, there are many people living with their own affectionate memories of Revd and Mrs Newson and, consequently, a fuller picture emerges of the impact this couple had on village life in Guarlford. It is of a dynamic couple who, like their predecessors, were totally committed to the pastoral care of the people of Guarlford and were fully involved in all aspects of village life and beyond. The Rectory had an ever-open door, but in the midst of their busy lives they also raised four children of their own as well as taking in as many as twenty evacuees during the Second World War.

In the early years, Revd Newson travelled round the parish on a 'Red Indian' motorcycle and sidecar, and on one occasion he ended up in the pond outside Grange Farm. Mrs Frances Newson also used the motorcycle combination and would frequently offer lifts in the sidecar. She could often be heard singing at the top of her voice as she sped along the country lanes. Later, they changed to pony and trap, and Revd Newson would be seen in the Glebe Field trying to catch the pony. Finally, he changed to a motor car which, needless to say, was freely available for the benefit of all.

There are numerous stories of the kindness and generosity of Revd Newson, even though he was a man of very limited means. He would often pay off the debts of those parishioners who found themselves in dire circumstances such as risk of eviction, even on one occasion selling his own furniture to do so. If parishioners appeared in court, he would often be there, using his legal training to defend them. He had a great sense of fun; he enjoyed arranging and acting in amateur dramatics, and his concerts in the village hall were always very popular. At the annual Harvest Supper, he provided much of the entertainment himself - always singing 'Widdecombe Fair'.

His church services had a relaxed air of informality. For well over forty years, he would play the organ for the hymns as well as conduct the service; and he rarely used the pulpit for his sermons, preferring to stand by the front pews. Often he would rest one foot

Figure 5.7 Revd F J Newson in later life

on the pew and reminisce at length, until a discreet cough from Mrs Newson brought him back to the text. There is a poignant minute from the PCC meeting of March, 1964, when the PCC requested that he continue to play the organ for as long as his failing eyesight allowed - but sadly it was not to be for long.

In 1922, the Rural Dean, on a visit to St Mary's, observed that the many items, which had been donated to the church over a number of years were displayed without the required faculty approval of the Worcester Diocese and, therefore, in contravention of Church Rules. Revd Newson would not agree to their removal and consequently, he and his churchwardens, Mr Brewer and Mr Absalom Bradshaw, found themselves the following year appearing before a Consistory Court at Worcester. After due consideration, the court gave retrospective approval for the items to remain with the exception of the statue of Madonna and Child, which had to be moved from its position beside the altar to its present location above the font on the west wall. Eventually, in 1964, fading eyesight and infirmity forced Revd Newson to reluctantly resign the living at Guarlford and he and his wife retired to Newland. He died the following year and is buried just opposite the church door at Guarlford.

From the day of their marriage in 1920, Frances May Newson became fully immersed in village life. She supported her husband with his church and pastoral duties and even, when required, tended the antiquated church boiler for Sunday services. She gave active support in other aspects of village life - Sunday School with its attendant outings and parties, Guarlford Women's Institute, summer fetes and dancing classes in the village hall. On retirement to Newland, she diverted her considerable energies to the community there. During the war years, she joined the St. John Ambulance, in which she eventually became Superintendent of the Malvern Division. In 1980, she was made a Commander of St John at the Grand Priory Lodge in the City of London. The *Malvern Gazette* reporting the occasion stated: "Mrs Newson seems to have a most remarkable knack of fitting more into sixty seconds than most people." In 1996, at her funeral at Guarlford, the St John Ambulance Malvern Division formed a Guard of Honour. She is laid to rest with her husband opposite the church entrance. Nearby, is a commemorative

Figure 5.8 Mr R H Smith, Mrs F M Newson and Mr S W Medcalf celebrating St Mary's 150th Anniversary.

seat to the Reverend and Mrs Newson, provided by their family. Visitors to the churchyard, using the seat, can enjoy fine views of the Malvern Hills.

In 1965, Revd Hartley Brown came and stayed for fifteen years. He was to be the last full-time Rector of Guarlford. 'Father' Brown and his housekeeper, Miss Frith, are remembered with great affection by the people of Guarlford. He can best be described as a quiet, gentle man, very active with the pastoral care of his parishioners and in the life of the village. He would be seen driving around in his 'Reliant Robin', sometimes at alarming speed - he once finished up in one of Bill Medcalf's fields. He nearly always wore his cassock and distinctive beret, and he would always have time to stop and talk. He was also accident-prone. Miss Joan Bradshaw remembers herself and Miss Joan Newell riding their horses down Rectory Lane when Father Brown, rushing from the church to talk to them, jumped from the churchyard wall and tore his cassock to an embarrassing length. Mrs Meriel Bennett remembers him standing in front of an electric heater during a Sunday School and setting fire to his cassock. Meriel, who was teaching the infants at the back of the church, remembers wrapping him in the church carpet to extinguish the flames. The children found it all very exciting. Then there was the village fete incident remembered by many, when the bench he, Miss Frith and others were sitting on in the Rectory garden tipped over backwards, arms and legs going in all directions much to the great amusement of bystanders.

During Father Brown's time as Rector and in memory of Revd Newson, the chancel rail was extended to its present full width; the church organ received a major refurbishment, also in memory of Revd Newson; and the church was rewired and redecorated. He retired in 1980 to the Beauchamp Community at Newland. Miss Frith cared for him until he died in 1982, and she died a year later. They are both buried in Newland Churchyard.

From the forming of the ecclesiastical parish until the retirement of Father Brown, the rectors and, if married, their wives, were central to the many aspects of village life. Their presence and influence were very apparent. However, by 1981, the Church of England policy that priests should retire at seventy combined with a decline in the recruitment of new priests inevitably resulted in significant changes. Small parishes such as Guarlford would no longer have the luxury of their very own pastor.

A Benefice was formed consisting of the three parishes of Guarlford, Madresfield and Newland, and its first Priest in Charge was the Revd David Martin, known affectionately by some at Guarlford as "the boy David". He took up residence, with his young family, in the Rectory at Madresfield and divided his time between the three parishes. Sundays were particularly busy with the maintenance of services in all three churches. In Guarlford he was still known as the Rector. Inevitably, the pivotal role in village life played by his predecessors could not continue. For example, he soon had to give up his seat on Guarlford Parish Council. Guarlford, like many other parishes, had to get used to having a part-time parish priest. The Rectory at Guarlford was sold.

Revd Martin in his own quiet way worked hard to bring the three parishes of the Benefice closer together. He established a Benefice Junior Church, which met (and still does) in Madresfield School, and he revived the joint parish magazine, now called *The Grapevine*. As before, it covered the three villages of Guarlford, Madresfield and Newland and, at the time of writing, this is still going strong. He also revived the Guarlford Youth Club. For two consecutive years, he co-ordinated his three parishes into a summer village 'ride-about' event, and he was also instrumental in the formation of an informal benefice choir known as 'The Parish Singers'. He also initiated the practice of house discussion groups across the benefice during the season of Lent. In 1991, he left to take up a new post at Alvechurch.

After an interregnum period, the Revd (later Canon) John Green became Priest-in-Charge of the United Benefice in 1992; but the Worcester Diocese was still going through a period of change and allocated to him extra Diocesan duties which were to take up at least half his time. Inevitably, this meant even less time for pastoral care for the three parishes, and involvement in other village activities became very difficult. After a time, the number of parishes was reduced to two when Madresfield and Newland merged to form the ecclesiastical parish of Madresfield with Newland, and Newland Church became the Chapel to the Beauchamp Community.

It was during his time in this post that Canon Green established links between the Benefice and the Diocese of Masasi in Tanzania, an extremely poor country. Visits were exchanged and these continue. Fund-raising efforts resulted in the provision of a 'Land Rover' for the community in the remote region of Rondo and the funding of a teacher there. At the time of writing, this latter funding continues, the money being raised at the annual harvest supper auction. Canon Green will also be remembered as a cheerful man with a great sense of fun and an insatiable appetite for travel; he left in 1999 to take up full time Diocesan duties and the Rectory at Madresfield was sold.

In 1999, there was yet more change. The ecclesiastical parishes of Guarlford and Madresfield with Newland merged to form a single parish. At the same time, this new parish was united with the Parish of Powick, which includes Callow End, to form the new Benefice of Powick and Guarlford and Madresfield with Newland, with one priest overall, the Revd David Nichol, who resides in Powick. He divides his time between the two parishes, each having two churches. In one respect history has repeated itself, because Revd Newson, many years previously, used to help out with services at Callow End.

There were interregna, then, following the departure of Revds Brown, Martin and Green. In these cases, it is usual for the churchwardens to conduct the day-to-day affairs of the church and for retired priests to take temporary responsibility for church services and pastoral care. At Guarlford, these duties were performed by Revds Overton and Richards, and, for two interregnum periods, by the Revd Beverley Colman. They are all remembered with affection by Guarlford parishioners. Beverley Colman had a particularly interesting ministry, which included service as Army Chaplain in Egypt, and then in Malaya during the Communist emergency there, followed by ministry in Indonesia - but that is all for another book. In 2005, another interregnum begins in mid June, with the departure of Revd David Nichol to become Vicar of Holy Trinity North Malvern and St James' West Malvern.

Churchwardens and Layreaders

The office of churchwarden has been in existence since the thirteenth century, and by the fifteenth century churchwardens were elected annually, all adult parishioners having a vote. A parish church usually has two churchwardens, and their main duties concern the care, maintenance and preservation of the fabric of the church and its contents, support to the incumbent, and the maintenance of order in the church and churchyard.

It is not possible to list all the churchwardens who have served Guarlford because no formal record has been kept and not all minutes of past PCC meetings have been traced. Some churchwardens served for many years. For most of the twentieth century, and spanning three generations, one of the churchwardens was from the Medcalf family of New House Farm.

Ronald H Smith of Guarlford Court Farm was churchwarden for forty-five years. In 1993, while being interviewed by BBC Hereford and Worcester about his retirement as churchwarden, he was asked who was taking over his duties. He replied that his daughter would be the new churchwarden. Then the young female reporter asked him what he thought about that. He replied that his daughter had her head screwed on and would do a good job, but he did not approve. When asked why, he said he agreed with the view of St Paul that the women in church should be silent. This brought the interview to a close. Some churchwardens were great benefactors to the church: for instance, John Stapleton, Edward Archer and Thomas Need. Other churchwardens in recent times were Miss Meriel Smith (now Mrs Meriel Bennett), Mr Clifford Hayes, Mrs Elizabeth Tidball and Mr David Masters. The current warden (2005) is Mr Donald Hill.

Two particular layreaders are worthy of mention. During the incumbency of Revd Hartley Brown, a Mr Ken Smith of Woodshears Road was of great

Figure 5.9 Mr and Mrs S W Medcalf.

assistance in his capacity as a layreader, and he often conducted the Evensong service. He and his housekeeper, Miss Dunford, were well-liked in the village and always supported parish events. The other layreader well-known and held in great affection by many was Malcolm Russell of 'Tanhouse'. He was born in Salford in 1939 and, after attending Durham University, he took up teaching, first in Llangollen, then in Zambia, and eventually at the nearby Chase High School, before establishing his nursery at 'Tanhouse'. Besides teaching, he took an active interest in scouting, an interest, which he maintained all his life. On becoming a layreader, he took many services at St Mary's, Guarlford, and also at other churches in the Benefice. He will be remembered for his relaxed and informal manner, his unbounded enthusiasm and optimism, and his generosity of spirit and goodwill to everyone. He died in 2001, and his ashes and a memorial stone to Malcolm and his mother, Mary Bruce, who lived at 'Tanhouse' in her later years, are situated near the bell in the tree, which Malcolm would ring prior to Sunday services. Beneath an oak tree nearby is 'Little Mary's Seat', which Malcolm had made for his mother when she lived at 'Tanhouse'.

Fetes, Bazaars and Outings

Throughout the life of the church there has been a continuous round of fund-raising and social events - outings for the Sunday School, choir and Mothers Union, summer fetes, Christmas bazaars, harvest suppers, concerts and pantomimes.

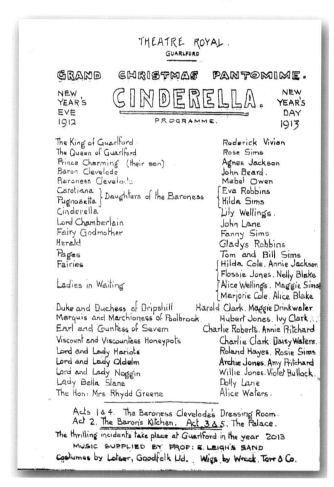

Figure 5.10 Cinderella Pantomime poster, 1913.

The summer fete has been a consistently popular event, and it remains an important fund-raiser for the upkeep of the church, as well as fostering community spirit. In the earlier years it would take place on the Rectory lawn, with events such as dog obedience trials and donkey rides in the adjacent glebe field. In the days when few ordinary people had transport and hence had limited access to diversions further a-field, events such as the fete were something to look forward to and the fete still is, in spite of the many competing attractions nowadays. There would be the usual mix of stalls, teas, amusements including 'bowling for a pig' and races for children and adults. It was usually organised by the ladies, with the men being urged to help with the setting up and any other heavy work.

Excerpts from early parish magazines give a snapshot of some of the other activities, such as the 1906 September issue's 'Choir excursion to Llandudno'. Members arose at 2 am to catch the excursion train to Llandudno, arriving there at 9 am, fully ready for breakfast. There followed a day of seaside entertainment: "There is the sea wherein to swim and whereon to sail - The pier provides a good sea breeze and a first class band. - We spent a small fortune in playing miniature games of cricket and football and racing. Then we had our photograph taken - price One Penny. An entertainment on the pier, a row on the deep, and supper completed a delightful day. The return train left at 7.30 pm and landed the party at Malvern in the small hours."

In the 1907 January issue, 'Parochial Tea' records the family party in the schoolroom on St John's Day: "About eighty sat down to a Tea provided by many kind friends in the Parish. Evensong followed at 7 pm after which we all returned to the Schoolroom for a 'Social'. There was dancing, with restful intervals for music. A carol party sang two or three Christmas Carols, whilst songs were given by Miss Olive Bedington and Mr J Woodyatt. Musical Chairs (and the floor) provided seats for young and old, and, of course, Mrs Panting triumphantly won the last chair, as usual".

Figure 5.11 The Guarlford Fete, 1911.

Then the 1907 August issue has the 'Parochial Fete': "The chief attraction was the Athletic Sports. The competitors, if backward in coming forward, were in earnest and strove manfully for the valuable and unique prizes. The course was in perfect condition, the greasy pole was very greasy, the obstacles dreadful hindrances in the races, and the starter an object of terror with his formidable pistol. The bicycle races were fast and furious, with the exception of the Tortoise Race, which was excitingly slow. Heroic ladies even competed in the bicycle obstacle race. The Tugs of War, especially that for ladies, were exhibitions of amazing strength. Sir Edmund Lechmere, kindly acted as judge, Mr G Wall as starter, and Mr Medcalf, nominally the treasurer, was the pivot upon which the whole evening turned. Later in the evening dancing was indulged in on the Rectory lawn, the music being kindly supplied by Messrs Stanhope, Burston and Cameron."

In the 1909 August issue there is 'Guarlford Olympic Games and Marathon Races': "We did not see why we should be overshadowed and dwarfed into insignificance by greater places and grander communities, so we thought *we* could have our own Olympic Games and Marathon Races. The Church of England Men's Society acted as committee with the help of Mr Medcalf; Mr Bladder lent his field and the Rectory garden was thrown open."

Then, "At six o'clock the crowds began to pour in. Carriages, motor cars and perambulators rolled up. Poor Mr Bradshaw Junior was besieged by eager competitors wishing to enter their names and pay their fees. There was Mr Wall, the starter, and at the winning post, Sir Edmund Lechmere who had kindly agreed to act as judge. With him was Captain Allen-Hoblyn, and the Rector was in at least twenty places at once. Only those who were present can form an idea of the keenly contested tugs-of-war. Then there were the bicycle contests and the obstacle races in which competitors started in costume appropriate to the arduous task ahead but finished in the very latest Parisian modes. There were races and tugs-of-war for both ladies and gentlemen, and a game of musical chairs by bicycle. You could throw at coconuts, kick footballs, you could roam the garden searching for treasures or you could listen to the band. Lady Lechmere presented the prizes, which were both useful (e.g. a kitten; a pair of braces) or ornamental (e.g. a bucket, a half hundredweight of coal, a pat of butter). After everybody gave three cheers for a wonderful fete we all parted company."

Finally, the 1909 August issue has 'The Mothers' Outing': "Carriages and pairs were in waiting at the Rectory Room early in the afternoon. Into these Sister carefully packed the mothers 'this side up'. Then off we dashed! A beautiful drive through Malvern Wells, past British Camp to Eastnor to visit the church. Then on to Holly Bush for tea. After tea the young and active scaled the surrounding hills before returning to the waiting chariots which bore them home across Castlemorton Common, through Welland and Hanley Swan to Guarlford once more. Kind friends contributed to the expenses and every Mother will join in thanking them for a delightful afternoon."

The Rectory

When the building of the church was finished in 1844, a house for the incumbent was built nearby. Again, leading Malvern residents were generous with financial help, one donation alone being one hundred pounds. A year after the Parish of Guarlford was formed in 1866, the house became the Rectory. When Revd Hartley Brown, the last full-time Rector of Guarlford, retired in 1980, the Rectory was sold to a Captain Leveratt, RN, who carried out extensive refurbishment, and later to Mr Michael Huskinson who is the Worcester Diocesan Registrar and a parish councillor.

In 1907, Lord Beauchamp gave permission for an outhouse in the Rectory grounds to be adapted for use as a Parish Room, later known as the 'Rectory Room', the chief purpose of which was to establish an 'Evening Club' where men could "receive instruction and partake in mutual discussion". This work was completed in 1909. The Sisters from Malvern Link made use of it for their Guarlford 'Mothers Meetings', and for their 'Boot and Clothing Clubs'. The Reading Room was to be open every night of the week. Members had to be over sixteen years of age and the subscription was four pence per month. Mr Christopher Robathan agreed to be its secretary. A year on

Figure 5.12 Children dancing in front of the Rectory at the 1911 Fete.

it was proving to be a great success; besides being open for reading and recreation and for the Sisters' activities it was used for Sunday School and by the 'Church of England Men's Society'. During World War Two, the room became known as 'The Point', being an assembly point for Air Raid Wardens. First Aid classes were held there, and later there were a flourishing youth club and numerous jumble sales.

Other Places of Worship in the Parish

The Rhydd Chapel

The parish magazine of October, 1906, gave notice that Sir Edmund Lechmere, on his return to Rhydd Court, had re-opened his private chapel for Services, and it was planned to have monthly communion services at 8 am for communicants living in the Rhydd area. In St Mary's Vestry Book there are records of occasional early morning communion services until the end of 1914, but nothing afterwards.

The 'Tin Tabernacle'

The Old Elm Chapel, or 'Tin Tabernacle' as it was often called, stood near the junction of Hall Green and Guarlford Road. It was a corrugated iron structure, built on the initiative of a Mrs Brocklebank, wife of a shipping magnate, who lived at 'The Firs', Malvern.

Many people thought it was a Methodist Chapel, but it was, in fact, a Brethren Chapel. The Plymouth Brethen was founded in 1830, and later split into 'Open Brethren' and

Figure 5.13 The Tin Tabernacle.

'Exclusive Brethen'. Guarlford Chapel belonged to the former.

Various retired missionaries acted as pastors at the little chapel, and Mrs Brocklebank herself used to visit, arriving by landau complete with grooms. Members of the chapel were expected to give a portion of their income to fund maintenance and running costs and provide special treats for the children. Children who attended St Mary's were reportedly a little envious of those who went to chapel, because the chapel outings always seemed much grander.

Besides Sunday Services and Sunday School, there were Women's Meetings with knitting, sewing and Bible reading on Monday afternoons, and on Wednesday evenings there were services and Bible study for children and adults.

During the Second World War, the Old Elm Chapel was taken over by the 'Andrew League', an organization that existed to give holidays to school children. During this time, no services were held in the chapel. After the war, the building was sold to property developers and demolished to make way for the housing estate that now stands around the site.

The Church Today

For over 160 years St Mary's has stood at the centre of the village. During that time, there have been many baptisms, weddings and funerals. Loved ones are buried in the churchyard. Each year parishioners have attended the festivals of Easter and Christmas, together with other festivals and occasions such as Harvest Thanksgiving and Remembrance Sunday. Week by week services have repeated the acts of worship of the Anglican Church being performed throughout the country and beyond, maintaining here in Guarlford a continuity stretching around the world over two millennia.

Thus, St Mary's and, at different times, the chapels have been at the heart of Guarlford's life over the generations. Church life today is different in many ways from 1844, when St Mary's was originally built as a district chapel. In recent years, there have been successive re-organisations of the parishes, and parish priests have to share their time between several churches and congregations. There are widely dispersed parishioners

nationwide to supplement those already in existence. School Boards could charge up to nine pence a week and had to guarantee that children aged five to thirteen years would attend: a School Attendance Officer was appointed to enforce this. Then came the 1891 'Free Education' Act, when the Government took on the responsibility for providing education, which was compulsory for children aged five to ten years. The 1918 Education Act raised the compulsory school leaving age to fourteen.

There are references in the Log Book to 'aid grants', the amount given depending upon pupils passing certain tests. Between 1898 and 1901 Guarlford National School received on average twenty pounds per annum in aid grants. The Parish Council records also refer to the 'Lloyds Charity', the income of which was shared between Great Malvern and Guarlford. In 1896, Guarlford's share was £4-12-9d (£4.64) "… of which one pound was for the education of poor children"; the members of the Parish Council decided that the education money should be passed to the School Manager.

The Buildings

The school and 'School House' stood between the Church and the Rectory, side-on to the road. When the 'School House' was sold after the school closure, the conveyance included a document regarding an 1843 deed of gift of land for the building of the Church and Rectory from Mr Edward Thomas Foley and the Vicar and Churchwardens of the Parish of Great Malvern.

There were two separate playgrounds, one for the boys, and another for the girls and infants who entered the school at the front, via a cloakroom, which led into the main classroom with its high-pitched ceiling. This classroom measured 33ft by 18ft. The boys had a separate entrance and cloakroom at the back of the school, also leading into the main schoolroom, from which a door led into the smaller classroom (20ft by 10ft), which the plans show with a gallery, later removed. The 1867 plans also have drawings of the "girls' and infants' privies" and these, with those used by the boys, were just outside in the playground.

Mr Kenneth Woolley, born in the 'School House' in 1925, remembers that at the school "… there was a pump in the girls' toilets, from which Mr Clark, the caretaker's husband, would fill a large header tank from the well, then open a valve to give the toilets a daily communal flush. The day's 'takings' would then proceed past an inspection cover just inside the School gates – we were never able to discover the final destination. Progress was often blocked by tennis balls and other objects. Clearance was often part of the headmaster's duty."

A flue for the stoves was built into an internal wall, and in 1903 concern was expressed about the lack of ventilation, as the windows had been made without any 'hoppers', that is, small opening windows for ventilation; but it was not until 19th August 1910 that there is a reference in the School Log to the great improvements in the school building after alterations to the windows had been made in the spring of the year.

Figure 6.2 The School and School House.

Thomas Hayes: a Pupil in Victoria's Reign

There are few early written records about the school. The surviving School Log Book runs from 1900 to 1946, and there is also an exercise book from 1890 in existence belonging to Thomas Hayes of Clevelode, grandfather to Clifford Hayes. Thomas could only have been about twelve years of age (and so one of the older pupils); his book is remarkably neat with beautiful copperplate handwriting. Parsing sentences (analysing the structure and naming all the parts of speech), dictation, transcription and some composition work form the English syllabus. A composition from July 15th 1890 reads:

"On Saturday I went to Worcester, first I went to the Museum, and I saw different kinds of birds, a child's skull, a big tiger, Chinese shoe, monkeys, birds eggs, horse's and cow's skeleton, mammoth's tusk, leopard, a young deer, thrushes nests and their eggs, skeletons of birds, snakes skin, ferrets and their young ones..... I went from the Museum to a coffee tavern and had my tea, then I went to the Cathedral while service was on, one boy sang by himself. I looked round and went back home by train."

In Mathematics young Thomas was tackling exercises in vulgar fractions, decimals, simple interest and various other problems, all sums clearly and neatly written. Geography consisted of drawing detailed maps of England and Wales, Scotland and Ireland without any border across the country. Thomas wrote essays about these and also life in Canada. Any empty spaces on the pages are filled by handwriting practice, using quotations from poems and 'wise sayings'. All this written in ink with remarkably few mistakes and blots!

The Log Book

The only Log Book available is kept in the Worcester Records Office and covers the years 1900 to 1946. It begins with commencement of Mr A E Martin's time as Headmaster, starting on February 5th 1900. The school consisted then of the two rooms and two classes, with seventy children in the 'Mixed School' and fifty in the 'Infants Room', where Mrs Martin was the teacher, together with an assistant. Joan Bradshaw's mother, Miss Price, taught at the school before the First World War. The mixed class, taught by Mr Martin, had pupils from seven to thirteen and, later, fourteen years of age.

Figure 6.3 Miss Price and the Class of 1910.

Several times Inspectors state that the school should really have three teachers, and assistants of varying talent and attendance filled the gap. There are many references in the early part of the Log Book to the 'migratory' character of the pupils. This was presumably because agricultural workers often moved to find work as the seasons changed. In November 1908, the Headmaster notes that within seven weeks ten children had been admitted and nine had left. The classes may seem to be very large, but early Log Book entries point out the erratic attendance of the pupils, mainly because of bad weather but also because children stayed at home to help with work on the farm and in the house. Indeed, significantly, special notes are made of times when most of the pupils are actually present. Childhood illnesses were rife: for example, in January 1904, the school was closed for five weeks because of an outbreak of measles, and it is recorded that throughout the lifetime of the school snow and floods kept some children at home, especially the little ones. The 'catchment area' was large, and Alf Young of Hall Green recalled that, when he attended Guarlford School from 1928 onwards, the school also used to take its pupils not only from Guarlford village and Hall Green but also from Clevelode, Hangmans Lane on the road to Upton, and as far as the Old Hills at Callow End.

The necessity for the able-bodied of all ages to help with the Harvest was recognised and the summer holidays were adjusted accordingly, with two weeks in July and then the whole of September (for the hop-picking), something which continued well into the twentieth century. Even so, an His Majesty's Inspectorate (HMI) report in 1912 makes particular reference to the fact that there were still too many absences, which can easily be understood, given that even later in the century children were tempted to help in the fields instead of going to school.

The highlight of the school year at that time was the summer outing, which would be to the Old Hills at Callow End, where the children had sports and a tea party. The journey was made in a harvest wagon belonging to Mr Bradshaw, who farmed at Guarlford Court Farm. Mrs Lil Gilroy was one of the large family of Morris children, eleven in all, who lived mostly at Clevelode. Mrs Gilroy went to Guarlford School in 1917 at the age of ten and remembers that every year at Christmas there was a School Concert; she recalls singing 'Three Old Maids of Lee', with friends Amy and Annie. Evidently, in freezing weather, Mr Martin used to throw water down to create for the children a frozen slide running from the playground into the lane, and every time the Hunt met the children were taken to the corner by the church to see the horses and hounds.

The Curriculum

During Mr Martin's time as Headmaster, the subjects studied included English (much Grammar), Arithmetic, Religion, History, Geography, Needlework, Drawing and Singing. Intriguingly, in 1908, an Inspector suggested that in the Infants class the practice of reading sentences backwards should be abolished. Behaviour is generally noted as good, but, characteristic of reports on many rural schools in those early years, country children could be very reserved, so oral work was difficult. There are references to 'Drill', but most surprising is the fact that on March 19th 1901 chemicals and apparatus for Science lessons were received, and Science was taught to the whole school, including "lessons illustrating the properties of oxygen, hydrogen, nitrogen and chlorine; the chemical character and constituents of pure air, and the nature of the impurities sometimes found in it." Sadly, there is in the Log no record of how the pupils responded.

Figure 6.4 Mr and Mrs Martin and the Class of 1920.

Alf Young said that his father and uncle, who attended Guarlford School in the early decades of the century, told him that, during the First World War, boys could leave school at about the age of thirteen, because they were needed to work in place of the men who had gone to war. They were interviewed by Miss Severn Burrows of the Malvern District Committee, and she decided whether they had had enough education. The School Log Book has an entry for April 1915, which says that, because of a shortage of farm workers, all the boys over twelve years of age, except one, had been given leave to go to work. In June 1915, the authorities even allowed boys under the school leaving age to work with the harvest, and the headmaster found it difficult to make some return…

Mr Woolley: Headmaster 1923 - 1941

The Log Book records that on April 16th 1923 Mr Clarence William Woolley became Headmaster of the School, and it is from pupils of his era that the most vivid memories come. Mrs Phyl Bayliss shared her school life with Mrs Rene Sims (then Waters) from 1921 to 1930 and says, "I loved Guarlford School; I didn't want to leave a bit!", a sentiment echoed by many. Pictures of the schoolrooms are fresh in the minds of ex-pupils still in the village today, a common experience and one echoed in many literary accounts of schooldays. Particularly remembered in Guarlford's case is the fact that at that time the big room was divided by a curtain about five feet in depth to create two classrooms. If you were in favour, you were allowed to draw the curtain for lessons after Roll Call and Prayers. There were large 'tortoise' stoves, one in each room. Some former pupils remember that the large room didn't get warm until they were going home. Mrs Clark, the caretaker, lit the stoves on winter mornings. In *Cider With Rosie*, Laurie Lee describes the stove in his own village school:

"It was made of cast-iron and had a noisy mouth which rattled coke and breathed out fumes. It was decorated by a tortoise labelled 'Slow But Sure', and in winter it turned red-hot"(p48), a description which would have been familiar to many who attended Guarlford School, where at times the fumes from the stoves made the classrooms distinctly foggy, particularly before the ventilation was improved. Mr John Little remembers, in the late thirties, the chill being taken off bottles of milk by placing them on the stoves.

Figure 6.5 Miss Cope and the Class of 1930.
Back row L-R: 3rd Charles Bladder; 5th Sam Beard.
Front row seated L-R: George Fisher; Joyce Clark and Ernie Clark far right.

Before the introduction of free school milk, Mr Woolley thought that children should have something at playtime to sustain them and he used to make 'Horlicks' for them, heating milk on the stove – the 'Horlicks' was mixed laboriously with a 'plunger' gadget. Mr Woolley was evidently a 'kindly disciplinarian' and is praised in Inspectors' Reports for overcoming the country children's natural reticence. He continued to teach the basic subjects soundly and to broaden his pupils' experience: there are references in the Log Book to trips to the 'Malvern Assembly Rooms' and the 'Picture House' to see plays by Shakespeare, travel films and even *Ben Hur* in November 1927, together with other excursions. Ken Woolley remembers one such excursion, which was a conducted tour over the ex-German liner 'Berengaria' – he thinks in Southampton. Sam Beard says, "Over a period of time Mr Woolley firmly fixed life's educational requirements and good manners into our largely unreceptive minds."

Miss Cole and Miss Cope: Class Teachers

Figure 6.6 Miss Cole and the Class of 1935.

The school became a three-teacher school for a time, with Mr Woolley as Headmaster and teaching Standards Five and Six (the seniors aged eleven to fourteen). A Miss Lindsay has been mentioned as a teacher, but most people recall that in the 1930s Miss Cope, daughter of Police Inspector Cope of Upton, taught the Junior Class (Standards Three and Four), and Miss Cole, daughter of the wheelwright in Chance Lane, reigned supreme in the Infants Class (Standards One and Two). As Pamela Fairhurst (nee Newson) recalls: "My memories really start at the Village School next door to the Rectory; one small room was my world – the Infants room – presided over by one of life's natural teachers, Hilda Cole, who taught generations of children to read and write and made it all seem like fun. And, oh, the wonderful smell of the corner cupboard full of plasticine, blunt scissors, raffia, beads and other delights, which came out after all the hard work had been finished – and the lovely round stove which gave out a tremendous heat and was surrounded by a circular guard to stop little hands getting burned. We won't dwell on the outside lavatories, the girls off one playground and the boys off another, cold, miserable but necessary places." Stoves as well as smells seem to loom large in memories of schooldays.

The School Day

The school day began with assembly and prayers for the classes all together, occasionally being led by the Rector. The ringing of the school bell marked the sections of the school day and was a useful 'timepiece' for others working in the fields and houses around the village. The school was lit by oil lamps, and water from the pump at Mrs Clark's cottage nearby was used for drinking purposes at the school. A popular duty among the pupils was to collect the water in the galvanized two-gallon water cans and place them on the windowsills, with the enamel mug provided. For a long time, the pump water from the school and 'School House' was considered unfit for drinking, because of the proximity of the churchyard; but, according to the Log Book, in May 1940 the water from the school pump was analysed and finally pronounced fit for drinking.

> ### Playground Games
>
> *The games children play in the playground are an essential part of school life, and Margaret Omar recalls games that will be familiar to many: skipping games (some girls were very proficient at these!), conkers, marbles, hoops and so on, as well as 'Nuts in May', 'The Farmer's in his Den' and 'What's the time, Mr Wolf'.*

Derrick Bladder, who was a pupil at the school from about 1927 to 1936, says, "We did the usual lessons, (the basic 'three Rs', History, Geography, Nature Study). We used to play sports and on a Friday afternoon we boys used to work on the vegetable patch. We loved going out instead of being in school, especially when the season was right. Happy days." The children also enjoyed nature walks around the lanes and up to Wood Street and Ox Hill, walks still fondly remembered today.

Evidently, Mr Woolley, in common with his predecessor, liked introducing the older pupils to scientific experiments. Mr Woolley taught the children gardening by maintaining a school garden in the field by the Rectory. Kenneth Woolley remembers plum trees, vegetables, flowerbeds, even rose arches and that "Dad was keen on his marrow beds; we collected leaves to make leaf mould". The soil was heavy Worcestershire clay and all water had to be brought from the 'School House' by Mr Woolley. In the 1930s, the older children spent one day a week at Great Malvern School, where the boys were taught woodwork and the girls cookery.

Some extra holidays are also recorded in the Log Book, such as those for Royal Weddings: the Duke of York's (later to be George VI) in 1923; the Duke of Kent's in 1934; and the Duke of Gloucester's in 1935. On January 28th 1936, "the scholars and teachers attended the Parish Church for a Memorial Service" to mark the funeral of George V. Alf Young remembered that on Armistice Day, November 11th, the children would march to the War Memorial by the church gate.

After Guarlford School

Before the Second World War children either stayed at Guarlford School until they were fourteen or went to one of the Grammar or High Schools in Worcester, Hanley

Castle or Tewkesbury at ten or eleven. The Secondary Modern Schools in Malvern (later state comprehensive schools) were not built until the 1950s. The Chase, now a College of Technology, opened in 1953, and Dyson Perrins C of E School in 1958. Those who stayed at Guarlford School until they were fourteen entered employment, for example on farms, as did Derrick Bladder and Lil Gilroy; or they became apprentices in local businesses, such as Phyl Bayliss's needlework apprenticeship, while Alf Young was apprenticed as a carpenter to Thomas Powles at the top of Wood Street (where the firm of 'Walsh' is now).

Wartime

Very little appears in the Log Book about the progress of the two World Wars outside the village. The girls, as well as the boys, helped with 'war work' in the First World War, and within a fortnight in August 1914 the Upper Standard Girls made thirty-nine shirts and six pairs of socks for the Army. There is a poignant reference to the school being closed to enable children to attend the funeral of a young man who had himself been a pupil just a few short years before. Several times the words "no coal, so no school" appear in the winter of 1917.

Memories are, however, still clear about events in the parish in the Second World War. There is a description of how, before the Second World War, the 'Gas Van' came to the village, and Mr Woolley had to supervise the youngsters trying out their gas masks. They went into the van, where tear gas was turned on, to test if the masks were all right and being worn correctly. And Margaret Omar (nee Lane) recalls: "We had to walk down the lane with our gas masks in boxes. I remember sitting there and we had to try to see if we could breathe in. Some of the younger children had 'Mickey Mouse' masks and I was just too old to get one. I was quite upset."

The Lane Children

The Lane children (Edwin and Margaret) and others were very involved in salvage collections: "We had to bring stuff in for salvage; it was going to be judged who brought in the most valuable stuff. They divided us into four groups, one in each corner of the playground; we were in the same group as the children from The Rectory. Our Dad found an old motorbike that he had scrapped and thrown in the pit up at the house. So we dragged this old motorbike out, took it down to School and found that part of the engine was aluminium - they regarded that as valuable." So Edwin and Margaret's group won the prize!

Margaret also remembers that she and her friend were sent to the girls' cloakroom to try to make shelters with the cardboard mats used for exercise: "If there was an explosion and the blast was blown in we would have used these mats to protect us. I don't think they would have had much effect, but we thought it was quite funny at the time. We also had to knit things, socks for sailors and so on."

Guarlford School supplied many ex-pupils to the war effort: as Sam Beard says, "When World War Two came along, Guarlford School pupils were well to the fore and included one Wing Commander and two or three pilots (RAF) and two Warrant Officers (Royal Artillery)", as well as other men, together with Land Army girls and Wrens.

The main effect of war on the school was the arrival on November 29th 1940 of twenty-three evacuees from Selly Park School, Birmingham, with their teachers, Miss Gosling and Miss Morris. In 1939 the authorities had considered closing Guarlford School and transferring the children to Madresfield, as the building was deteriorating and also, by May, the numbers had dropped to fifty children between the ages of five and fourteen. This was partly a result of smaller families, but also the fact that, as mechanisation increased, there were fewer labourers working on the land and occupying the tied cottages. However, as the probability of war increased, it had been decided to keep the school open to welcome evacuees. Mr A R Rose was one of these evacuees and he described his memories of the village school: "I remember the 'Brummy' kids thought the country accent was a bit funny, no doubt the Guarlford kids thought our accent was funny too. We were not very scholastically inclined at the village school; we were more interested in the ferrets and things kept by the son of Mr Woolley, the schoolmaster, and the superb model planes made by his other son."

The Woolley Family

As Mr and Mrs Woolley lived in 'The School House', they and their family were prominent in the life of the village. Mrs Lucy Margerie Woolley trained as a nurse in the Manchester area before marrying in 1914 and, after bringing up her children, she practised privately in Malvern. Margaret Llewelyn (nee Woolley), the youngest of the six children says, "My father was a good, hard-working man and conscientious teacher. For fourteen years he was also a Captain in the Church Army, serving in Cromer, Plymouth, Eccles and Chard, before moving to Hallow and Guarlford. To us he was a loving father and devoted husband."

John was the eldest of the six, born in Chard in 1915. After leaving Guarlford School, he went on to Worcester Grammar School and was a keen member of Guarlford Football Team and the Tennis Club. He worked in the Worcestershire Education Department until he joined the RAF Volunteer Reserve before the outbreak of the Second World War.

In 1916, David was also born in Chard. David, a keen cyclist, cricketer, tennis and bowls player, was a friend of Colin Bradshaw, brother of Joan. He had a private tutor at home and then trained as a pharmacist in Malvern and Taunton, being sponsored through college by a Taunton chemist. David served in the Army during the War. He finally owned three chemist's shops and an optician's in Bristol.

Then came Monica, who was born in Crewkerne in 1918. Monica, who had been slightly disabled in childhood by infantile paralysis, went to Tewkesbury High School and became a teacher. Miss Monica Woolley was a familiar and popular figure to many in Malvern, as, after teaching firstly in Birmingham, she became temporary head of Hanley Swan School when war began, and finally taught for forty-two years at Malvern

Figure 6.7 Mr and Mrs Woolley with, L to R, David, baby Peter, John and Monica, c.1923.

Parish School, also known as Mill Lane School. During the war, Monica was in charge of the evacuee children being sent to escape the 'blitzing' of Birmingham, and when she died in November, 2003, the *Malvern Gazette* tribute remembered her "kindness and truly dedicated teaching".

Next was Peter, born in Hallow in 1922. He went on to Hanley Castle Grammar and trained as an engineer, working at 'Archdales' in Worcester and then at the Royal Radar Establishment (RRE) in Malvern. After him came Kenneth, who was born in Guarlford in 1925, was educated at the Village School and then at Hanley Castle Grammar School. He joined the RAF in the Second World War and afterwards, like his father and sisters, he became a teacher, at Pershore Abbey Park Junior School, and finally retired as a deputy headmaster. He continued to fly in peacetime, enjoying his hobby of gliding. The youngest child, Margaret, who like Kenneth, has supplied many memories for this history, was born in the School House in 1929 and, after following her sister to Tewkesbury High School, taught in Dartmouth and Australia. In the photograph of Miss Cole's class of 1935, (Figure 6.6), Margaret is the happy little girl standing front left, as she describes herself, "all knobbly knees and gappy smile".

The School House was not large, but was home to the family of six children and their parents. Margaret recalls, "The house was usually cold and damp. The tiny sitting-room, the 'room' as it was called, had a fireplace, but I only remember the fire being lit at Christmas. The bedrooms had small fireplaces, but you had to be near death before one was lit and then the smoke nearly finished you off! The only carpet in the house was in 'the room'. Hall, kitchen and scullery were brick-floored and looked lovely when first washed. Runners of hardwearing material provided some protection, but little warmth. Linoleum covered the three bedroom floors as well as the stairs. Rag rugs were some small comfort beside beds."

Margaret described how the School House was always full of pets. At one time after the Second World War, there was even a monkey at the School House: "I came across him in a pet shop in Manchester. When he put out his little cold hand for me to hold and pleaded 'Get me out of here' I was hooked. Mother was always a sucker for animals and people in distress, so she gave permission for me to bring him home. Pete built a big cage in half of the brick-built henhouse in what were originally the boys' toilets. Kim, as we called the monkey, had a heater and two boxes into which he could retire day or night. He had strong branches to climb, hens to pull faces at, and Mother who fed him grapes and bananas through the bars. They were great pals. In winter Kim could be found sitting on her knee before the fire, while in summer he played around her feet. When he had long out-lived his wild brothers and Mother could do no more for him, she called the vet. But Kim had beaten him to it. They found him curled up as though asleep in his night-compartment."

Figure 6.8 Mr Woolley and the Class of 1935.

Kenneth says that the family had little spare money as such, but they were very happy. The children all had their 'tasks' to do in turn. Both Margaret and Kenneth remember having to fetch milk from the Medcalfs at New House Farm every afternoon or evening after school. For Kenneth, it was eerie coming back through the churchyard, expecting every minute that something would jump out from behind the yew trees lining the path. His father was earning just £20 a month before the war but, as has been seen, ensured that his children had the best opportunities available. In those days, even if you won a scholarship, there were still expenses to be met.

During the early years of the war, Mr Woolley himself was also an Air Raid Warden, "determined to do his bit": he had a whistle and a rattle (in case of gas attacks), gas-mask and helmet, and when the sirens sounded, he would disappear for hours – the family didn't know where.

Tragically, in 1941, great sadness came to the happy family living at 'School House'. John, the eldest son, who had been very involved in village life, had joined the RAF and his plane did not return from a mission on June 19th 1941. Then, just six months later, on December 12th, Mr Woolley died of kidney failure at the age of sixty-two. However, his influence and memory still live on in the many pupils who remember him today. He is buried in Guarlford churchyard.

The family stayed on in the School House. Peter Woolley was very much the handyman around the house. After the war, the old range was removed and Peter built a brick fireplace. There must have been an earth closet next to the washhouse originally, because Margaret can remember the excitement when the flush toilet arrived and she can also remember helping Peter with building work: "The small brick building to the left of the gates was our garage. Ken had some electrical training and he rewired the house at some stage. People were resourceful then – they had to be."

Mrs Woolley purchased The School House in February 1951, living there until her death in 1971 at the age of 81.

Closure

The death of Mr Woolley brought a great change to Guarlford School. On 9th January 1942, nineteen Senior pupils (i.e., those aged eleven to fourteen) were transferred to Great Malvern Parochial School in Manby Road, which is now known as Malvern Parish School. This left two classes at Guarlford School in the care of Miss Cole and Miss Gosling, the latter becoming temporary Head of the school. School events continued to be recorded in the Log Book: for example, on 16th December 1942, "…a wireless receiving set was set up in the school"; and on 19th July 1944, "…the children were taken to the Church corner to watch King George VI and Queen Elizabeth pass by after their visit to Malvern". By 15th August 1944, most of the evacuees had returned to Birmingham with their teacher, Miss Gosling, and Miss Cole was left as sole teacher.

However, there had already been discussions in July 1944 at Madresfield about moving the Guarlford Junior children to Madresfield School, and the Madresfield Senior Elementary children to a school in Malvern Link, where they would receive a more appropriate education. Guarlford School is described in one Madresfield record as being without a Head Teacher and the school building in bad repair, something echoed in other documents of the time. Margaret Omar also recalls "…a large hole in the roof in the Infants Room. When it rained the water was collected in a big bath and older boys used to have to come and empty it. By 1943 the floor in the corner of the large room was rotting and had to be barricaded off." Eventually, it was agreed that, as there was to be a new Church of England Senior School in Malvern Link and the school-leaving age was to be raised to fifteen in 1945, it would indeed be better for the Madresfield Seniors to move and the Guarlford Juniors to take their place. So, on 2nd October 1944, sixteen children from Guarlford, between the ages of seven and eleven years of age, were entered onto the Register at Madresfield School, among them three evacuees who later returned to Birmingham. Other pupils, having reached the age of eleven plus, moved on to Secondary education elsewhere, leaving just fourteen Infants at Guarlford School in the sole care of Miss Cole.

It was at this time that a school bus began to run from various parts of the parish and then via Chance Lane to Madresfield and back, something, which continued almost to the end of the twentieth century. The influx of Guarlford children also provoked discussion about the provision of school dinners at Madresfield, as they could "…not be expected to go home for their dinner" and eventually a kitchen was provided.

The Guarlford School Log Book ends on January 16th 1946, but nowhere is there any record of exactly when Guarlford National School closed. The Madresfield School Register records the fact that, on 2nd April 1946, ten children from Guarlford, between the ages of five and seven years, were enrolled at Madresfield. Money raised by the sale of Guarlford School was used to improve the facilities at Madresfield and Miss Cole rejoined her pupils when she was interviewed in November, 1946, and appointed as an assistant teacher at Madresfield School; she later married Mr Wall of Madresfield.

Many children from the parish still attend Madresfield Church of England Primary School, as Guarlford is in its catchment area; but no longer do they wait for the school bus in lanes and by the church, picking up conkers on autumn mornings as their forebears did. Guarlford School and 'School House' have gone, demolished in the early 1970s, and two semi-detached houses have been erected on the spot where many still in the area today spent their childhood; but the memories remain, for, as Sam Beard simply but eloquently says: "Guarlford was their starting point and they could not have wished for better".

Chapter 7

The Impact of War

Early Conflicts

The Civil and Other Wars

Little is known of the impact of early conflicts in the part of Worcestershire which was to become the parish of Guarlford but, for example, the considerable Civil War activity in this area must have made life for the local inhabitants both hazardous and difficult. One of the earliest actions of what is referred to as the First Civil War took place at Powick in 1642, just south of Worcester, a parish now part of the combined benefice to which Guarlford also belongs; and then, in 1651, another battle, this time in Worcester itself, brought defeat for the Royalists, whereas in 1642 they had prevailed, in spite of inferior numbers. The Civil War came close to Guarlford, too, in the settlement's proximity to the River Severn crossings, particularly at Upton, which were crucial to the strategic movement of Royalist and Parliamentary forces across the county.

In the following centuries it is probable that men from Guarlford served in the Worcestershire Regiment but it is not possible to identify them from the regimental archives. The regiment was not involved in the Crimean War (1853 - 1856); but two regular battalions and elements of its volunteer and militia battalions served in the Boer War (1899 - 1902).

In the twentieth century the two world wars touched the lives of many people in this country and around the globe, including families living in small parishes such as Guarlford. In both wars, Guarlford men saw active service, some were wounded, some were captured, and some died. Their families and all those remaining at home suffered varying degrees of anguish and hardship.

The First World War

Military Service

When German forces invaded Belgium in 1914, Great Britain, because of treaty obligations, had little option but to declare war against Germany. History shows that throughout the country there were great waves of patriotism and jubilation and a confidence that a just victory would be achieved in a matter of months. Few envisaged the long war and horrific events ahead.

Nationwide, a major impact on normal life was the absence of those men enlisted into the armed forces. In the early years these were reservists, the Territorial Army, and massive numbers of volunteers. By 1916, the jubilation and optimism had faded; voluntary recruitment did not meet the country's requirements and was replaced by conscription. All of this was reflected in life at Guarlford. For example, Tom Hayes from Clevelode was enlisted into the Worcestershire Regiment in May 1917, just one month short of the age of thirty-eight years. He was sent straight away to Devonport for training, and then on to active service in France. From his Army Pay Book, we know his daily rate of pay was one shilling and sixpence, from which he would have had to support his family in Clevelode. It is not difficult to imagine the anguish of his wife, Edith, when, in July 1918, he was reported missing. However, the Red Cross eventually confirmed he was a prisoner of war, and he was repatriated via Hull in January 1919.

In April 1917 Guarlford Parish Council received a letter from Lt General Robert Scallon in which he requested the council to convene a public meeting so that he could explain the details of the National Service Scheme to the public. The Parish Council declined on the grounds that the scheme had already been explained, and the majority of those men remaining in the parish were already engaged in work of National Importance. Consent was given, though, to a separate request to form a local Committee for the Parish of Guarlford under the National Service Scheme, its purpose presumably being to review individual cases for exemption from conscription.

People were very worried about their nearest and dearest family members, and testament to this is the framed list of names in the church, most likely made up of those away on duty for whom families wished to offer prayers. The list was compiled

Figure 7.1 Some of Guarlford's WW1 Servicemen.
Clockwise from top left: 1. Jim Probert RA, Jack Beard, George Beard RA, Sam T
Beard Rifle Brigade, Lizzie Probert and daughter, George E Beard Worcestershire
Volunteers, Rosina Beard and Emily Beard; 2. L/Cpl Thomas Hayes; 3. T W Panting
RA; 4. Capt. Revd F J Newson, the Rector; and 5. P C Panting.

sometime from 1916 onwards. The suffering and anguish caused by the war could take many forms. Mrs Phyliss Bayliss, for example, recalled that her father, George Bedington, was called up for war service on the 26th May 1916, the day she was born, and throughout the war he carried with him a photograph of his baby daughter. Her father was wounded and hospitalized when part of his calf was shot away.

First World War Casualties

Three men from Guarlford families are known to have died during the First World War. They were Lance Corporal Frank Scrivens, brother of Rosina Beard of The Malthouse Cottage and the Panting brothers who were the sons of the widowed Mrs Ellen Panting of The Heriots, Clevelode. Frank Scrivens, a regular soldier with The Worcestershire Regiment, died of his wounds at Etaples, Pas-de-Calais, France on 1st May 1917, aged 31 years. He is buried in the Military Cemetery there.

> **The Worcester Regiment**
>
> In 1922/23 His Majesty King George V conferred a total of seventy-two Battle Honours on the Worcester Regiment relating to the Great War. Of these, ten were selected to be displayed on the King's Colour of each Battalion. These were Mons, Ypres, Gheluvelt, Neuve Chapelle, Somme, Cambrai, Lys, Italy, Gallipoli and Baghdad.

Thomas William Panting was educated at Guarlford School and was a Gunner in the Royal Field Artillery. He served in France and Egypt, but, at the age of twenty-one, after a painful illness, he died in the Military Hospital at Woolwich on the 10th May 1917. His body was conveyed by train to Malvern, where, by kindness of the Wireless Depot of the Royal Engineers at Worcester, a military funeral was arranged. The coffin draped with the Union Jack was brought from the station to Guarlford Church on a gun carriage with a firing party in attendance. After the service, at the graveside, three volleys were fired and the Last Post sounded. Thomas Panting's Commonwealth War Grave can be seen in the Guarlford churchyard.

Philip Charles Panting was Thomas's younger brother, and he was also educated at Guarlford School before going to work in Dudley. He was then conscripted as a Private into the Duke of Edinburgh's Wiltshire Regiment. After only nine months service and only one month in France, he was killed in action on the 1st June 1918, at the age of twenty. He is remembered on the British Memorial at Soissons in France. The Memorial stands in the main square of Soissons,

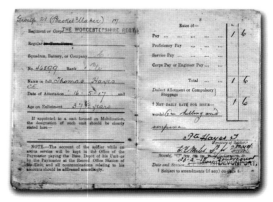

Figure 7.2 Tom Hayes's Pay Book.

Figure 7.3 The Funeral of Thomas William Panting, Royal Field Artillery, 1917.

and commemorates nearly four thousand war dead from 1914 - 1918 who have no known graves.

The Malvern News at that time commented on the wave of sympathy for the brothers' widowed mother, and also for their grandmother who had lost husband, son and two grandsons within eighteen months, and yet had managed to knit over one hundred pairs of socks for our soldiers. Reg Green, another of her grandsons, said she was constantly knitting, and when her eyesight failed in later years she would judge how the sock was progressing by feeling it.

Village Life

With the passage of time, there are no first hand accounts of village life during these troubled times; but Charlie Williams, relating stories passed down to him, said the army requisitioned all the good horses, leaving the lame, 'left-handed', and mares with foals. All the hay was also requisitioned, except one rick per farm. Wounded soldiers on convalescence would arrive with a steam engine and baler to bale the hay and ship it off to France. With the shortage of men and the need to produce as much as possible from the land, life in the farming fraternity would have been very arduous; the services of schoolboys and women were enlisted to work as farm labourers. There was also a great deal of knitting by the ladies to provide comforts to those on the front line. After the war Captain Bullock hosted a 'Welcome Home' celebration at Mill Farm for the returning men.

The Second World War

Military Service

The outbreak of war in 1939 resulted in the mobilization of reservists and territorial forces, but this time there was conscription from the outset. Again, Guarlford men departed on active service. To name just a few: three brothers from the Woolley family, John, Ken and David; Derrick Bladder; Sam Beard, who joined the Territorial Army in 1938, served in the Worcestershire Regiment from 1939, then the Royal Artillery and was demobbed in 1946 in the rank of Battery Sergeant Major; Alf Young; Keith and Paul Chester; Colin Bradshaw, who was an RAF pilot. Charles Bladder, in later years auditor of the Guarlford WI accounts, was evacuated from Dunkirk on the ship 'Ivanhoe' and was lucky to survive when it was hit by a bomb which killed forty men; he was later at El Alamein, and, in 1944, was Mentioned in Dispatches for distinguished service, finishing his military career with the rank of Battery Sergeant Major. Harry Jackson was wounded and taken prisoner, and there was, of course, Commander Ratcliff, a prominent member of the village community, some of whose contributions are described in Chapter 10, 'The Village Hall'. Two other people who served in the Second World War, but who came to Guarlford later, were Major Monty Smyth MBE and Major Geoffrey Boaz MBE. Major Smyth was a prisoner of war (POW) of the Japanese in the notorious Changi camp in Singapore, where he said he had his appendix removed on a barrack hut table. Major Boaz, who kept a flock of Merino sheep - a quieter occupation - when he retired to Guarlford much later, served in North Africa, Greece, and North West Europe.

> ### The Second World War
>
> During the Second World War various Battalions, both regular and Territorial, of the Worcestershire Regiment fought in France (1940), Eritrea, North Africa, Burma and North West Europe and one Battalion served briefly in Iceland.

Two Men Died

Sergeant John Gordon Woolley, RAF Volunteer Reserve, the son of the headmaster of Guarlford School, was reported missing in June 1941, when his aircraft went down in the North Sea. He is remembered on the Runnymede Memorial in Surrey for airmen lost in the Second World War with no known grave.

Figure 7.4 Some of Guarlford's WW2 Servicemen and Servicewomen.
Clockwise from top left: 1. Dorothy Panting, WRNS; 2. Battery Sergeant Major S G T Beard, RA; 3. Rene Sims, Postwoman; 4. Leading Stoker J Probert, RN and Pte S G T Beard; and 5. Derrick Bladder, RAF.

Private Dennis Alfred Jackson of the Worcestershire Regiment died from his wounds in August 1944, at the age of twenty, in No. 4 Canadian General Hospital, Farnborough. His coffin was conveyed to Malvern and laid to rest in Guarlford churchyard. The funeral service was conducted by the Revd Newson and the Revd Townsend, Vicar at the Wyche, where the family was living at the time. The Jackson family used to live in Clevelode Lane next to The Homestead, but, according to Keith Chester, son of Captain Chester, the house was demolished in the 1930s. Dennis Jackson's Commonwealth War Grave can be seen in the churchyard next to that of 'Harry Boy' Jackson.

Women on the Home Front and Wartime Farming

Women were vital to the 1939 – 1945 war effort, and Miss Joan Newell was one of many who served in the ATS (Auxiliary Territorial Service) and drove the length and breadth of the country delivering military vehicles. Dorothy Bick, nee Panting, joined the WRNS and served in London. Guarlford Women's Institute provided a focus for

Figure 7.5 Joan Newell, ATS. Front centre.

many commendable activities in support of the war effort; these are described in detail in Chapter 9, 'Clubs and Societies'.

Then there were the Land Army Girls, such as Miss Joan Bradshaw and Mrs Phyllis Bayliss, working long arduous hours on the land and doing work normally considered more suitable for men. In the summer, with double summer time, it was not unusual for the girls to work from 7 a.m. until 11 p.m. to bring in the harvests. (Charlie Williams remembers haymaking until about 1 a.m. and then starting again about 4 a.m.) Many girls came to the countryside from Birmingham; some worked at Guarlford Court Farm, and Mrs Dorrie Smith found them to be very pleasant and hardworking.

Mrs Vi Clarke from Penny Close remembers much of the common land and other fallow land being used to grow vegetables. Root vegetables were preferred because they could be stored. She remembers that the land from the village pond to the Rhydd was used to grow potatoes, swedes and carrots; turnips were grown along Clevelode Road. There were vegetable store 'hides' along the Guarlford Road; but most of the land bordering Guarlford Road as far as Mill Lane provided extra grazing for cattle. Cereals were grown on land now occupied by Penny Close and vegetables were grown on that which is now Penny Lane. Bamford Close stands where there was once a productive orchard of apples, pears and cherries. Charlie Williams recalls Guarlford Court supplying large quantities of potatoes for the sailors at HMS Duke in Malvern.

Italian and German POWs were used on the farms, but reports indicate that, perhaps understandably, their hearts were not in the work.

Dorrie Smith recalled that food shortages for families such as hers were not so bad because they had their own milk, eggs, fruit and vegetables, poultry, and sometimes a pig, an advantage for farming families, which Chapter 2 also refers to.

Evacuees

Guarlford had its fair share of evacuee children, mainly from Birmingham. Many of the children, up to ten at a time, were housed in the Rectory with the Newsons; but evacuees also went to other families. In November 1940, twenty-three children from Selly Park School, Birmingham, joined Guarlford School with their teachers, Miss Gosling and Miss Morris. Miss Morris lodged with the Medcalfs and another teacher, Miss Garstang who taught at Hanley Castle Grammar School, lodged with the Smith family at Guarlford Court. Dorrie Smith said she stayed for three years, and after the war kept in touch for many years. Eventually, she became head teacher at a large comprehensive school in Lancashire. Dorrie also said they had two evacuees from Bournville who stayed with her for about eighteen months. They were very unruly and disruptive, for example, letting out the livestock and tipping farm tools into the pond. Nevertheless, they kept in touch for many years after the war. A Mr A R Rose from Solihull, himself an evacuee at the Rectory

Figure 7.6 Joan Newell celebrating her 80th birthday driving an HGV in 2003.

from 1940 to 1942, recalled some years ago that they were very well fed and cared for, in spite of rationing. Blackberry and apple puddings were a particular memory. He also had memories of helping with harvest at New House Farm and hop picking during the summer holidays, as well as tending his own vegetable plot at the Rectory; each evacuee had a little plot.

Figure 7.7 The Second World War Listening Post, Rectory Lane.   Crown Copyright.

The Listening Post

The near derelict building in the field near the sharp bend in Rectory Lane was a radio listening post, which was built to monitor enemy radio traffic. It was jointly operated by the Telecommunications Research Establishment (TRE), Malvern, and the RAF. Edwin Lane can remember it being built. The location was reportedly chosen because it had the best radio reception that could be found in the area. It was self-contained, with water and septic tanks, and it was connected to four large lattice radio aerials. It was a secretive place, surrounded by a high wire fence and with an armed guard. The story goes that locating the German V2 missile base to Peenemunde came, in part at least, from information gathered from the listening post.

After the war all the equipment was removed and the building left vacant. It was then occupied for about two years by Ernie and Vi Clarke. Vi said that she and other girls (including her future sister in law, Nina Clarke) came from Wales to the Guarlford area, just before the war, to work as housemaids at Madresfield Court. She and some of her friends lodged in one of the Medcalf cottages. Vi met Ernest Clarke of Guarlford, a soldier in the Gloucester Regiment, while he was on leave from Scotland, and eventually they married; but Vi continued to lodge with her friends until the end of

Figure 7.8 The Listening Post interior view showing the receivers.   *Crown Copyright.*

the war. Then, having no place of their own, Derrick Medcalf allowed them the use of the radio hut for a small rent, and they made part of the surrounding field into a self-sufficient smallholding. Her first son was born there. In 1947, they moved into one of the first council houses to be built in Penny Close, where Vi still lives. Since then, the hut has been used as a stable and chicken coop. It still stands as a prominent, if derelict, physical reminder of the dark, intense wartime years and their impact on Guarlford life.

Bombs

The late Alf Young recalled and Edwin Lane remembers, too, the bombs dropped in a row across the Guarlford Road in 1941. The story is that a German bomber, being pursued by an RAF fighter, jettisoned its bomb load. Alf Young said there were twenty-one bombs, but none exploded. One apparently went through a bay window. They were all dug up, taken away, and detonated.

Civil Defence

Many Guarlford people were involved in Civil Defence Duties: Captain Chester was in charge of Air Raid Precautions (ARP) for the whole of the Upton Rural District; Mr Ron Smith, Mr Bradshaw and Mr Woolley were ARP wardens for Guarlford. Edwin Waters, Keith and Paul Chester, amongst others, were in the Home Guard; they paraded on Sunday mornings at the Morgan Works. Rene Simms did plane-spotter duties on Worcester Beacon. The assembly point for ARP Wardens was the Rectory Room known as 'The Point'. The original enameled ARP sign which was mounted on the wall of The Point can now be seen on the wall of the Old Smithy, at the home of the late Mr Alf Young.

Figure 7.9 The Rectory Room, 2004.

Mr Charles Williams BEM and the Crashed Beaufighter

During the war Charlie was a young farm worker employed by Mr Ron Smith of Guarlford Court. On the 22nd April 1944, he was working in a rickyard when he saw an RAF Beaufighter, apparently in difficulties, fly low over South Wood, crash in a field

Figure 7.10 The ARP Sign.

beyond, and then burst into flames. He ran through the woods to the aircraft where he found one of the crew, an RAF sergeant, with a badly broken shoulder, sheltering behind a crab apple tree. Asked if anyone was still in the plane, the sergeant replied, "Yes, the pilot, but you won't save him." Charlie ran to the plane and found the pilot, badly injured and trapped in the cockpit. Charlie later recalled, "I was young and strong. It was too hot to mess about, so I put my arms through and ripped him out, seat, parachute, the lot." As he got clear of the aircraft, its ammunition began to explode. Charlie's father and Mr Wall from Grove House got the pilot to the relative safety of a nearby ditch, while Charlie ran for an ambulance. "Young Williams undoubtedly saved the pilot's life," said Mr Wall. "Three minutes later and he would have been burned to death." The pilot was an Australian named Bob Morris. Charlie received a letter of tribute from an Air Commodore, as did

18-year-old Miss Christine Chester, daughter of Captain Chester, who helped comfort the pilot in the ditch.

The RAF sent men to guard the wrecked aircraft. Mrs Dorrie Smith related how she invited them into Guarlford Court for a meal and afterwards they all stood round the piano and sang the songs of the day; then the airmen slept the night on the dining room floor. Later, Charlie Williams went to Buckingham Palace to receive the British Empire Medal from the King in well-deserved recognition of his bravery.

Bob Morris made a full recovery from the incident, after spending nine months in hospital suffering from a broken pelvis and serious burns. Before returning to Australia with his English wife, he visited

Figure 7.11 Charlie Williams and Stanley Morris.

Charlie and later, from Australia, sent him a cable on the occasion of Charlie's twenty-first birthday. Bob Morris died in 2002. In 2003, his son Stanley travelled to England, and exactly fifty-nine years after the Beaufighter incident he met Charlie and presented him with the wallet his father carried during the crash and the last photograph taken of his father with his grandchildren around him. "These are the people to whom you gave life," said Stanley.

The Beaufighter

The British Beaufighter was a two-seat, twin-engine war-plane, which came into service with the RAF in 1940. It was the most heavily armed Allied fighter of the Second World War and gave outstanding service, particularly as night fighter and torpedo bomber.

Homecoming

In 1946 there was a presentation of engraved tankards to those men who had served in the war. It took place in the village hall and Cdr Ratcliff made the presentations with Revd Newson in attendance; but, unfortunately, only those living in the civil parish received a tankard, those living within the ecclesiastical parish but outside the civil parish were excluded, even though many had attended Guarlford School and had been very much a part of village life. The reasons for this are not at all clear but, not surprisingly, it did

Figure 7.12 The cups presented to Mr Keith Chester and Mr C Fisher.

create both discontent and unease for some time. No-one seems to remember who funded the purchase of the tankards, but it is thought to have been by public subscription. Mr Keith Chester has kindly donated his tankard to Guarlford.

Figure 7.13 A post Second World War British Legion Parade.

In the following years the veterans of the Second World War swelled the ranks of the British Legion, and the Guarlford Branch, founded in 1929, was no exception. The Armistice Day parades from Hall Green to Guarlford Church took on extra poignancy when the fallen, now from two world wars within three decades were remembered.

Post the Second World War to the Present

The United Kingdom has been involved in numerous conflicts since the Second World War – Korea, Malaya, Afghanistan, Iraq and others - but Guarlford does not seem to have been affected very directly, except, of course, for one or two individuals who served in the armed forces, but there was not the wider and deeper impact of the twentieth-century's two world wars. Two members of the Guarlford community known to have served in later conflicts are the Revd Beverley Colman, who was an Army Chaplain in Malaya in the 1950s during the emergency in that South-East Asian country, and in 1982, Dr Peter Mayner who saw active service during the Falklands

In Guarlford's case, the Civil Parish, when it was first formed, was much larger than both the ecclesiastical and the current civil parish, extending into Great Malvern and including Pickersleigh Road up to and beyond Pickersleigh Court. As a consequence, the Council was to consist of nine councillors rather than the seven we have today.

Mr Lambert started the meeting by calling for nominations for the nine posts of councillor. In all there were fifteen nominations from those present. However, two of these nominees withdrew and, there being no request for a poll, the following councillors were elected by a show of hands:

Edward Banford, William Barratt, John Bullock, William Busk, Harvey Garfield, Stephen George Medcalf, John Tomkins, Roland Tummey and the Reverend John Bateman Wathen.

In the beginning, the councillors only served for a year and the elections were held each year at the Annual Parish Meeting; it was not until June 1898 that the Parish Council petitioned the Local Government Board to be allowed to have the elections decided by secret ballot rather than by a show of hands at the Annual Parish Meeting. Not surprisingly, it took some time for this change to be agreed; the first ballot was not held until after 1946.

Figure 8.2 Revd J B Wathen.

Figure 8.3 Mr S G Medcalf.

The first meeting of the newly elected council was held two weeks later, on the 19th December 1894, in the School Room, when the Rector, the Revd J B Wathen, was elected Chairman, and Mr S G Medcalf was elected Vice Chairman. The first item of business was the hire of the School Room for meetings; the Council decided to offer the School Manager a fee of two shillings and sixpence (12.25p) for each Council meeting, the fee to include heating and lighting. However, the School Manager clearly felt that this was inadequate and countered with a request for five shillings (25p) a meeting; negotiations to agree a fee for the use of the School Room went on for some time, eventually a compromise being reached and a fee of three shillings (15p) a meeting was agreed. The Council also decided to purchase some lamps, presumably to supplement the lighting provided by the school.

The Council also resolved that the Rector should administer and distribute Guarlford's annual charity income to deserving cases within the parish. In 1787 Joseph Lloyd left £100 to be invested and the income to be distributed to the poor of Great Malvern. Great Malvern Charities administer this and eight similar bequests, which cover church maintenance as well as poor relief. Guarlford, as a former part of Great Malvern, was due a proportion of this income and, consequently, the new Council raised the question as to how this income should be allocated now that Guarlford was a separate parish. The Clerk was asked to obtain information about the number of poor within the two parishes in order to provide a basis for allocating the funds. He established that in 1891 the population of Great Malvern was 7779, whilst that of Guarlford was 671. There were 370 cottages rated at £8 and under in Great Malvern and 107 in Guarlford, 52 adults received parochial relief in Great Malvern and 20 in Guarlford. It was eventually determined that Guarlford should receive one fifth of the income set aside for relief of the poor.

> ### Mr S G Medcalf
>
> *Mr Medcalf was born in 1862 and spent his early childhood in Sussex, where he attended the Brighton Grammar School and then, later, the Cowper's School in Finsbury. After some experience on a farm in Berkshire, he moved to Malvern in 1883 and worked at the Court Farm, before becoming tenant of Lady Foley at New House Farm in 1884.*
>
> *In 1910, when the Foley Estate was sold, he purchased the farm from Sir Henry Foley Grey, the then owner.*
>
> *Mr Medcalf held many posts; among these were, Overseer, Parish Councillor, District Councillor and Guardian. He was also a Churchwarden, Hon Sec to the Hereford & Worcester Hop Growers Association, and a sergeant in the Worcester Yeomanry.*

In 1896, Guarlford's share of the income from the Lloyds and the other Charities was £4.12.9 (£4.64), of which £1 was for the education of poor children and the remainder for distribution of bread to the poor in the parish. At the meeting it was agreed that the education money should be passed to the School Manager and that bread should be purchased by Mr Portman and be distributed by Councillors Mr S G Medcalf and Mr W Busk.

The Council continued to receive donations from the Lloyds and other charities until 1984, when the Great Malvern Charities decided to manage the local charities centrally rather than distribute small amounts to the individual parishes. In recent years the Parish Council used the funds to make a number of small gifts each Christmas to elderly parishioners. However, as the parish became more affluent, it became more and more difficult to identify anyone who might need such help, and now the practice has been discontinued. Consequently, although the Council no longer receives any charity income, there is still a small amount left in the charity account for use in an emergency.

Finally, the last item of business in this first meeting was the decision to create a set of Standing Orders; the Clerk was instructed to draw up the rules for conducting the Council's business for approval at the following meeting.

A few meetings later, in April 1895, the Council appointed John Partington and Henry Bladder as Overseers for the forthcoming year. At that time, each parish was responsible for the poor within the parish; the task of the Overseers was, once the amount of money required for poor relief was determined, to collect it from all the parishioners and then distribute to those in need. They were also required to collect the precept levied by the Council. The precept is the amount of money required by the Council to pay the clerk and its other running expenses. Nowadays, the precept is set by the Parish Council and provided by the Malvern Hills District Council. Because of this Poor Relief responsibility, parishes were very reluctant to allow anyone to move into their parish unless they could show that they had the means to support both themselves and their family.

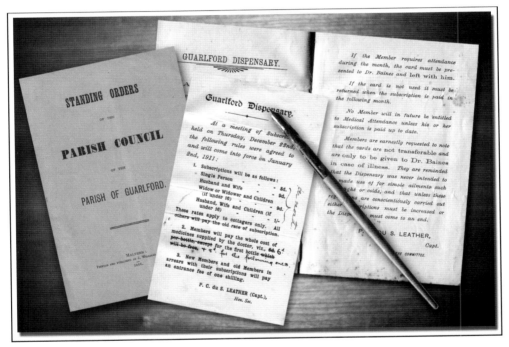

Figure 8.4 The Original Standing Orders and Dispensary Rules.

In these early years, most of the Council's time was spent in dealing with such problems as the 'foul' ditch in Mill Lane, the excessive speed of motorcars through the village (little appears to change), the poor state of Blakes Lane, and the unauthorised enclosure of land at Clevelode. However, over the following years there were a number of more pressing matters that the Council had to resolve, such as the management of the Great Malvern Burial Ground, changes to the parish boundary, the provision of fire cover to Guarlford by the Malvern Fire Brigade and the introduction of sewage, water, electricity and telephone systems.

It is interesting to note that major national and world events receive very little mention in the Council's minutes. This is not surprising as the Council only deals with local issues, which are usually rarely influenced by national or global events. Another feature is that the Council's minutes, from which this account is drawn, only record decisions and actions, with little or no discussion as to why a particular course of action was thought necessary or, in some cases, what the outcome was. Perennial problems that occupied the Council for many, many years were pollution of Hanley Brook (later renamed Pool Brook) by the Malvern Sewage Farm, complaints about smoke from the Electricity Works at Sherrard's Green, management of the allotments, bus services, and the need for speed restriction or warning signs in the village centre.

The Middle Years

Fire Cover

In February 1900 the Council decided, "…that it was desirable that the services of the Malvern Fire Brigade should be available to extinguish fires that may occur within the parish". As a consequence, the Clerk was instructed to write to the Malvern Urban District Council (MUDC) offering the sum of £5 per annum to entitle the parish to such a service. Malvern did not accept this offer and required that the annual payment be based on the assessable value of the whole parish, including land and buildings; eventually the Parish Council accepted this arrangement in April 1901, which resulted in an annual fee of £16.9.6.

Unfortunately, some time later the MUDC failed to send in its account for a few years, and when the account did eventually arrive in 1911, the Parish Council found that it had insufficient funds to pay the bill and was unable to raise the money by issuing a retrospective precept to the Overseers. In April 1912 the Council agreed to pay £14.2.0, a proportion of the outstanding account. This did not end the matter and a further account of £16.13.3 for the period up to 31st March 1912 was received. The Council regretted that it had received insufficient information about the rates paid by other councils and decided to defer payment until the MUDC provided the requested information. This account was eventually paid in August 1912. Negotiations continued for some time, and the MUDC then offered fire cover for a flat rate of thirteen guineas a year. The Parish Council thought that this was too high and suggested a figure of ten and a half guineas, which the MUDC rejected.

In April 1913 the MUDC proposed that the agreement of 19th April 1901 be terminated and cover be provided for the next five years at an annual cost of £12; after some delay the Parish Council, by a small majority, voted to reject this offer, giving as its reason the cost to the ratepayers. It appears that the Chairman of the Malvern Council made some scathing remarks about this decision, to which, not unnaturally, the Parish Council took great exception. It may seem odd that, to save just two pounds a year, the Council were prepared to deny the parish the services of the Malvern Fire Brigade. However, it must be remembered that at today's prices £12 is equivalent to at least £300, which even today the Parish Council would regard as a significant proportion of its precept.

This matter came to light at the Parish Meeting in September 1924. A report of the meeting in the local paper states that Mr A Bradshaw said, "Protection from fire was a matter that had kept him awake at night" and he asked, "What protection did the Parish Council have in the case of fire?" The Chairman, Mr G C Wall, explained why the Malvern Fire Brigade no longer provided cover but said, "That there was a fire engine in Upton-upon-Severn". It is not clear from the minutes of the meeting whether or not Upton-upon-Severn had actually agreed to provide fire cover and, if it had, what the cost might be. It was not until June 1929 that the Clerk was instructed to write to the Upton-upon-Severn Rural District Council (Upton RDC) to ask it to support the Upton Fire Brigade, so that its services might be available for Guarlford.

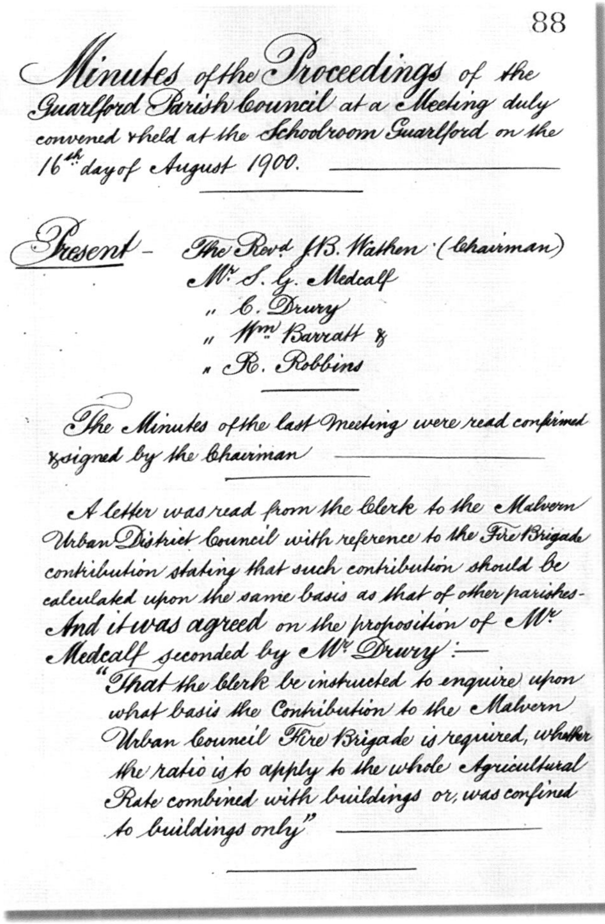

88

Minutes of the Proceedings of the Guarlford Parish Council at a Meeting duly convened & held at the Schoolroom Guarlford on the 16th day of August 1900.

Present - The Revd J B. Wathen (Chairman)
Mr S. G. Medcalf
" C. Drury
" Wm Barratt &
" R. Robbins

The Minutes of the last Meeting were read confirmed & signed by the Chairman

A letter was read from the Clerk to the Malvern Urban District Council with reference to the Fire Brigade contribution stating that such contribution should be calculated upon the same basis as that of other parishes. And it was agreed on the proposition of Mr Medcalf seconded by Mr Drury:—

"That the Clerk be instructed to enquire upon what basis the Contribution to the Malvern Urban Council Fire Brigade is required, whether the ratio is to apply to the whole Agricultural Rate combined with buildings or, was confined to buildings only"

Figure 8.5 Parish Council Minutes, August 1900.

The Parish Boundary

When the Guarlford Parish was first created it extended well into Malvern and consequently, the newly formed parish was required to contribute to the running and maintenance of the Malvern Cemetery; Guarlford Parish Council also had to provide two members of the Great Malvern and Guarlford Joint Burial Committee.

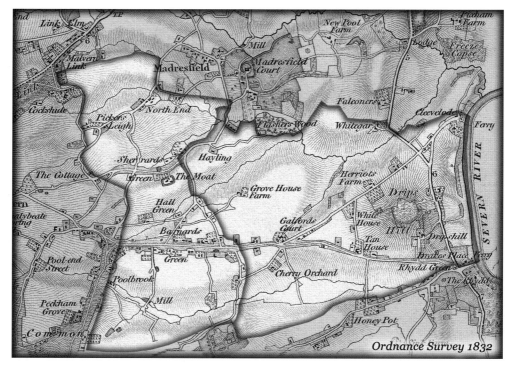

Ordnance Survey 1832

Figure 8.6 The original civil parish boundary and the current smaller boundary superimposed upon the 1832 Ordnance Survey map.

In October 1899, Great Malvern proposed and Guarlford agreed to extend the cemetery by purchasing eight and three-quarter acres at £250 an acre. It may have been because the parish was split into two completely different sections, the northern urban area known as Upper Guarlford and the main southern and rural Lower Guarlford, together with the cost of expanding and maintaining the cemetery that led the Council to try and hand over the northern area to Great Malvern Urban District Council.

The Council first proposed this in June 1904 and again in June 1908, but nothing came of it. The County Council raised the issue again in 1931 and the Parish Council called a public meeting to review the County's proposed changes. At this public meeting, which was held in the Pickersleigh Road School on 6th February 1931, the parishioners present decided, with only one dissident, to oppose the proposed changes.

It is not clear why there was this change of heart. However, the parish's objection to the proposed change was placed before the County of Worcestershire when it commenced its Parish Boundary Review later that year. Guarlford's objections, though, were not accepted; but, later in this review, the MUDC proposed that, because of both the national crisis of the Great Depression and local economic reasons, it

Capt. F E Chester

Capt. Chester enlisted in the Sherwood Foresters in 1915 and was commissioned in 1917 and served at Passchendaele. After the war he became a small-holder at the Homestead, Clevelode Lane.

He served for many years on both the Parish Council and the Upton Rural District Council and became Chairman of the Upton RDC.

was not an opportune time to extend its boundary. Consequently, it was not until 1933 that the review eventually took place and the boundary was changed to its present state. The new Council, now with seven councillors, was elected in March 1934. Shortly afterwards, due to the reduced size of the parish, the Council reduced the Clerk's salary to £12.10.0 pa (£12.50). Apparently the clerk accepted this cut in salary with good grace!

Even after the boundary change, Guarlford still participated in the management of the Malvern Cemetery and contributed to its running costs. It was not until March 1954, after lengthy and detailed negotiations, that the Council was able to withdraw and receive £100 recompense. As the Guarlford churchyard was now to be the main burial site there was talk of increasing its size by using some of the glebe land, but lack of money and legal difficulties made that impossible.

Introduction of Mains Services

Guarlford was long without mains water, electricity, telephone and an effective sewage system. In 1926, the Council asked the Shropshire, Worcestershire and Staffordshire Electricity Company to extend their electricity supply to Guarlford; the Council repeated its request again in 1928, 1929, 1930, 1931 and 1932. In 1933, as there was still no supply, the Parish Council wrote to Stanley Baldwin, the local MP and former Conservative Prime Minister, to ask him to intervene.

Mr Baldwin replied that he had established that the current delay was caused by the executors of Mr S G Medcalf's estate being unwilling to grant the electricity company a wayleave for the overhead line across its farmland. The Council then proposed that Cllr D W Medcalf and the Clerk should have a private meeting to resolve the matter.

The Minutes

The minutes shown in Figure 8.5 are a good example of the very attractive copperplate script used at that time. However, not every clerk was able to emulate this standard of handwriting.

The minutes continued to be handwritten until the mid 1980s when a very old typewriter was introduced. Nowadays all the council's agendas, minutes and letters are produced using Microsoft Word and other software on an Apple Macintosh computer.

A month later, Cllr Medcalf reported that the problem was that the electricity company could or would not guarantee to provide a supply to New House Farm within a year of receiving a wayleave. He continued that it was not unreasonable that the Medcalf estate were unwilling to grant a wayleave on those terms. However, he said a subsequent meeting between the parties concerned had now resolved the matter. The electricity supply finally arrived in the village centre in 1935. However, discussions on extending the supply further east towards Clevelode and the Rhydd were still taking place in 1945, and work did not start until after 1948.

Figure 8.7 Cllr Capt. F E Chester and Mrs Chester welcoming Princess Margaret to Upton–upon-Severn in 1953.

Sewage disposal was a topic that occupied the Council for many years and aroused considerable feelings, not it might be supposed because of the lack of an effective system but rather due to the cost of the comprehensive system proposed by the Upton-upon-Severn Rural District Council (Upton RDC). The first mention of a proposed new system for Lower Guarlford was in 1910; and the Council referred this proposal back to the Upton RDC for clarification as to whether this system was instead of the Upper Guarlford system or in addition to that system. Later that year, the Parish Council approved the proposed scheme, as defined by the Madresfield and Guarlford Joint Sewage Committee, and asked the Upton RDC for a copy of the plans. The proposed system consisted of sewers from Guarlford Rectory and Harrisons Cottage, Madresfield, to the Disposal Site at Orles Coppice, with branches from Rectory Road and Madresfield Court.

The next mention of the scheme was at the Parish Meeting on the 1st May 1913 called to consider Upton's proposal. At this meeting, there was a unanimous decision that the Parish Council should oppose the scheme at the forthcoming Local Government Board meeting. There is no indication in the minutes as to what had brought about this opposition by the parishioners, but presumably they thought that it would be expensive, however, this opposition was successful in causing the scheme to be postponed.

All appeared to go quiet until 1924, when the Upton RDC introduced a new proposal that included all three parishes, Newland, Madresfield and Guarlford. At the Guarlford Parish Meeting held on 22nd September 1924, Mr W Brewer, one of the parish representatives on the Upton RDC, said, "Madresfield's sewage system was in a poor state and had to be attended to, therefore Guarlford had been brought in to help pay for it". Mr G C Wall, the Guarlford Parish Council Chairman, said, "…if the scheme were carried out it would mean a very heavy expenditure, about £15,000 to £20,000, which would have to be borne by the ratepayers."

After some heated discussion, it was proposed that, as many of the houses in Guarlford had an adequate system, the proposal should be strenuously opposed; this was carried unanimously. It was later reported, in March 1925, that the Upton RDC had rescinded its earlier decision. Although discussions on this topic were still taking place in March 1926, the scheme was never implemented and, consequently, there are still houses in the village without the benefit of mains sewage disposal. The construction of the Penny Close houses in the early 1950s with a small sewage farm at the end of Penny Lane, provided a limited solution.

Lack of mains water was also a problem; it was not until September 1945 that the Council asked if the water main could be extended to Guarlford Court and the other nearby houses. In 1947, Cllr Capt. Chester, who was also an Upton RDC councillor, reported that the Upton RDC had signed the contracts for providing water supplies to various portions of the district and that Guarlford was to be given first priority. Nevertheless, mains water is still not universally available throughout the parish, or indeed even in the village centre, one house, at least, still relies upon well water.

There is no mention in Council minutes as to when the telephone system became available in Guarlford; but, in September 1946, the Council, at Cllr Mrs Newson's suggestion, agreed to request the installation of a telephone kiosk in the village adjacent to the church. By 1953, after several further requests, nothing had happened. However, Cllr Capt. Chester reported, "…that at the recent meeting of the Upton RDC it was announced that two kiosks had been allocated to the county and that he was hopeful that one of these might be secured for Guarlford". It was not until 1955 that Guarlford actually got its telephone kiosk at a cost of about £240; and the next battle the Council embarked upon was to have a light installed in the kiosk. Also, in more recent times, the Council had another minor victory when it successfully resisted the British Telecommunications' proposal to remove the kiosk because it was 'uneconomic'. This was a welcome result as the kiosk is not only useful but also a classic design that enhances the village centre. Some years later, the intervention of the local MP, Sir Michael Spicer, helped to secure the repair rather than the replacement of the Victorian post box in the church wall, after it had been severely damaged by thieves.

Penny Close Housing

In early 1945, the need for new houses was a national issue and Upton RDC was considering where its new housing should be built; the initial plan was to have eight houses in Guarlford and six in Madresfield. This was shortly revised to having all the houses in Madresfield with a view to providing community centres and other amenities in the same location. The official view was that the wives and children of the tenants were the first consideration in order to attract people to live in the country and that the husband's distance from work was not of the first importance.

Naturally, the Council did not accept that it was not to receive the promised eight houses and protested strongly to Upton RDC, which eventually reversed its decision and agreed to eight houses in Guarlford. However, two years later, no houses had materialised and the Council then lobbied the War Agricultural Executive Committee and County Planning Office for some action.

These houses were urgently needed. Cllr Capt. Chester said, "…that there were eight houses scheduled for demolition in the parish of which agricultural workers occupied six. There were also fifty applicants, including twenty-one agricultural workers from Guarlford and neighbouring parishes for these houses." As a consequence of these representations, the Upton RDC purchased some additional land and eventually twelve semi-detached house were built in what became Penny Close. Today many of these houses are privately owned and none is occupied by people involved in the farming industry.

Figure 8.8 Mrs Smyth and Mrs Lockley distributing the Jubilee mugs.

Recent Years

The Silver Jubilee

In February 1977, the Council set up a parish-wide committee, chaired by the Rector, Revd Hartley Brown, to organise the parish's Silver Jubilee celebrations. As it was the Queen's wish that the celebrations should not be paid for out of the rates, the Rector stated that the objective of the committee was to raise sufficient funds to provide, firstly, a children's party and each child with a Jubilee mug, secondly, a village commemoration, such as a group of trees, and, finally, a donation to the Queen's Jubilee Appeal.

All the children in the civil parish up to school leaving age would be invited as well as parishioners of 65 years of age and over. At the kind invitation of Major and Mrs J M Smyth, it was agreed that the party should be held in the grounds of Dripshill House. In all, about sixty children attended what was a very successful party.

Figure 8.9 Handing over the donation to the Queen's Silver Jubilee Appeal. From the left: Cllr the Reverend Hartley Brown, Cllr Major J M Smyth MBE, Cllr Mr T G Boaz MBE, Sir John Willison and Cllr Mr J Guise.

Figure 8.10 Clockwise from top: 1 Tidy Up Group. Back Row: Major J M Smyth MBE, Mrs H Browning, Sir John Willison, Cllr Mr J Guise, Dr E H Jones, Front Row: A N Other, A N Other, Amanda Skinner, Sian Browning, Bernadette Kirton and Jane Kirton. 2. The Jubilee Plaque and 3. The Church Pond Renovation.

To cover the costs of providing the picnic and mugs, the Committee organised a variety of fund-raising events that included a gymkhana, a bowling competition, a coffee evening and a barbecue. With the money raised, the Committee was able, after covering all its expenses, to donate £75 to the Queen's Silver Jubilee Appeal. To commemorate the Jubilee, the Committee planted three trees, a Copper Beech (later replaced by an oak) at the Rhydd Green, an English Oak at Clevelode and a Worcester Black Pear in the village centre. The latter was donated by Major Smyth, the Chairman of the Parish Council. The Council also erected a plaque adjacent to the post box, on the churchyard wall to commemorate the planting.

Finally, the Committee organised a 'Tidy Up' campaign with the Church Pond as the main target. The work was carried out with the help of a group of volunteers and the Worcester Conservation Group. Figure 8.10 shows some of the volunteers, who, with the help of the 'Keep Britain Tidy Campaign', were responsible for tidying up the village centre. The barn in the background was badly damaged by fire and demolished some years ago.

After the success of the church pond renovation, the Jubilee Committee, before it closed down, set up a separate Amenity Committee, made up of Dr E H Jones, Miss J Newell, Mrs H Browning, Revd Hartley Brown and Mr J M Skinner to continue looking after the village environment. This committee later become the Guarlford Association, which continued to operate for several years, and held barn dances in the village hall, with music provided by 'Hodge's Dump', to raise funds.

Figure 8.11 The Village Sign.

The Village Sign

In March 1981, the Parish Council, which then consisted of the Chairman, Major J M Smyth, Mr R H M Bartleet, Mr T G Boaz, Revd Hartley Brown, Mr S W Medcalf, Mr A H Pettigrew and Mr R H Smith, decided that a sign, which illustrated the name 'Guarlford', would be a desirable addition to the village. However, research by the Chairman and consultation with local and other experts was unsuccessful in producing any information on the derivation of the name Guarlford that could be represented pictorially. As a consequence, the Council opted for a wrought iron sign showing the name only. The sign, which incorporated the Parish Council's Black Pear logo, was designed by the Clerk, Michael Skinner, and built by Mr Dennis Morgan the well-known Barnard's Green blacksmith.

Village Hall Restoration

The Village Hall is a charity administered by its trustees, the Village Hall Committee, which has the sole responsibility for maintaining it as a parish amenity.

In 1990, both the Village Hall Committee and the Parish Council were concerned to learn that the Village Hall did not meet the local Fire Brigade's health and safety requirements and, consequently, could not be granted a licence for public functions. The Village Hall Committee also believed that if the hall were not brought up to the required standard it would become unsafe and unusable for private functions and would have to be closed.

Mr S W Medcalf

Bill Medcalf (1926-1998) was the only child of Derrick William and Ethel Medcalf. He attended St Cuthberts, Malvern Link, and then went on to King's School, Worcester. He married Edna Charley in 1952 and they had two children, Susan and Andrew.

He was a member, Chairman and finally Director of the Madresfield Agricultural Society. He was also for many years Church Warden, Chairman of the Village Hall Committee, Chairman of the Parish Council, and Governor of Madresfield Primary School.

After consultations with the Rural Community Council's Village Hall Advisor and its consultant architect, the Hall Committee had produced a renovation plan, which it was estimated would require the Committee to raise £10,000 pounds. It was suggested that one solution would be for the Parish Council to raise the required loan at a reduced rate from the Public Works Loan Board. However, concerns were raised about the cost to the parishioners of servicing such a loan, possibly increasing each individual's poll tax by about £6 a year for twenty-five years.

As this was an important issue, it was decided to consult the parish by holding a Parish Meeting, which was held on Monday 25th June 1990 and chaired by Cllr Mr R H Smith. Mr S W Medcalf, Chairman of the Village Hall Committee, described the proposed renovation plan and its estimated cost. The meeting, which was very well-attended, was then thrown open for general discussion in which the pros and cons of repairing the hall or building a new one were discussed at length. Eventually, it was decided that the best way to proceed would be for the Parish Council to hold a referendum. This was duly held and had a very good turnout, eighty four percent of the parish voting. Seventy-six parishioners supported the loan, whilst 101 opposed the loan, and, consequently, the plan was abandoned, leaving the Village Hall Committee to maintain the hall from its own fund-raising activities, which it has managed to do very successfully.

Mr R H Smith

Mr R H Smith (1909-1997) came to Guarlford in 1939 when he took on the tenancy of Guarlford Court Farm. He married Dorrie in 1941 and became involved with the church and village organisations. He was a co-founder of the Malvern Branch of the 'Young Farmers Club', and he was also a member of the Madresfield Agricultural Show Committee.

Figure 8.12 Mr R H M Bartleet, Major J M Smyth MBE, Mr R H Smith and Mr T G Boaz MBE.

The Retirement of Long-Serving Parish Councillors

Guarlford has been well served by its councillors over the last hundred and ten years, many serving for long periods. In 1991, four of some of Guarlford's longest-serving councillors retired; between them they had served as members of the Parish Council for ninety-nine years: Mr R H Smith for thirty-six years, Major J M Smyth MBE for twenty-seven years, Mr R H M Bartleet for twenty-four years, and Mr T G Boaz MBE for twelve years.

Major Smyth was also a County Councillor, and both he and Mr Smith, in turn, had served as Parish Council Chairman for many years. Mr Bartleet was also a longstanding member of the Board of the Malvern Hills Conservators, a body founded by his grandfather.

To mark this occasion, the Parish Council held a presentation evening in the Village Hall on 25th June 1991, and the Chairman, Mr S W Medcalf, presented each of the retiring councillors with a plaque to commemorate his service to the parish.

The Millennium Church Pond Restoration

The Council decided that to commemorate the Millennium it would initiate two projects, first, the restoration of the Church Pond and, second, the planting of several trees. Although the pond had been cleared in 1977, it had by this time become seriously overgrown and in urgent need of restoration.

The County Council had launched its Aqua Vitae 21 partnership project in December 1998 to provide advice and support for pond renovation throughout the county, and the Parish Council was able to take advantage of this support from the County Council and its partners.

Figure 8.13 Janet Lomas leading the pond restoration.

The pond is 75 metres long, 8.5 metres wide and 600mm deep. A survey prior to the restoration found four adult great crested newts, two crested newt tadpoles and eight smooth newt tadpoles. The restoration programme had to be timed so that it would not disturb the life-cycle of the legally protected great crested newts. Janet Lomas, the Parish Trees Warden, was appointed project manager, with the task of liaising with the County Council and its partners, arranging a pond survey, obtaining expert advice on drainage, hiring contractors and co-ordinating the work of the parish volunteers. The volunteers, including all the councillors and officers, helped with removing the debris and were also responsible for painting the pond rails, mowing the grass verges and planting the daffodils donated by Mr David Masters.

The restoration was very successful and the Council entered the project as part of its Church Yard and Village Centre entry in the Worcestershire County Council's 2002 Community Pride Competition. Guarlford came second in the competition with a prize of £300, which the Council has used to support the production of this history of the village.

The Millennium commemorative trees were a field maple planted at the Rhydd, a black poplar planted at New House farm, in memory of Mr S W (Bill) Medcalf, and two rowan trees planted in the village centre. The latter two were donated by David Masters, the parish's representative on the Board of the Malvern Hills Conservators. A plaque listing these trees was placed on the churchyard wall adjacent to the Silver Jubilee plaque.

Figure 8.14 The Millennium Plaque.

Figure 8.15 The Restored Church Pond in 2002.

The Golden Jubilee

Although it was known that the annual fete in July 2002 would be extended to become a Jubilee Fete, the Council thought that the parish should have a celebration on the actual Jubilee date of the 4th of June. Thus, the Parish Council Jubilee Picnic was conceived. It was to be a collaborative occasion, in which everyone brought a contribution to a communal buffet. This, of course, proved to be excellent, the Guarlford ladies being well-known for the quality of their catering. In all, it proved to be a very enjoyable afternoon, with games for both children and adults. At Dr and Mrs Peter Mayner's invitation, the event was held in the grounds of Cherry Orchard and proved to be a splendid venue that was very well supported by over a hundred parishioners.

The Parish Council Today

The parish has been well served by its Council over the last hundred years; it has fought long and hard with the District and County Councils on many occasions to ensure that the parish and parishioners are treated fairly and that the village amenities are not only maintained but also improved. Howkins may argue that parish councils have

Figure 8.16 The Parish Golden Jubilee Picnic held on the 4th June 2002 at Cherry Orchard.

little power, and this is true; but they do have influence, and a determined parish council can make a measurable difference for its parishioners.

The role and workload of parish councils is changing at the present time as a result of numerous Government initiatives being promulgated, the recently imposed complex and detailed financial regulations involving additional audits, and the increasing desire of the District and County Councils to delegate more functions to parish councils. Furthermore, it is the Government's stated intention that parish councils should play a larger part in local government and, consequently, will be required to become more professional in approach and encouraged to achieve 'Quality Status'. Clerks, in particular, are being encouraged or even put under pressure to gain qualifications in local government; indeed, councils cannot achieve Quality Status until the clerk has such qualifications.

It would be very difficult to argue against having competent councillors and professionally-qualified clerks, but it does represent a significant change in emphasis. Clerks may no longer regard their work as a service to the community, but, rather, as a professional occupation, which, with its increasing workload, responsibilities, and the requirement to observe the new Local Government Code of Conduct, deserves a commensurate reward. All of these changes, if implemented, particularly the acceptance of additional functions, will inevitably give rise to an increase in the parish precept. Moreover, Councillors, who have traditionally given their time and commitment freely out of a sense of social responsibility and community spirit, may feel in the future that trust and a certain dedication have been dismissed in favour of more bureaucracy and Government diktat.

The Guarlford Parish Council has decided that, for the time being at least, because Guarlford is a small parish with only 242 electors, it would not be cost-effective to seek 'Quality Parish' status or to take on any of these additional functions. Nevertheless, it is inevitable that there are changes to come as parish councils and their functions and responsibilities are required to evolve over the coming years.

Parish Council Chairmen

The Councillors who have been elected Chairmen of the Parish Council from 1894 to 2004 are:

1894 Revd J B Wathen
1904 Mr S G Medcalf
1919 Revd F J Newson
1922 Mr G C Wall
1925 Mr C Thompson
1931 Cdr F J Ratcliff
1942 Mr D W Medcalf
1972 Mr F J George
1976 Maj. J M Smyth
1987 Mr R H Smith
1991 Mr S W Medcalf
1996 Mr M G Huskinson
2001 Dr P E Mayner

Chapter 9

Clubs and Societies

As They Were

The Rectory Room

There were many flourishing clubs and societies in this self-contained community a hundred years ago, before television took over so much leisure time in the second half of the twentieth century. Guarlford was a busier place, day and evening. Moreover, when work was over for the day, leisure activities tended to be social occasions, which generally brought people together outside the home. As well as at church, neighbours met at various places both indoors and out. Now only the WI remains of all the clubs and societies which prospered not so very long ago.

In the first decade of the twentieth century, Sister Elizabeth and Sister Gabriella from the 'Convent of the Holy Name' at Malvern Link assisted in the parish. They had their headquarters and Mission Room in part of the stables at the Rectory, which became known as 'The Rectory Room', later named 'The Point' or 'First Aid Point' in the Second World War. Here the Sisters held various classes and 'Mothers'

Meetings', suspended in August and September for hop-picking. The Sisters also ran a 'Clothing and Boots' Club' and a 'Dispensary'.

'The Rectory Room' was open in the evenings from 7 until 10 p.m. for meetings of the 'Reading and Recreation Club'. Mr C Robathan, then of 'The Homestead', was Honorary Secretary and the subscription was fourpence (2p) a month. In 1901, a course of four lectures by J Gold M.R.C.V.S., on Veterinary Science, was held in the schoolroom: "They were well supported and much appreciated." Classes for "…woodwork, rough carpentry and wood-carving were held in Mr Bradshaw's barn" (now 'The Granary'). The ladies had an 'Embroidery Guild', which met weekly on Wednesday

> ### Football Teams
>
> *Mrs Bayliss has a framed photo of the football team of 1938 - 39, and she can recall many names of those in the picture: "Owen and his brother, who also lived at Hanley; Mr Beard; Cdr Ratcliff, who lived at Dripshill; Mr Tommy Clark; two Davises from Callow End; the blacksmith from Barnard's Green, who hasn't long retired; Gussy Holt; John Woolley from the school, the eldest son of the Headmaster; Jones from Hanley; Brown, a Lowe, Dovey; two young boys called Phipps from Hanley. That was Sunshine Carty from Barnard's Green - he was the goalkeeper, a tall chap. There was a big family of them. Then that was Mr Wilks, who lived at the farm along the bottom road".*

afternoons at Mrs. Luscombe's house at the Rhydd. In 1909, they "…contemplated the working of a banner of Our Lady, designs for which have been made by William Bucknell, Esq.". The banner is still in St. Mary's Church, Guarlford, today. Apparently, the Guild collapsed after a while, as a meeting is recorded at the Rectory on April 24th 1915, with a view to re-starting it.

The Cricket and Football Clubs

In the first decades of the century, the 'Guarlford Cricket Club' played on one of Mr Medcalf's fields. Their Captain was Mr Shinn of Guarlford Road and Mr A Martin, son of the then Headmaster, was their Honorary Secretary. Miss Joan Bradshaw's history notes describe how "…the season of Guarlford Cricket Club ended with a match against the Ladies, the Club using broomsticks as bats".

According to Joan Bradshaw's records, on October 7th 1907 'Guarlford Football Club' was formed; the first 'kit' was a white shirt and a green sash. Mr Bob Stanton was Captain and Mr O V Bradshaw of Guarlford Court was Honorary Secretary. A decision was made to purchase a new ball and have the old ones repaired. The 'Football Club' played its first match on October 26th 1907 on a field at Guarlford Court, the granary there being their changing room. On October 8th 1908, the 'Guarlford Football Club' records that thanks were extended to local farmers Messrs Medcalf and Bladder for their gifts of goals and the field.

Mr Edwin Lane has an old minutes book for the 'Football Club', 1923 – 28, when Mr Holloway resigned as Secretary, and Edwin's late uncle, Mr George Lane, was elected

Figure 9.1 Gentlemen versus Ladies cricket match, 1910.
Standing on the left Mr Victor Bradshaw and, seated in front of him, his future wife
Miss Florence Price.

to the office. The last meeting that was recorded in the book looks as though it was the folding up of the club for a while. They decided to give the goalposts away and funds remaining in the bank account totalled £3.3s.4d. Somebody proposed a resolution that this should be given to the hospital, which was voted on and turned down. The minutes book ends there. The Club obviously started up again later on, because it flourished from the 1930s to the 1950s.

Phyl Bayliss's husband, Owen, was in the Guarlford football team in the late 1930s. One year they won three cups in a season. Owen's family lived in Hanley Swan and Phyl met him through football: "I watched Guarlford play football and he was in the team. They wore blue shirts with white sleeves and played on one of Mr Medcalf's fields up Rectory Lane." Mr Derrick Bladder remembers later shirts as quartered blue and white, while Mr Sam Beard recalls "Charles Bladder was the doyen of Guarlford's football team and an impressive record they had." According to Mr Ken Woolley, Charles was much respected at Hanley Grammar School as a fine sportsman and was School Soccer Captain when Ken himself played for the First XI. After the Second World War, a new Guarlford football team was formed in 1947. Mr George Lane of Woodbridge Farm looked after the goalposts, as well as paying for and looking after the nets. At

Figure 9.2 The Guarlford football team, 1919-20.
Standing L-R: 1st Mr George Beard, 2nd Revd Newson and 6th Mr George Lane.
Seated on the right: Mr Frank Jarrett.

half time, he would bring hot tea across from his farmhouse for the two teams. Derrick Bladder says that the football team of that time also won several cups: the 1950-51 Malvern Hospital Secretary Cup; the 1952-53 Ogilvy Cup; and Malvern and District Association Amateur Football League.

The Tennis Clubs

Early in the twentieth century, there were three tennis courts at farms in the parish. On April 22nd 1912 a meeting was held to form the 'Guarlford Tennis Club'.

The Committee members were:

President: the Rector; Secretary: Mr Victor Bradshaw; Committee: Mr Jack Medcalf, Miss Bradshaw, Miss L. Hobbs, Mr Healey, Mrs. Healey (replaced by Mr Robathan).

The subscription was three shillings and sixpence; members had to be over fourteen years of age, visitors over sixteen. There was much discussion about what to charge visitors, and sixpence a day was decided upon. New winding posts and seating were to be bought and hearty thanks were expressed to Mr Bradshaw, who was giving the use of the court free. The 'Guarlford Tennis Club' was also playing on the Rectory lawn in 1912.

Lists of Rules were drawn up at different times: for example, players had to wear proper tennis shoes; players must retire on completing a set if other members or visitors are waiting to play; the court should always be available on weekdays, except after seven p.m. on Fridays if required for mowing; lost balls should be found or replaced.

Phyl Bayliss and Derrick Bladder both remember playing tennis at the Rectory during the 1930s. Derrick says, "We asked the Rector, 'Do you mind if we play on a Sunday?' and the Rector said, 'Any time you like, but not

Figure 9.3 Tennis at Guarlford Court, c.1914. L-R: Gladys Beard, Victor Bradshaw, Miss Larkworthy and Violet Bradshaw.

while there's a church service on'. In those days you didn't do things on a Sunday. I remember Farmer Atwood, farming at Dripshill; he did some haymaking on a Sunday, and my grandfather said, 'You'll never do any good working on a Sunday' – but he got his hay in before it rained!"

Tug-of-War Team

What Charlie Williams describes as "the fat bacon and cider brigade" decided to form a tug-of-war team at the end of the Second World War. The team included Charlie Williams, Bernard Clarke, Dennis Clarke, Bill Sims - who lived in Penny Close - and his cousin, the other Bill Sims, who worked at Portocks End Farm for Colonel Wiggin, the two Mounslows, and Tom Sims as coach. The team enjoyed much success at local fetes.

The Men's Club

Anyone walking past the village hall today, can still see the faded notice on the wall which says 'Guarlford Men's Club'. The club flourished for about fifty years. There was a bar in the first floor room nearest the lane, where members played crib, darts and other similar games. Some wooden steps led up to the higher room, the old drying floor, where a large billiard table took up most of the room. The large room where the men met, with a bar in it, was used on other occasions as a refreshment room. The billiards room was the changing room for the entertainments held in the large room at the back, the drying floor of the old malt house, now the village hall.

Derrick Bladder has good memories of the club and of one particular friend, Ray Barrett (who, Don Hill says, audited the church accounts for many years): "We had happy times as lads down at what we used to call 'The Men's Club'. We used to have a snooker team, crib team, darts team, everything. At one time they opened about three times a week (Monday, Wednesday and Saturday), then Friday as well. The local landlords didn't take much to that, because it took their trade away. The club beer was cheaper than the pub, only a penny or so - but a penny was a penny in those days. I always remember Ray Barrett, whose father kept the 'Plough and Harrow'. We used to keep in touch during the war – he was in Germany. I said, "We'll meet up at the club." And he said, 'No way!' Then the penny dropped! It was excellent to have a place to go. The club would provide the bar for all the village things like the Harvest Supper, and the hall wasn't partitioned off then." Mr Clark was Club Steward, and his wife washed the Guarlford football team strip. The Men's Club closed in the mid 1980s.

The British Legion

Figure 9.4 A British Legion Dinner in the Village Hall in the sixties.
Back row L-R: 2nd Mr Bill Sims
Middle row L-R: 3rd Mr Fred Holland, 4th Mr Fred Tummey
Front row L-R: 1st Mr Derrick Medcalf, 2nd Mr Ron Smith, 3rd Mr Ernie Clarke and
4th Mr Harry Jackson.

of a group meeting in March 1979 the Guarlford President, Mrs Margaret Earp, apologises to the other institutes for the "bowls and buckets dotted about the room, as the rain was leaking through the roof"! It was at the same meeting that "…the Hall was twice plunged into darkness, until the electricity meter was fed with more coins". This is something that many residents will remember happening at events in the village hall.

Every year the ladies of the WI celebrate with a birthday party, often in the village hall, as in this photograph of Mrs Ethel Medcalf in May 1969. Perhaps readers can recognise some other faces, too.

Banners

There are various WI Banners to which members have contributed over the years. Mrs Margaret Earp stitched a picture of Guarlford Court for one Worcestershire Federation Banner, and Mrs Rosemary McCulloch cross-stitched sections for the Malvern Hills Group Banner in 2000 as well as a new Worcestershire Federation Banner in 2001, showing, set in the churchyard wall, the Victorian post-box, which was later sadly smashed by vandals one night in the spring of 2000. Thanks to the intervention of Sir Michael Spicer M.P., on behalf of the Parish Council, it was repaired by the Post Office. Above the post-box can be seen a small plaque which refers to commemorative trees planted in 1977 to mark the Queen's Silver Jubilee, an English oak, a copper beech and a black pear, all of which are represented on the Guarlford WI Banner section, together with the sweet and horse chestnut trees, source of much pleasure to many children over the years.

In January 1970, another commemorative tree, an oak, was replanted beside the road to the Rhydd, just below 'Danefield'; it had been planted in November 1969 to celebrate the Worcestershire Federation's Golden Jubilee.

Not Just 'Jam and Jerusalem'

Guarlford WI has always been concerned with local and national matters, although, as one national Resolution in 1943 stated, at meetings there should be "no sectarian or party political matter" but "topics about the social and spiritual welfare of the nation should be discussed". Each WI debates the Resolutions to be discussed at the national Annual Meeting. Resolutions propose campaigns, often to be brought to the attention of the government of the day. The Resolutions from 1943 sound remarkably modern; they dealt with topics such as "the need for training in home-making for girls and boys" to be included in the school curriculum; compulsory showing of a clean bill of health by both parties before marriage – "as a measure against venereal disease"; the raising of the food blockade to allow some food and medical aid to reach children and expectant mothers in the occupied countries; help for small producers, and - the labelling of jam!

As already mentioned, Guarlford WI members always enjoy a party – and good food! It is reported that, in 1943, "Mrs Waters' daughter, now Mrs W Sims sent along four chocolate iced sponge cakes as a gift to celebrate the Birthday Meeting", which is now held in June each year. The WI has always had a good reputation for catering. Ninety guests from the group enjoyed an 'Italian Evening' in the spring of 1999, and a good sum was raised that autumn for the village hall when it was repeated. In addition, Phyl Bayliss has fond memories of many outings with the WI, including one to London for 'The Ideal Home Exhibition', which was followed by a visit in the evening to see *Camelot* in Drury Lane – they were very late home that night!

Obviously, the WI minutes record only what happens at the monthly meetings, but outside events are occasionally mentioned, as when speakers were unable to attend because of arctic weather in February 1947, floods in 1952, or petrol rationing during

the Suez crisis in 1956. Sad events are recorded, such as the death of George VI, foot and mouth disease in 1968, and the moments of silence on September 11th 2001, remembering those killed when the 'Twin Towers' in New York were destroyed. But there has also been joy, as when a garden party at Dripshill ended with the singing of 'God Save the King', because it was June 6th 1944, 'D-Day'. What a day that must have been for the ladies of Guarlford WI! Topics covered at monthly meetings have been very varied throughout the years, as for example in March 1970, when the ladies of Guarlford prepared themselves for a great change by having a meeting about decimal currency.

Staying true to the national WI motto 'For Home and Country', Guarlford WI continues not only to keep interest in traditional domestic crafts such as cookery, gardening and handicrafts alive, together with travel and nature, but also to take a keen interest in the wider world, always ready to look at new ideas as seen in recent meetings on the topics of 'Tai Chi' and 'Reflexology'. Three times there have been speakers from BBC Radio: Leslie Halward (resident of Guarlford for a time and writer of short stories and plays) spoke to the ladies in October 1949; Vera Ashe ('Mrs Scobie' of 'The

Figure 9.7 Guarlford WI's 60th Birthday. Guest Speaker, Mike George of BBC Radio Hereford & Worcester, and Mrs Elizabeth Johnson, Chairman of Worcestershire Federation of WIs, with Mrs Edna Medcalf cutting the cake.

Archers') came in October 1958, and, in 2001, Mike George, of BBC Radio Hereford and Worcester, was the guest speaker. There have been no television 'personalities' as yet, although in August 2004 Mrs Maureen Mercer organised a very successful

'Members' Evening' based on her appearance as part of a team on 'Family Fortunes', with Les Dennis as the host.

As the year 2004 draws to a close, Guarlford WI is still the only 'club' in the village; but the members hope that their Institute is more than just a club and contributes to the life of the village and the community at large – and long may it do so!

Figure 9.8 The Guarlford WI Christmas Party, 1999.

Standing L-R: B Harrison, E Watts, B Hill, J Ashcroft, E Medcalf, M Bruce-Morgan, A Deam, D Lloyd-Jones, E Tidball, M Sargeant, M Rutter, S Clifton, J Cameron.

Seated L-R: M Boaz, M Rayner. R McCulloch, P Jones.

Chapter 10

The Village Hall

Introduction

According to Action with Communities in Rural England (ACRE), a national charity whose purpose is to support sustainable rural community development, there are currently about 9000 village halls in rural England. The presence of halls in villages seems to have evolved without any set pattern; some were, and still are, church halls and some were built as Memorial Halls after the two World Wars. They all vary considerably in style, size and usage, depending largely on the population and degree of isolation of their supporting communities, as well as the existence or not of nearby alternative venues and attractions. Prior to the second half of the twentieth-century, they were, in general, well-used and for many people, because of lack of transport, provided the only social venue suitable for all the family.

The advent of motorised public transport in the early twentieth-century would have widened the horizons of some villagers; but it was not until well after the Second World War that car ownership became widespread and gave ordinary families the opportunity to look further afield for their leisure activities. Consequently, the village hall became less important to them. In Guarlford, prior to 1922, the school was used as the venue for social events such as the annual Christmas pantomime. This chapter tells the story of how a small group of enthusiasts converted part of a disused malt house into a village hall and how, over the years since then, the hall has been improved.

The Malt House

The old Malt House in Penny Lane was built about 1870. Large quantities of malt are used in the brewing of beer and it is very probable that the malt from Guarlford was supplied to local breweries. Local farmers grew most of the barley and the malt house provided employment for local men; there are entries in the church baptism register showing that some fathers' employment was 'maltster.' By 1911, all malt production in Guarlford had ceased and the building was left without tenancy for several years. Mr S G Medcalf, writing in the *Madresfield Agricultural Society Quarterly* in 1911 reported, "Barley, at one time grown to a considerable extent in the locality, is now conspicuous by its absence. The fact that there were two malt houses doing a good business in the district, both of which are now closed without tenants, speaks for itself."

> **Malt**
>
> *Malt is derived from germinated grain, usually barley and is used in beers, beverages and food. The grain is softened in water and allowed to germinate. This activates enzymes which convert the starch to malt sugar (maltose) and the grain is then kiln dried. All these activities took place in the malt house.*

The malt house with adjoining cottage and gardens was acquired in 1920 by Mr C F Robathan when he purchased Cherry Orchard.

Throughout the history of the old Guarlford malt house, the adjoining Malt House Cottage had various occupants; one of the earlier tenants was George Beard

Figure 10.1 The Malt House, 2004.

(grandfather of Sam Beard) who not only worked in the malt house but was also sexton at the church. Then there was the Waters family; Mrs Waters was well-known for her excellent laundry services and the plucking and dressing of poultry. The family lived at the cottage from about 1922 until the mid-1960s. Rene, the Waters's daughter, lived at the cottage until she married Bill Sims about 1942. Bill was a bar steward for the Men's Club for many years, and Rene was a postwoman during the Second

World War. The cottage was altered and improved over the years. In the middle of the 1960s, it was purchased by a Mr Cambridge, together with surrounding land; he extended and refurbished the cottage and, at the same time, built the adjacent two semi-detached houses. Gordon Earp, a retired headmaster, and Margaret, his wife, purchased the cottage around 1971, and lived there for in the region of twenty five years, during which time they also carried out extensive renovations, a process which has been continued by the present owner, Mrs Jacqueline Ward.

> ### Commander F J Ratcliff
>
> *F J Ratcliff (1889-1979) joined the Royal Naval training ship HMS Britannia at Dartmouth at the age of fourteen; he was commissioned in 1908 and served on a variety of ships in World War One and was present at the Battle of Jutland. In 1920 he retired from the RN in the rank of Commander (Cdr) and by 1922 he was farming at Dripshill. On the outbreak of World War Two he rejoined the RN and was subsequently taken prisoner in Bergen, Norway and interned in Germany. He was repatriated to England in 1944 and continued his naval service until 1946 when he returned to Dripshill.*

The Memorial Parish Club

In May 1922, a Parish Club was formed in Guarlford by way of a Memorial for Peace after the Great War. Its premises consisted of the building previously known as the Malt House, less the adjoining Malt House Cottage. These premises were eventually purchased from Mr Robathan by the newly-formed Parish Club Committee with money raised by public subscription and augmented by a mortgage from a local building society. Commander F J Ratcliff RN (Retired) acted as sponsor and guarantor for the loan. Most of the conversion of part of the malt house into the village hall as it is today took place over the periods 1922 to 1940 and 1946 to 1952, and was entirely due to the foresight, enthusiasm and efforts of Cdr Ratcliff and a small group of dedicated villagers.

The Guarlford Men's Club is Formed

Part of the building was reserved for the use of the men of the parish as a club. One of the earliest events organised by this club was the annual Guarlford Club Marathon, which was actually just three and a half miles long. There was a cup, which changed hands each year, and Cdr Ratcliff also presented the winner with a personal silver miniature. In 1924, the winner was Mr W Sims of Penny Lane and he won it again in 1929. His daughter, Mrs C Lockley, is now the proud owner of the miniature cups. Another winner was Mr D Bladder. There was also an annual tug-of-war competition.

This Men's Club, being the only regular tenant, gradually took control of the whole of the building except Malt House Cottage; and in June 1931 it officially took charge with responsibility for the existing mortgage debt. Cdr Ratcliff, D W Medcalf, and F George were appointed trustees and what was originally known as a Parish Club became

Figure 10.2 Cdr Ratcliff.

known as 'The Guarlford Men's Club', with a working committee elected annually. A licence to pull beer was obtained for certain nights known as 'Club Nights'. All the traditional club games such as darts, quoits and bar skittles were available, and eventually there was a full size snooker table. On Club Nights the whole premises were necessarily closed to the general public, but on other nights the committee would let the premises for entertainment and general purposes.

Considerable additions, alterations and decorations were undertaken by the committee to enhance the value of the rooms for hire, resulting in frequent lettings to the public. This state of affairs continued until the early years of the Second World War, when the large upper room was let separately to Messrs Winwood as a Furniture Repository for the duration of the war, at a rent of £115 per annum. This tenancy carried on until mid-1946. Meanwhile, the Men's Club continued to meet throughout the war in its original part of the building which was locked off from the main hall. The income from the letting enabled the club to pay off the mortgage on the whole building.

Guarlford Village Hall is Founded

After the war the Men's Club, whilst still enjoying the income of £115 per annum from letting the main hall, felt that it should make it available for public use, since it was urgently needed to fulfil the purpose for which it was originally purchased in 1922, that is, to be a Memorial Parish Club. The Men's Club let it be known that it was willing to offer the public access to the building, subject to the safeguard of its own existence and finances.

At this point, a Provisional Parish Hall Committee was set up to pursue these matters. Its chairman was Cdr Ratcliff, the secretary was the Revd Newson and its members were drawn from the War Memorial Restoration Committee. The members of the latter committee were representatives from each public

Figure 10.3 The Guarlford Marathon Trophies won by Mr W Sims.

TO THE WHOLE VILLAGE COMMUNITY
OF GUARLFORD.

The Committee of Guarlford Village Hall ask your careful consideration of the facts here placed before you. A Meeting of all interested in the welfare of the Parish will be held shortly. Your presence and the benefit of your opinion will be welcomed in dealing with the situation set out below.

The Village Hall Committee have negotiated for the purchase of that portion of the Malt House now used as a Village Hall, together with the ground floor premises below it.

The Hall as it now stands has proved inadequate and unsuitable. An improvement scheme has been worked out, which, together with the purchase cost is estimated at £1,500. The National Council of Social Service will give half the cost, viz., £750. It will also advance on loan, free of interest, £500, repayable over seven years. The Parish would be called upon to raise an initial deposit of £250 before the gift and loan can be negotiated.

Briefly the proposed improvements are these. New entrance on ground floor, entrance lobby, cloak rooms, lavatories and W.C.'s, store room, bicycle store, all on ground floor. Stairs leading to upper Hall. Kitchen with serving hatch at end of room near present entrance steps. Division of Hall by movable partition to provide small Hall or Committee Room as required. Provision of stage, electric fittings throughout, complete redecoration, removal of beams to provide clear view of stage, improved ventilation, reversal of floor boards to form new smooth surface for dancing, complete walled up separation of Hall from Men's Club premises. Hall available for use at all times, unhampered as at present, by consideration of beer license. Building to be a Village Hall administered by duly elected Trustees. Representative Management, including all parties and creeds. Hall available for hire by private parties, large or small. Town water supply and drainage available shortly.

You will appreciate the importance of an up-to-date Village Hall. Guarlford has reached a point when it must either expand and bring itself up-to-date or sink into insignificance and become absorbed. The village life, in order to maintain its present social importance and sporting prestige must move with the times or die.

It is obvious that a scheme of this proportion cannot go forward without the goodwill and whole-hearted support of the whole community, supplemented by all friends of Guarlford far and near.

The Village Hall Committee appeals to your love for Guarlford and to your public spirit for authority to carry out this scheme which they have evolved after two years of careful thought and many meetings to perfect their plan.

May we then be assured of your presence, your advice and your criticism, even if adverse, at the Meeting to which you will be called within a week or two?

For the Guarlford Village Hall Committee,

(Commdr.) F. J. RATCLIFF, Chairman.

(Rev.) F. A. NEWSON, Hon. Secretary.

Figure 10.4 The Village Hall Consultation Notice.

body in the parish and were, therefore, considered eminently suitable to serve on the Provisional Parish Hall Committee.

In May 1946, a public meeting was held in the school to discuss the Men's Club offer and elect a Parish Hall Committee with authority to negotiate the details of the scheme. After a period of negotiation, the Men's Club agreed to transfer to the Parish Hall Committee most of the rooms that make up the Village Hall as it is today. These rooms were to be made available, free from the costs of rent, rates and repairs, for a period of one year to give the Village Hall Committee time to investigate a more permanent arrangement. In September 1946, after public consultation, it was agreed that the rooms taken over from the Men's Club would collectively be known as 'Guarlford Village Hall' and on the 26th September 1946, there was a Grand Opening by Lady Beauchamp followed by a well-attended whist drive and dance.

Entertainment and Events

Figure10.5 The 1969 Harvest Supper with the Reverend Hartley Brown.

Whist drives were very popular in those days, and the minutes of meetings record in great detail the purchase of whist tables, chairs, playing cards and scorecards. The

Men's Club agreed to share the proceeds from its annual Poultry Whist Drive with the village hall, and this arrangement went on for several years. Dancing was also popular and the hall was let free of charge for one hour each week for the purpose of dancing lessons, under the tutelage of Mrs Newson. This was for the benefit of the young men and girls, so that they could better enjoy the regular dances - how times change! There was also old time dancing with Mrs Margaret Johnson. There was, at one time, a village dance band whose members included Edwin Waters, Charlie Williams, Duddy Sims and Frank Jarrett of Clevelode on the piano. Harvest Suppers were well attended, and a regular entertainer was the Revd Newson with his renditions of 'Widdecombe Fair', with everyone joining in the chorus; and then there was Mr Ron Smith with his 'stories' and, of course, there was other homespun entertainment. There were, too, the annual suppers of the Guarlford Branch of the British Legion. The ladies of the Guarlford Women's Institute also met regularly from 1946; in those early days they usually met in one of the smaller rooms on the lower floor which was heated by two oil heaters loaned by Captain Chester. The main hall was heated by coke stoves. Later, in the mid-1970s, there were fund-raising events such as beetle drives for the forthcoming Queen's Silver Jubilee celebrations.

Registered Charity Status and Continuing Improvements

From November 1946 onwards, enquiries were made into the availability of grants with a view to the possible purchase of the Village Hall premises from the Men's Club and implementation of ambitious but costly major improvements. In May 1948, there was a diversion from these activities when the vendors of Guarlford's school, which had closed, invited the Village Hall Committee to explore the possibility of purchasing the school building for use as a village hall. The committee sought more time from the vendors to explore the viability of the offer, but being pressed by the Board of Education for an immediate sale, the vendors declined and sold the school property to another party.

Efforts were then re-directed towards the original plans, although the proposed improvements were scaled down for cost reasons. A financial arrangement for the purchase of that part of the Malt House in use as a village hall, including the ground floor premises below it, was made with the Men's Club, and in December 1948 this was put to a public meeting together with the revised proposals for improvements. With the aid of grants and loans, the purchase went ahead and improvements were started. The next major event occurred in September 1949 when the village hall became a registered charity. The first Management Committee was formed and its members also became the Village Hall Trustees. The members were:

Cdr F J Ratcliff	British Legion
Mr R Smith	Parish Council
Mr F Tummey	Men's Club
Mr R Vivian	Football Club

Mr R Bladder	Youth Club
Mrs A Webb	St John's Ambulance
Mrs Newson	Women's Institute

Cdr Ratcliff lived at Dripshill House, and besides being chairman of the Village Hall Committee he was also chairman of the Men's Club and president of the Guarlford Branch of the British Legion. He clearly took a great interest in the welfare of the village, and he was also a generous man. He would frequently advance funds to enable repairs or alterations to the village hall to go ahead, accepting repayment as and when funds became available.

Figure 10.6 The Tummey Family circa 1914.
Standing L-R: Arthur William, Mary Agnes, Henry Martin, Ethel May and Frederick
Sitting L-R: Rowland Henry, Jessie Mabel and Sarah.

During 1950, there was much activity with the improvements programme and a continuous struggle with the Ministry of Education for the release of the necessary grants. At this time, the country was still in the grip of severe austerity following the Second World War, and the securing and releasing of grants would have been difficult. Hall improvements included provision of new cloakrooms with proper sanitary

Appendix 1

Historical Events and their Local Effects

DATE	MAIN INFLUENCES ON AGRICULTURE	LOCAL EFFECTS
Early settlements	First records provided by tenth century Saxon charters and the Domesday Book, 1086.	Main settlements were at Powick and Hanley with hamlets and farms in wooded wastes, probably surrounded by their own field systems.
Norman conquest	Designation of the Malvern Chase as royal hunting preserve.	Administered by forest law, rather than common law, giving protection to game, and to some extent, from development.
1200-1400	Increase in population until the Black Death in 1348, when it fell to barely 3.5 million in England, Scotland and Wales. During this population expansion, woodland clearance took place and more land was cultivated.	Through this period, the Priory became the area's principal landowner. Guarlford was specifically named as a Priory estate in 1291. At the end of the thirteenth century, the Priory had 500 acres of arable land in the manor of Great Malvern, 360 in the manor of Guarlford and 240 each in Newland and Woodsfield.
1400s	Ninety per cent of the population lived in villages, small towns or on farms. The rural populations were comprised of landlords, large tenant farmers who employed labour, and small tenants who did not, freeholders (large or small landowning farmers), smallholders, cottagers and squatters, who had no legal title to land but possessed customary rights to make use of common and waste ground.	Ridge and furrow at Cherry Orchard, and names of local fields such as Troughbridge and Stamperfield indicate that strip farming took place under the medieval open fields farming system. A farmer would own one or many scattered strips in open arable fields, and the stock would be grazed on common land. The move away from the open farming system was gradual over the centuries in the Malvern area, and much of it was already enclosed by the time of the Enclosures Acts of the late eighteenth-century and early nineteenth-century.

1536-1540	Dissolution of the Monasteries. Population growth (3.5 million in England, Scotland and Wales in 1520 growing to 8 million by 1650) led to food price inflation, and population migration to the towns and social unrest.	Land owned by Malvern Priory reverted to the Crown and was gradually sold: many of the yeomen and peasant tenants in the Malvern area found they had new landlords; some tenants were able to purchase their farms. Records show that wheat, oats, barley and much fruit were grown in the area. Cattle and swine were the main livestock, but few sheep.
1664	Charles II sold hunting rights in exchange for one third of the common land, which he then sold.	The best of this common land became enclosed, often depriving small livestock farmers of a living. Over the next two hundred years, much of the remaining common land became eroded by enclosure by large landowners, cottagers and small farmers alike, until the 1884 Malvern Hills Act was passed, as a result of which the Conservators were set up. The Hornyold family of the Blackmore Estate purchased land from the Crown at this time, and the estate grew until the end of the eighteenth-century. Hopyards are recorded in Worcestershire by a map dated 1636.
1700s	Further expansion of the population, with Industrial Revolution from 1760-1850. Efficiency of arable production improved with the invention of the seed drill. The total arable acreage expanded rapidly, much of it into previously uncultivated land. A four-course rotation including forage root crops was introduced by 'Turnip' Townsend. Stock could be fattened over winter, making fresh meat available for the first time for most of the year. Gradual enclosure continued leading to consolidation of holdings. This squeezed out the small independent farmers and rural poor without legal title.	As a result of population explosion after 1750, rural poverty increased. Records show that in 1744 overseers of the poor were distributing a bread charity from the tithe barn at Baldenhall. A shortage of workforce, with increasing migration to the towns during the Industrial Revolution, drove increased mechanization on farms. In 1741, Thomas First Lord Foley, a wealthy industrialist who had made his fortune in the Black Country and was owner of the Stoke Edith estate, purchased the manor of Great Malvern. The Foley estate grew, and by 1800 comprised more than 3,000 acres; 1,363 acres lay within the Malvern area.

1760-1830	The Enclosures Acts saw the completion of the transformation of the open fields, commons and much of the waste land into a pattern of enclosed fields. This was a move to further improve agricultural efficiency. When land was enclosed, it was allocated to landowners who thereby had lost farmland.	Disafforestation of the Chase had already resulted in enclosure of some common land. Commoners' rights were allocated to local cottages, allowing the cottagers to continue livestock farming.
1800-1851	Population in UK rose to 21 million. Over 50% of the population now lived in towns. The Corn Laws were introduced in 1815 to protect farmers from international trade. This led to higher bread prices.	Steam-driven threshing machines now began replacing other methods.
1836	In 1836, the Tithes Commutation Act meant that payment of tax by produce was replaced by a money payment relating to acreage of land farmed. It led to the drawing up of tithe maps and awards, which show who farmed the land, and what was grown.	Lord of the Manor, Edward Foley, planted young elm trees along the Guarlford Road. (These died of Dutch Elm Disease and were replaced 100 years later). In 1841, the Great Malvern tithe apportionment was drawn up (encompassing the area which became Guarlford parish). This shows that the 4,022 acres of the parish contained 1,700 acres of arable land, 1,613 acres of meadow and pasture (this acreage would have included orchards), 628 acres of commons, 36 acres of woodland and 48 acres of hopyards. Oats was the largest grain crop grown. All but the smallest holdings in the Guarlford area were farmed by tenants. Landowners' estates varied in size, from that of the Foley Estate, which owned approximately one third of today's Guarlford parish, to Richard Benbow's 26-acre farm, Cherry Orchard, which was farmed by Walter Haynes.
1846	Abolition of the Corn Laws to allow grain imports to feed a growing population whose staple diet was bread.	This led to a move away from growing corn to more dairy, meat and fruit and vegetable production, which had ready local markets unaffected by imports.

1850-1875	Further improvements in agricultural methods: drainage; and improved plant nutrition. Horse-drawn reaper arrived in 1860, followed by the reaper/binder. British farmers became at least twice as efficient as their European contemporaries. 80% of food consumed was produced in the UK.	
1880	The Great Agricultural Depression: after a series of bad harvests, grain imports arrived from Canada, and meat from Australia, New Zealand and Argentina arrived with the invention of refrigeration, severely depressing prices. Workforce moved to the towns.	Madresfield Estate planted most of South Wood for recreation, including shooting, and created employment for gamekeepers and woodmen. Some parishioners of Guarlford are able to pass down the memories of their grandparents who suffered the great hardship experienced by the rural workforce at this time.
1887	Around this date, the First Edition Ordnance Survey maps of England were produced, providing a detailed picture of field boundaries and other landscape features.	Dripshill Wood was the only large area of woodland in the area when the tithe map was produced in 1840 (it was in the Madresfield parish at the time), but by 1887, the First Edition OS shows the similarly sized South Wood (planted 1880, enlarged between 1912-1918). Cabinet Wood and Garter Wood were planted in 1912 and 1916 respectively.
1900-1914	Urban population of 80%. Death duties and land taxes brought about land sales. A period when many farmers declared bankrupt.	Foley Estate sold in 1910 to pay Death Duties. Many farms were purchased by the Madresfield Estate, and many by sitting tenants, leading to more land in owner-occupation. The closure of the malting business at the Malt House (now the Village Hall) just before the First World War may have affected local demand for growing malting barley.
1914-1918	First World War. By 1914, almost all the corn harvest was cut mechanically, reducing harvest labour requirement.	The war increased demand for home-grown food as imports collapsed. Virtually everyone in the parish was involved in farming in one way or another. Women were employed in the fields doing seasonal jobs: hoeing, fruit-picking, hay-making, and at corn harvest time.

1917	Price support for agricultural produce introduced.	A return to more arable farming.
1919	Forestry Commission set up to encourage woodland planting to reduce timber imports bill.	Death duties force sale of land on Madresfield Estate. Land and many houses were sold to new owners as well as to sitting tenants, increasing further the owner-occupation of farmland in the parish. The Hornyold Estate was sold up in 1919. G Lane, A Bradshaw and D W Medcalf were tenants on land on that estate in Guarlford parish which came up for auction.
1920s	Return to free trade led to rapid rise in imports and decline in the agricultural industry. Many move away from producing corn towards livestock farming. Marginal farmland was abandoned. Farmers, who could afford to, invested in intensive methods. The late 1920s saw the first battery hens, and pig fattening houses.	The 1927 OS map shows 26 acres of orchards at Cherry Orchard, New House Farm, Guarlford Court and the Homestead. In 1920, Edward Corbett describes Guarlford at that time as "… mainly pasture, devoted to dairying; and the principal tillage crops are wheat, beans and roots". Joan Bradshaw records that hop growing in the parish had ceased by the 1920s.
1929	World-wide recession: further collapse in prices. Other European countries introduced agricultural price protection.	Locals recall that, so poor were the returns from farming, Madresfield Estate was unable to let five of its farms, including Clevelode Farm, Pixham Farm and Upper Woodsfield. So the estate opened up shops where they sold the produce from these farms, which were farmed 'in hand', i.e., run by the estate.
1930s	England introduced import controls and price support to help farmers through the worst times. Marketing Boards set up for milk, pigs, potatoes and hops. Milk production increased by 30% between 1933 and 1938.	Hardship is recorded in the parish by many who grew up in this period. There were many cases of depression and suicide amongst the farming community, including one suicide at Cherry Orchard.
1935	World economy recovers: prices improve.	
1936	The Tithe Redemption Act released obligations to pay tithes.	

1939-1945	Second World War began. Difficulties in importing food, caused by the war, led to food shortages, and rationing. Four million acres of grassland came under the plough in the 'Dig for Victory' campaign.	German and Italian prisoners of war worked on farms in the parish, as well as Land Army Girls. Local people who lived close to the land found they were better off for food than those in the towns. The Ministry's local War Agricultural Executive Committee, based at Hanley Swan and Deblins Green, provided machinery and contractors, who carried out the work at cost, to help farmers increase productivity.
1947	The Agricultural Act was brought in to increase food production. The Marketing Boards were re-established, and 'Deficiency Payments' were introduced to support cereals.	Improved confidence led to higher capital investment and uptake of new technology. Hand milking was gradually replaced by a system of suction of milk into buckets. More and more work was carried out by tractors.
1947-1952	Agricultural output grew by 20%. By 1960, another technological revolution was underway, as government policy strived for increased output and greater security of supply.	The last person to plough and cut corn using horses in Guarlford was Charlie Williams. Charlie refused to replace the horses he loved with the little Fergie tractors, which appeared after the end of the Second World War.
1950-1970	Low world prices, and increasing cheap imports lead to high cost of agricultural support. To reduce these costs, the government introduced minimum import prices on imported food, and farmers' deficiency payments were cut on over-produced food.	A change began whereby the farms, which had all been mixed farms producing many different crops and with a variety of livestock including a few dairy cows, began to specialize. Direct sales of milk to the customer from milk floats came to an end. Gradually, the dairy farms were producing more milk from larger herds, and the milk left the farms in churns, and eventually in the tanker lorry.
1967-68	Food and Mouth Disease led to the slaughter of cattle, sheep and pigs. Ninety-four percent of confirmed cases occurred in north-west Midlands and North Wales.	The disease came as close to Guarlford as Kempsey, where infected livestock were slaughtered.

1973	Britain entered the European Economic Community. Increasingly, small-scale production became uneconomic. This led to further specialization and enlargement of holdings.	Guarlford's farms gave up milking cows one by one. By the end of 2001, the last dairy farm in the parish, New House Farm, had ceased milk production. More and more from the 1970s onwards, progressive farmers enlarged their holdings as others retired.
1992	The MacSharry Reforms introduce arable production control in the form of 'Set-aside', and subsidies in new forms.	
2001	Foot and Mouth disease again: widespread outbreaks occurred, with two thousand and thirty confirmed cases between February and September.	Sheep grazing land on the Madresfield Estate, near the Old Hills, were slaughtered, bringing the threat of disease very close; and the countryside closed down for many months, affecting everyone. The Guarlford Farmers' Support Group raised £3,500 for the Addington Fund.
2005	CAP reform: the Single Farm Payment is introduced, decoupling subsidies from food production.	

Appendix 2

The Local and National Timeline

Date	Event
409	*End of Roman rule in Britain.*
757	*Offa becomes King of Mercia.*
1066	*Norman defeat of King Harold at Hastings.*
1085	Malvern Priory built.
1086	*Domesday Survey.*
1215	*Magna Carta; rebellion in England.*
c.1217	St Leonard's Chapel at Baldenhall built.
c.1250	Clevelode Chapel built.
1477	*William Caxton's first printed book in England.*
1509	*Henry VIII becomes King.*
1536 - 1599	*Dissolution of the monasteries.*
1558	*Elizabeth I becomes Queen.*
c.1560	St Leonard's Chapel at Baldenhall demolished.
1560	Clevelode Chapel falls into disuse.
1588	*Defeat of Spanish Armada.*
1611	*Publication of Authorised Version of the Bible.*
1613	Earliest known reference to Malvern's healing springs.
1642	*Civil War begins.*
1660	*Charles II restored.*
1674	Clevelode Chapel demolished.
1707	*Union of England and Scotland.*
1741	The Manor of Malvern bought by Thomas, 1st Lord Foley.
1775	Lane family purchase land at Great and Little Woodbridge.

1776	*Declaration of American Independence.*
1789	*French Revolution.*
1793	*War with France.*
1815	*Battle of Waterloo.*
1830	Princess Victoria visits Malvern.
1832	*Great Reform Bill.*
1842	Dr James Wilson and Dr James Gully arrive in Malvern.
1843	St Mary's Church, Guarlford, built as a chapel of ease.
1844	St Mary's Church completed and consecrated.
1851	*The Great Exhibition.*
1852	A new church is built at Madresfield.
1857	The Revd John Wathen appointed incumbent at Guarlford.
1859	Railway comes to Malvern Link.
1861	Railway comes to Great Malvern.
1866	Ecclesiastical Parish of Guarlford created and the Revd John Wathen becomes the first Rector.
1867	Madresfield church replaced with the present one. Guarlford National School built.
c.1870	The Malt House is built.
1870	*Forster's Education Act.*
1870s	*Agricultural depression.*
1871	Madresfield School built.
1877	New organ chamber and organ installed in St Mary's.
1888	*County Councils established.*
1891	Edward Elgar moves to Malvern.
1892	Memorial window to Edward Archer installed in St Mary's.
1894	*Local Government Act establishes 7000 parish councils.*
1894	Guarlford civil parish formed, first Parish Meeting held on 4th December to elect councillors followed by first Council Meeting on 19th December.
1895	Elgar gives Marie Hall a violin lesson.
1900	Lady Emily Foley died.
1901	*Death of Queen Victoria.*

1904	Malvern gets electric lighting.
1905	The Revd John Wathen dies; the Revd Hubert Jones becomes Rector.
1906 - 1907	Renovation of St Mary's, new West window installed; bell tower dismantled; bell mounted in tree and a new carved pulpit installed in memory of Revd Wathen.
1910	Sale of the Foley Estate.
c.1911	Malt House ceases production.
1913	Revd F Newson appointed Rector of St Mary's.
1914 - 1918	*The First World War.*
1919	Madresfield Estate sale.
1922	Malt House purchased for use as a parish hall as a memorial to peace.
1926	*General Strike.*
1929 -1931	*World-wide economic crisis.*
1929	The Guarlford Branch of the British Legion is formed.
1931	The Men's Club takes over the Malt House.
1933	Guarlford's civil parish boundary reduced to its present size.
1934	A new Parish Council, now with seven councillors, is elected.
1935	Electricity supply connected to Guarlford.
1936	*Abdication of Edward VIII; George VI becomes King.*
1939	*Outbreak of the Second World War.*
1940	*Battle of Britain.*
1940	November 29th, twenty-three evacuees arrive from Selly Oak.
1942	Children aged over eleven moved from Guarlford school to Mill Lane school.
1944	Sixteen juniors moved to Madresfield School.
1944	Charles Williams BEM rescues RAF pilot from burning plane.
1945	*End of Second World War.*
1945	Commencement of negotiations for Penny Close housing.
1946	Ten infants moved to Madresfield school. Guarlford school log book ends on January 16th 1946. Formation of a Village Hall Committee. Grand opening of the hall by Lady Beauchamp.

1947	Connection of mains water to the village centre.
1948	Connection of electricity to Clevelode and the Rhydd.
1949	Village Hall Committee becomes a registered charity.
1951	*Festival of Britain.*
1952	*Elizabeth II becomes Queen.*
1955	Installation of telephone kiosk by church in village centre.
1965	The Revd Hartley Brown installed Rector of Guarlford.
1966	Communion rail extended and organ refurbished in memory of Revd Newson.
1975	*Referendum confirms membership of the Common Market.*
1977	Silver Jubilee celebrations and restoration of the Church Pond.
1981	Installation of the village sign. Revd David Martin installed Rector of Guarlford, Madresfield and Newland.
1982	*Defeat of Argentina in the Falkland Islands Conflict.*
1982	Publication of 'The Grapevine', the parish magazine for Guarlford, Madresfield and Newland.
1991	*Gulf War against Iraq.*
1991	Retirement of Cllrs Bartleet, Boaz, Smith and Smyth.
1992	The Revd John Green part-time Rector of the three parishes.
1998	Sound loop installed in St Mary's through an anonymous gift.
1999	*Elections for Scottish Parliament and Welsh Assembly.*
1999	The Revd David Nichol becomes Rector of the new Benefice Guarlford, Madresfield, Newland and Powick.
2000	Millennium Church Pond restoration and planting of the commemorative trees.
2001	*September 11th attack on the World Trade Centre, New York.*
2002	Golden Jubilee Picnic.
2003	New church lighting installed in memory of Malcolm Russell.
2004	Organ renovated and overhauled in memory of Mrs Dorrie Smith.

Appendix 3

Sources and Select Bibliography

Local Guarlford Sources and Records

Bradshaw, Joan. *An Account of the Origins of Baldenhall and Guarlford* and other unpublished notes, undated.

Boaz, Geoffrey. *My Merino Story*, private publication, c.1992.

Green, Reg. *I Got on My Bike*, unpublished autobiography, 1983.

Parish Baptism and Burial Registers, 1844 to present.

Parish Council minutes, 1894 to 2004.

Parish Magazines 1906 to 1912.

Parochial Church Council minutes 1947 to 1964 and 1978 and 1988.

The Grapevine, Parish magazine, 1981 onwards.

Vestry Records, 1905 to 1922.

Village Hall Committee minutes, 1946 to 1953.

Village Hall Deeds, 30th August, 1949.

Women's Institute minutes, Tuesday, 13th May, 1941 to present.

Journals and Newspapers

Corbett, Edward. 'The Stroller' in *The Worcester Herald* in 1920s.

Malvern Advertiser, 13th October, 1877.

Malvern Gazette, 27th May 1944, 18th Oct 1979, April 2003 and other editions.

Malvern News, 19th May 1917, 2nd June, 1917, 10th Nov 1917 and 21st September, 1918.

Other Malvern and Worcestershire Sources

Covins, Frederick. *Malvern Between the Wars*, Malvern Books, 1981.

Foley Estate. *Sale Catalogue,* Ludlow and Briscoe, 1910.

Hall-Jones, Roger. *A Malvern Bibliography,* First Paige, 1988.

Holt, Gill. *Malvern Voices: Wartime,* Malvern Museum, 2003.

Kelly's Directory of Worcestershire, 1940.

Madresfield Agricultural Club, *Madresfield Agricultural Quarterly,* 1914.

Madresfield Estate, *Sale catalogue,* Mabbitt and Edge, 1919.

Nash's Worcestershire, John Nichol, 1781.

Noake, John. *The Rambler in Worcestershire: Stray Notes on Churches and Congregations,* Josiah Allen, 1848.

Worcestershire Historic Environment and Archaeology Service. *Map of Much Malvern property of Lord Foley,* 1744.

Worcestershire County Records. *Great Malvern Tithe Map and Apportionment,* 1841.

Worcestershire Historic Environment and Archaeology Service. Transcription of field names from Great Malvern Tithe apportionment by David Guyatt, 2001.

Worcestershire County Records. *Guarlford National School Log Book,* 5th Feb. 1900 – 16th January 1946.

Worcestershire County Records. *Guarlford Parochial Box,* (church documents).

Worcestershire County Records. *Madresfield Tithe Map and Apportionment,* 1840.

Worcestershire Federation of WIs. *Worcestershire Within Living Memory,* Countryside Books, 1995.

The Worcestershire Regiment Museum Trust. *Correspondence: The regiment's theatres of war 1853 to 1945.*

General Bibliography

Balchin, W G V (consultant ed.) *Living History of Britain,* Country Life, 1981.

Brown, Jonathan and Ward, Sadie B. *Village Life in England, 1860-1940,* Batsford, 1985.

Evans, George Ewart. *Ask the Fellows Who Cut the Hay,* Faber, 1956.

Friar, Stephan. *Sutton Companion to Local History,* Sutton, 2001.

Gwilliam, Bill. *Worcestershire's Hidden Past,* Halfshire Books, 1991

Harris, Esmond and Harris, Jeanette. *Field Guide to the Trees and Shrubs of Britain,* Reader's Digest Assoc. Ltd., 1981.

Howkins, Alun. *The Death of Rural England,* Routledge, 2003.

Hurle, Pamela. *The Malvern Hills,* Phillimore, 1984.

Leatherbarrow, J S. *Worcestershire,* Batsford, 1974.

Lee, Laurie. *Cider with Rosie,* Penguin, 1962.

Leicester, Hubert A. *Forgotten Worcester,* S. R. Publishers, 1970.

Lloyd, David. *A History of Worcestershire,* Phillimore, 1993.

Miles, Archie. *The Malvern Hills – Travels through Elgar Country,* Pavilion Books Ltd., 1992

Mingay, G E. *Rural Life in Victorian England,* Book Club Associates, 1976.

Nix, John. Hill, Paul. Williams, Nigel. and Bough, Jenny. *Land and Estate Management,* Packard, 2003.

Pevsner, Nikolaus. *Worcestershire,* Penguin, 1968.

Rackham, Oliver. *The History of the Countryside,* Phoenix, 1968.

Read, Miss. *Village School,* Penguin, 1960.

Smith, Brian. *A History of Malvern,* Alan Sutton, 1978.

Smith, Keith. *Around Malvern in Old Photographs,* Alan Sutton, 1989.

Stokes, John and Hand, Kevin. *The Hedge Tree Handbook,* The Tree Council, 2004.

Thompson, Flora. *Lark Rise,* O.U.P., 1959.

Trevelyan, G M. *English Social History,* Longmans, 1946.

Web Sites

www.acre.uk - Action with Communities in Rural England.

www.berrowsjournal.co.uk - Berrows newspapers.

www.1901.census.nationalarchives.gov.uk - 1901 census.

www.cwgc.org - Commonwealth War Graves Commission.

www.fleetwood-trawlers.connectfree.co.uk - HMS Lord Plender.

www.malvernremembers.org.uk - Malvern's Roll of Honour.

www.ourworld.compuserve.com - Leslie Halward.

www.raf.mod.uk - Royal Air Force.

www.thisisworcestershire.co.uk - Malvern Gazette.

www.ukagriculture.com - Living Countryside Ltd.

www.visionofbritain.org.uk - Historical information about Britain.

www.worcestershire.gov.uk - County history and archaeology.